Black Priest/ White Church

With A New Introduction By Judge Bruce McM. Wright

Africa World Press, Inc.

P.O. Box 1892
Trenton, New Jersey 08607

Africa World Press, Inc.
P.O. Box 1892
Trenton, N.J. 08607

First Africa World Press, Inc. edition, 1990

Copyright © Lawrence Lucas, 1989

First Published by Random House, 1970

Library of Congress Catalog Card Number: 88-71876

Cover Design by Ife Nii Owoo

ISBN: 0-86543-108-6 Cloth
       0-86543-109-4 Paper

To my mother, family, and Malcolm X,
who have made me black:
to Lorez Harden, fighter for good;
to Tom Buck, who urged me to write;
to Ann Brennan, friend and secretary;
to black Catholics wherever they are;
to all real Christians black and white and yellow
everywhere—this book is affectionately dedicated.

I

A NEW INTRODUCTION

By Judge Bruce McM. Wright

The availability, once again, of the impassioned cry of Father Lawrence Lucas will serve to introduce another and different generation to both the beauty and the flaws in the divine calling of the priesthood. An abrasive benefice when first issued, it remains in its melancholy revelations a harsh exegesis.

Not much has changed in the nearly two decades since this book burst like an ecclesiastical bomb upon archdiocesan sensibilities. The Church of St. Peter moves, if at all, like solemn costumed glacier. Popes, of course, have changed, but not the doctrine. Dissidents, who cling to Latin as the only proper expression of the eucharistic rite, have, now and then, been banished and flayed. The faithful must not dwell upon the possibilities of birth control or the heresy of women as priests. In keeping with the anti-feminist posture of the church, abortion must be zealously opposed by right-to-life sticklers who nevertheless passionately cry out for the death penalty. While Garry Wills may have deplored the bare ruined choirs of Catholicism, Father Lucas was a one-man Tractarian Movement in his own enthusiastic piety. That he remains a parish priest to this day, may have more to do with what Newman called courtesy, as opposed to sympathy. New expressions of old truths have never been welcome in Rome. Both the Church Eternal and Father Lucas continue in their difference of mystery and force.

And Father Lucas, the dissident author of his hard cover homily: has he changed through the years? In his Harlem parish and vicarage, The Church of the Resurrection, he has wrought an amazing grace. An Afro-Semitic Christ, in dark and moral serenity, looks down upon Resurrection's flock. Lucas utters preachments that engage the gritty issues of black survival. Lucas now presides where once there was an all-white clergy. The target of many a non-benefice for his impertinence, only John XXIII would have embraced him, had he come to Harlem. Pope John Paul, a strict constructionist of the scripture, in what many believe to have been a deliberate pastoral snub, ignored Resurrection when he stopped briefly during his Harlem progress. That is, he ignored Father Lucas. He elected, instead, with media ostentation, as though impersonating Christ at obscure Eboli, to shower public affection upon Father Emerson Moore. A convert, like Manning and Newman, Moore apparently warranted greater celebrity mileage for propagation of the faith among the ghetto benighted.

Despite such pious animadversion, Lucas remains the quintessential Stentor of the ghetto's liberation theology and, indeed, of a modernized almost surrealist Catholicism. The press has made much of the licensed weapon he wears beneath his vestments and of the Mercedes he drives. They find in such worldly luxuries a contradiction with his allegiance to a faith that many associate with vows of poverty. Others marvel that this protean mean of the cloth ever looked into a haunted mirror and accepted holy orders in a wedding to Jesus. Blacks, seminal, sensuous and hedonistic, have never flocked to either the priesthood or the sisterhood, despite a black love for ritual, ceremony and robes of office. Reluctant to forswear the touchable joys of sex, they remain suspicious of celibacy, equating it with a subversion of nature. They look with tolerant mistrust upon Harlem's Convent of St. Benedict (probably, The Moor) and its order of nuns and their seeming domestic service as The Hand Maidens of Mary. They are regarded as symbols of black bondage and remnants of Christianity's slave owning hypocrisy.

In many ways, Lucas is a spiritual clone of the "good" Pope, John XXIIII, and of a kind of armed *pacem in terris* in his sense of moral innovation. His church sails serenely on, an agitation to the archdiocese and a comfort to its black penitents. The cardinals who are his nominal superiors in the hierarchy, pay as little official attention as possible to this radical exhortations. By contrast, Pope John Paul urges a homiletics bearing close kinship with the most conservative reading of the scripture. No women, he insists, may ever grace the priesthood and homosexuals are to be frowned upon as a scourge of the faith. The Pope, in an *ex cathedra* pronouncement, having the stamp of a *bulla* in red ink, justifies the exclusion of women and their isolation from priestly orders by citing the all-male twelve disciples of Christ. That kind of rigid argument simply reflects that, the more things change, the more they remain the same, and that the rock upon which the church spiritual was founded, refuses to move.

The shortcomings of the Roman church reflect many of the same blemishes as those that taint the society from which its membership and its clergy spring. In 1939, as a black teenager, I applied for admission to Notre Dame University. I was told bluntly that the University had to respect the bias and prejudice of its Southern students and that, as a Negro, I could not attend. In an awkward gesture at atonement, but not of obligation, I was offered the placebo that Notre Dame's first president had freed his slaves before taking up his duties in South Bend. If bright ecclesiastics yield to racism and to the scandal of slavery, why should anyone expect better of their flock?

Finally, in 1945, Notre Dame admitted its First Negro student. He was, of course, a football player. With great fanfare and zealous hypocrisy, Notre Dame announced that it had never discriminated along racial lines.

The ancient faith has nevertheless survived and has never deterred Father Lucas. A devout radical and unafraid of being banished to the Index, he sees his faith as largely unresponsive to the special needs of black Catholics. He has sought to supply those needs. For too many years, when he was growing up in his native New York, the archdiocese was dominated and dictated to by a lace curtain Irish Mafia. It designated itself the "white" Catholics and the Italians as the "black" ones. In the meanwhile, in Harlem, the few Catholic churches there, posted signs in strategic places, enjoining the resident to "Become A Catholic." While the dry doctrine and alien liturgy had little with which the ghetto poor could identify, some found that for a limited number of grades, their children could get a better education in Catholic schools than the public ones.

It should not seem surprising that Catholicism's staid discourse and monitions have found little response among black descendants of Africa's oral traditions. The dark adaptation of Christianity prefers to shout, to dance with the Holy Spirit and to tremble with fervor and emotion. No personal or fiery magic leaps from the stiff parade to the altar, led by the burning censer's purifying fumes and priests dressed in fiddleback chasubles.

In a white and hostile world, Catholicism's *tableau vivant* of aloof dignity, seemingly doing socially distant missionary work among blacks, is far too devoid of the magnetism, the sweat and pulpit oratory that cajoles God and electrifies the body with screams of joy. And those blacks who prefer the Catholic pew do not appear to be the kind who do anything with pentecostal abandon or charismatic energy. Most Blacks seem to prefer their pastors to vivify the Bible with gestures and an athletic interpretation of The Word. Thus, it becomes quite understandable that Langston Hughes's Jesse B. Semple (known as Simple), learning that white churches had become integrated, said he did not want to go downtown to hear some typed-up sermon.

It is now unnecessary to travel downtown to hear the drama of the word. Father Lucas' translations into personal meaning are delivered for his Harlem parishioners. That there is a black Roman Catholic bishop from Harlem, is no doubt due to the existence of Father Lucas and the dedication of the archdiocese in teaching Lucas that it can be a rewarding experience to kiss the hem of appropriate diocesan garments.

Has the Lucas rebellion made a difference? Of course it has. It is a genuine revolution to compel the movers and shakers of an archdiocese to think in a way that includes some insight into the necessity for change. Churches love to shrink from the truth that they have capitulated to America's racism and its own brand of home-grown apartheid. But, whatever difference *Black Priest* has made, Lucas is that difference. He has not abandoned the faith, but continues to seek to make a difference from within. A main theme that his book makes is that any purported pillar of morality should, at the very least, strive to be a role model. The Roman Catholic church, itself a minority in what is essentially a Protestant society, should, with its claimed moral power and wealth, be a bold leader in eradicating racism, as opposed to an instrument of complicity in the national immorality of racism, both secular and religious.

A residue of racism is perceived in the closing of most of the Catholic churches in the depressed (read black) areas of Detroit. Black Catholics are told that they can travel to Grosse Point, a Mid-western capital of racial restrictive covenants and from where anyone black is often escorted forcefully as a presumed trespasser or worse. The black clergy in the archdiocese that includes Detroit simply expressed the "hope" that there would be some sensitivity to the needs of black congregations. Father Lucas has done more than express a hope; he has remained an activist in addressing the cultural and religious needs of blacks who find a degree of spiritual sustenance in Roman Catholicism, but who know that there is something more their church must confront.

Father Lucas is a trouble-maker, for which the Catholic Church should be grateful. Yes, he is angry, as well with an anger fed by the lumbering slowness of his faith to be more persistent in helping to civilize America the beautiful. That he remains true to the highest ideals of his faith, demonstrates that he is energized by hope, a hope that is dramatized by the love and support found in his own congregation. He has found room in his belief for both the wisdom and biting truths of a Malcolm X, as well as for the teachings of the Holy Scriptures. The Roman Church meanwhile, continues along its stolid way. When Pope John Paul II made his well advertised safari to the United States and addressed the multitudes in Boston, he never once cited with praise the role played by Judge W. Arthur Garrity, Jr. in integrating Boston's public schools, nor did he chastize South Boston's zealous Catholics for their racist opposition to the moral issues they defeated.

In effect, John Paul has closed the doors against the winds of the 20th century that John XXIII briefly opened with his saintly image. The availability, once again, of *Black Priest/White Church*, gives Roman Catholics an opportunity to rejoice in the pain of discovery as they confront, once again, their shortcomings and the hopes dramatized by Father Lucas in refusing to abandon his own vision of the faith. While his honesty often hurts, it provides prescriptions for a theological cure for self-inflicted wounds.

Judge Bruce McM. Wright
Harlem, U.S.A., 1988.

FOREWORD

VI

When a book is almost nineteen years old and has been out of print for over ten years, some natural questions arise; to wit, why bring it back into print; have not things changed a great deal in nineteen years to make this book outdated?

Answers to these questions are easily forthcoming. It's being brought back into print to counter the very reasons which caused it to go out of print so rapidly. Such a frank discussion about the Catholic Church by an ordained priest of the Church from the particular perspective of the author was never expected in the first place. In the second place, it is not desired to be widely disseminated.

As to the second question, the factual answer is that the book is not outdated, but is very much up to date. Things have not substantially changed but have gotten worse in degree. Moreover, the hypocrisy of the cover-up has been enormous. In short, the Catholic Church today in terms of the vast majority of its membership remains a bastion of white racism from within and a bulwark of support for white supremacy in the wider societies and in the world at large.

The brain washing is still strong enough to make the white jesus-honoring colored Catholics among the most irrelevant to the needs and conditions of the overall African communities. Changes have occurred primarily in areas of superficial preaching, costuming, dancing and singing in liturgies that fundamentally remain inside church buildings and low-budgeted and staffed "Offices of Black Catholics" functioning as public relations spaces and window dressing for the white institution.

White bishops are still making general statements about the African communities, to which they are complete foreigners, on the basis of a relative handful of colored Catholics whom they have chosen and isolated from the masses. When this book was first published, there was one Black bishop who was an auxiliary or assistant bishop. Now there are ten, of which two are ordinaries or bishops in charge of dioceses — Atlanta and Biloxi. The question here like elsewhere is which of these men, all chosen by white bishops, is making any difference or is exercising real leadership in the Black communities much less participating in the African revolution? White folks are still in control of and are the final determinators of those who come to us as black clergy and religious. White bishops continue to choose Black lay folks for titles, not real power, on the basis of distortion of mind, ignorance of our history, weakness of spirit, and irrelevancy in the Black community.

Bishops are still making great statements when places of worship of folks with money and power based on money get vandalized. Yet, they remain silent when Black folks get beaten and killed by white mobs, usually in Catholic neighborhoods. Catholic clergy, including bishops, when great notoriety is involved, are still to be found in abundance when one of the relatively few white police officers gets killed. But they are painfully silent and absent when white police kill Blacks from grandmotherhood to childhood. Our bishops seem and appear quite cozy with the richest thugs and political enemies of Black people as long as these are occupants of high office and/or possessors or controllers of large monies.

Parochial schools and parishes are still being closed in inner-cities for lack of funds and Catholic high schools are doing less educating and even closing when the number of African students reach a certain percentage.

African peoples, who may know little or nothing of particular issues or peoples in a given election, can still safely vote opposite the "Catholic vote" and be assured that nine and a half out of ten times they're helping African peoples or making the situation less harmful.

Diocesan newspapers can still carry ads during a major election supporting a candidate who verbally doesn't want to kill us, African peoples, inside the womb but is hellbent on destroying us from the moment we exit the womb and our visibility becomes clear.

In short, this book in substance is not outdated by a long shot. It is sorely needed within the Catholic Church especially in the United States to make us clear about all the pervasive reality of white racism, the only racism that really exists. Moreover, it is a reminder that racism is the major sin of our day and that anyone claiming to be Christian has a most serious obligation to identify, confront, and destroy it. To this end this book is sincerely dedicated.

Contents

Introduction

"Why is Father Lucas so bitter?" About a year ago a middle-aged Catholic lady asked this of a very close friend of mine. I was surprised because, although she had known me from childhood, it had been several years since we had been able to sit down together and talk. The basis for the question could only have been what she had been hearing from others. Somewhere behind this question were the words of some of the white missionaries in Harlem who really believe that Lawrence Lucas is a bitter young man.

From my point of view, there is no answer to that

question. Lucas is not a bitter man. He is angry and disappointed, but hopeful.

I do not believe that anger is a vice to be deplored or a virtue to be pursued. What determines its value is the reality of the believed wrong that arouses it, the circumstances that surround it, and the consequences.

We should not forget that it was partly the anger of some decent people at the horrors of slavery that led to the Civil War, which broke the back of slavery at least under one form. It was the anger of some American people at Cicero, Illinois, at Selma, Alabama, etc., that led to the passage of the 1964 Civil Rights Act. It is the anger of black people at the black experience in America that has led to the recent burnings and "riots" in our cities, which have in turn led to a realization by many Americans of the realities of this black American experience. Outraged anger spurred the initiation of so-called poverty programs on different levels of government and hopefully will lead or help lead to many and far more basic changes that as a nation we will have to make if we are to survive.

Anger, then, is no sin in itself, though uncontrolled anger is. The causes of anger are often far more sinful. People, strangely enough, get upset or say they do when we speak of black anger and outrage today. It would be odd indeed if any black man living in or under any of the white institutions in our society were not angry.

In the context of this book, I am angry and disappointed because I am a black man and a Roman Catholic priest. Being black and Catholic, like being black and anything else in America, is extremely difficult. Being black and a Roman Catholic priest today is an almost impossible combination.

I fully realize that many inimical to the Catholic Church on other grounds will attempt to use this book to attack the Church for their own ends. This is not unfamiliar. Man has attempted to misuse and abuse everything and everybody God has created almost since the beginning of time. Thus, I could not make my decision on the basis of possible misuse. Hopefully, there will be many others who will use this as a spur toward the reformation so badly needed. In their loyalty to the Church, it might well move them to make that Church what it is supposed to be. It is for these that this book is written.

I am not a convert to Catholicism. I am what many choose to refer to as a "born" Catholic. I am so by virtue of baptism received at the hands of a white Catholic priest thirty-seven years ago, but since then ratified by my own free choice. Except for the first two years of grammar school and two and a half years in graduate studies after ordination, my whole formal education has been in the Catholic system.

Today, also by my own free choice, I am in my eleventh year of the priesthood.

But, before becoming a priest, even before my baptism which took place several weeks after birth, I was a black man. It was a black infant who was presented to a white Roman Catholic priest for baptism. It was a black man who offered himself to serve Christ as a priest by ordination at the hands of Cardinal Francis Spellman.

I was born in Harlem. In fact, I came into this world rather unceremoniously in the back seat of a taxi midway between 132nd Street on Madison Avenue and Harlem Hospital. Nor did the family flee the Harlem scene at the earliest possible opportunity, so that I had to come back to establish such connection with Harlem as would be expedient for writing a book or making a movie or running for political office. I was raised there and have loved every moment of it in spite of what white people primarily have made of it. Only brief periods of my life have been spent away from here.

The reason why being black and a Catholic priest causes me anger and disappointment is that the Catholic Church in this country is a white racist institution: It looks white; it thinks white; it acts white.

As the black man matures and grows in appreciation of himself as an individual and as a member of a people, as he changes his goals and his methods of achieving these goals, the Church takes this period to exhibit more and more its whiteness and its racism. More and more, this Church is telling the new black man, "I have no understanding of you now; I have no sympathy for you; I feel no empathy with you; I am losing even what I still call my love for you. Either you behave and return to what or who you were in the past," says the Church to the black man, "or I will have no use or place for you. Moreover, if you do not cease this nonsense about freedom and equality, I will hinder you and obstruct you by silence, tokenism, apathy, subterfuge and indifference. If forced by you radicals and militants and communists who are trying to upset and change this wonderful society of ours, I will fight you directly to keep you in your place."

If the answer I am giving to the question of my supposed bitterness were limited to myself, there would be no need to write, nor any reason for anyone to read what I write. There are blacks and whites within the Church who are beginning to understand.

Black priests and religious, and black lay groups, are organizing across the country as a last attempt. Groups like Detroit's Black Catholics in Action and Chicago's Concerned Black Catholics all are out to change the "lily whiteness" of the Roman Catholic Church. The Church, they are convinced, must be awakened to the realization that black Catholics are fed up with being only a token part of the Church, supported only when the white structure agrees with them. They are determined to become an integral part of the Church, or they will desert that Church as it has already deserted them.

The purpose of this book is twofold. Its first aim is to examine the validity of the claim that being black and Catholic is almost impossible because the Church is a white racist institution. Its validity is of momentous importance to the life or death of the Catholic Church among black people and to the future of the Church itself in America.

Because of this answer, there is a rather basic but important point that must be made at the start. It may help others to read what I say without rage but with intelligence and calm honesty. When I speak of the Catholic Church as a white racist institution, I speak of its group picture, and a group picture does not reflect every individual in the group.

The sociologist, for example, is always interested in group pictures, in addition to other things. But he understands that a particular characteristic may be typical of the group as a whole though there may be many exceptions. If out of a hundred persons, sixty have red hair, it is possible to describe the group as "redheaded." It is incorrect to assume that this means all the students have red hair. Forty do not.

To assume that when I conclude, "the Roman Catholic Church in America is a white racist institution," I mean that all Catholics are racists, would not be true.

On the other hand, I do not say—nor should you

misunderstand me—that there are merely a few racists scattered here and there among the throng of absolutely marvelous people who constitute the Church. I am saying—and I hope to be understood—that the group picture or reality of the Roman Catholic Church, a group picture which represents the majority on all levels, is white and racist.

It would be unfortunate indeed if anyone were to be so blinded as to see this book exclusively or primarily as an attack. Certainly, it is not an attack on the American Catholic hierarchy. To say the American bishops are responsible for the racist Church in America, and that all that must be done is to throw out or change the bishops would be simplistic and naive. Such an attack would suggest that the American Catholic bishops as a group are leaders. I have no such illusion. As a group, they reflect the overall membership of the Roman Catholic Church. If you want to know about the Catholic Church in America, culturally, racially, ethnically, politically—economically may be the only exception—look at the bishops. Most American bishops are what they are because that is what their clients for the most part want them to be. It's a case of the sheep leading the shepherds. The sheep are generally happy with their shepherds and the shepherds are generally faithful to their sheep.

My second purpose, and the more important one, is to try to help solve the problem. In this sense, I suggest some general principles and offer some suggestions with a view to adding some coloring to the total whiteness of this Church, which I and many like me love.

While not autobiographical, *Black Priest / White Church* will speak primarily out of my own experience. It is not an apologia either directly or indirectly. On the other hand, this book will not be limited to my personal experience. It will be about the experience of black laymen, religious and priests whom I know all over the country. Yet it claims to speak for no one but myself.

In recounting experience, it will speak of the past as well as the present. Too often people are quick to say that so and so is rather negative. Father Lucas is always talking about the past wrongs, they say. Under this complaint lies the assumption that the past is really past. These wrongs no longer exist, they feel. We are sorry for what our parents did. We are different, so let's go on from here. Let's be positive. And with that, they are ready to discuss their nothing programs and their choice tokenisms for black people, tidbits which change nothing.

In the first place, these assumptions are false. These wrongs are not relics and remembrances of the past. They are the realities of the present. The hurting of black people by white Catholics and the White Catholic Church and the irrelevancy of the Church to black people is more real today than in the past. The reason for this is that black people are moving away from the sleep-inducing myths of the past. They are more sensitive, more aware of the inequities, and more attuned to what racism is than they were in the forties.

In the second place, we should not attempt to blind ourselves to the fact that the present is hardly understandable if we ignore the past. Many of the Church's past sins against the Negro help to explain the present condition of black people and their negative attitude regarding the Church. The fact that these wrongs persist cements the condition and attitude. It also reduces possibilities and dims future hopes. A careful look backward is necessary to understand the present and to look ahead for cures.

There is one overall assumption. Unless a man looks at himself honestly and sees himself as he really is, no matter how painful that may be, he cannot hope to change. In fact, he won't even suspect there is need for change.

1

Lawdy,
I Went Through
the Whitening Process

The best example I can give of how the Church makes black people white, or want to be, is myself. I say this without shame. Practically all black people in this country, regardless of what institution they belong to, have gone or will go through this. Some will make it through sooner, others later. Some won't make it out of the white man's bag. To the extent that I am out is due in no small measure to my encounter with Malcolm X. This relationship began a whole new way of looking at myself and others and things and events. It is impossible for me to forget that I am the product of the

Church's system that transforms black people into black-faced white people.

There is a twelve-by-fourteen picture, a gift from my sister, hanging over the desk in my study. It is a picture of Malcolm Little, better known as Malcolm X. He would have celebrated his forty-sixth birthday this year had he lived. When I look at that picture, I think of my first meeting with Brother Malcolm. He was not "brother" in those days, around 1957. Like most good Negroes and good Catholics then, I knew I wasn't supposed to listen to him. White folks had branded him a bad guy and a troublemaker. Good Negroes were for integration, were very law-abiding and nonviolent. Like white people, they were very anxious about Malcolm. They, too, feared Malcolm would poison their minds and endanger all that they had worked so long and hard to achieve.

Malcolm and I ran into each other on 126th Street and Seventh Avenue in Harlem one morning. I was dressed in the black-suit, black-tie and white-shirt uniform of seminarians. He stopped me to ask what I was about.

"I'm going to school."

"I surmise that," he retorted. "What are you doing there?"

"I'm studying."

"That's nice, what?"

"To be a Roman Catholic priest."

I'll never forget his expression. In those days most Negroes would have salaamed twice; here was an exceptional Negro whom white folks had accepted. Malcolm stood in his tracks, looked me straight in the eyes, and said, "Are you out of your God damned mind?" A few chats later I began to understand what he meant. Today I see the full, horrible truth.

The full, horrible truth is that the Church wrecks black minds. This is not unique to the Catholic Church, obviously; Christianity in America has hardly been geared to the black man's interests. The most devastating effect of Catholicism on Negroes has been the loss of their minds as black people.

By black people I am not speaking primarily or exclusively of color. "Blackness" in the context of American society spans the whole spectrum of life styles, experiences and their consequences—moral, social, psychological—to which people of color have been subjected. From the white viewpoint, being "Negro" or black in America has been less a biological than a social category. Negroes have been assigned a certain social role, have been treated distinctively, and directed into special areas of possibilities. This is true for their "superiorities" as well as their "inferiorities."

For the black man, "blackness" takes in the whole area of the black man's understanding and appreciation of himself as an individual, as a member of a group or community or a race; how he sees himself or his group in relationship to other non-black individuals and groups; the values he places on himself; his outlook on life and on events; the expectations he has for himself, his children, his brothers.

Until fairly recently the black man's whole conception, appreciation and understanding of himself was basically the white man's understanding of him. He saw himself and those who looked like him—he was not able to see them as his people—as the white man saw him and them. He saw the white man and spoke of him as the white man told him to. What he could look for in life, when he might expect what, what means, techniques and avenues were open—all had been dictated to him by whites. Whatever he said and did was controlled and ultimately determined by how some white person or group would respond, would feel, and whether it or they would like it or not. The white man controlled his mind, his heart, his will, his self-image, his aspirations, his thoughts and every movement.

When I say the Church made me white, or want to be, I do not mean that it encouraged me to think and act and behave like white people. America's racist society and all her institutions have never allowed black people in any numbers to act and behave like white people except in certain superficial ways. And certainly any racist institution would be upset if black people began to think like white people. The Church encouraged me to think about myself and black people the way white people think about black people; to view events and experiences as white people prefer to view them; to see the causes of my life experiences as white people imagine them or say they are.

The Church fostered and encouraged this racism. I do not mean she explicitly taught it in her doctrines. Rather it was a question of how and when she applied doctrines or did not, when she chose to be silent. The way it taught doctrines, the racist culture it handed down, was part and parcel of the religion. It's the way people of the Church behave and the attitudes they express. Nothing, I think, brings what I am saying into focus as easily and clearly as my experience in the system, especially in the parochial school system. It's amusing, now as I think back, yet it's very tragic when I contemplate all those mornings I woke up imagining that I was white, and really wanting to be. This experience seems to have been rather common among black people. If you have a system which makes members of one racial group wish to be something other than they are and makes them strive to be so, you can be certain you have a racist system. Nothing brings this out more clearly than the Church's schools.

I was born in Harlem in 1933. At this time the exodus of white people from Harlem had long been in full swing. They were seeking a new and better way of life. The blacks were moving in. Most of the remaining but retreating whites in the immediate neighborhood were of Irish and Italian backgrounds and members of All Saints Church, the parish in which I was born. On my mother's side, Catholicism went way back. Her family were staunch Catholics as only those from the West Indies could be. In Jamaica they had the "faith" implanted by no less than the Jesuits themselves. My father never converted nor did that part of his family I knew. Even then they had a basic distrust of organized religion.

All of us children were duly baptized within three weeks after birth. I am not sure to this day why I was baptized at St. Mark the Evangelist Church even though we had at no time lived out of All Saints parish boundaries. But St. Mark's, founded in 1907 as just another Harlem parish, was turned over a few years later to the Holy Ghost Fathers, whose work is among the colored. That was to be the parish for colored folks because white Catholic Christians were not welcoming the newcomers with open arms into their white churches. Their welcome was so cordial and humane that in the late thirties in one of the eight parishes in Central Harlem the pastor stood on the steps with a bullwhip, chasing the niggers away. Another church closed down for almost two years rather than let them in.

By the time I was six and could remember, All Saints did not exclude blacks. I recall my mother in church holding me up in her arms so I could see what was going on. All Saints had these big, beautiful, hand-carved wooden benches which simply hid little children. It was ten times worse if the little kids had to stay in the back, and that's where colored folks were told to stay. I came in on the end of all that—Negroes sitting in the back and Negroes approaching the altar last for the Sacrament of Christian unity, the Eucharist. This wasn't the bad, bad South; it was the good, good North. The Catholic Church, especially when it comes to black and white, always manages to be a part of the society in which it is. Unlike the Christ Whom it is supposed to be, it does not challenge, disturb, or rock the boat. In return, it enjoys peace, security and prosperity.

When it came time for school, the lesson that white was better began to be taught and learned in earnest. Negro parents had already accepted this belief and were instilling it in their children. Integration à la America was the great goal. It was the era when the "skin improvement" or whitening products were in their heyday. As for marriages, complexion was often the determining factor in child/parent relationships, as well as family, school and business relationships.

My two older brothers, Joseph and Alvin, were already in public school, not because there was no room in the parochial school but because All Saints School, directly across the street from where we lived, "was not taking colored." Even though the Council of Baltimore obliged Catholic parents to send their children to Catholic schools, Catholic schools in Harlem did not take "colored" Catholics.

We had thought when my turn came to start school, things would be somewhat different. My mother was quite friendly with the Sisters of Charity, who ran most of the Harlem parochial schools before the neighborhood became dark and they took wing. She was particularly close to the principal, Sister Theresa Marietta, a good soul, now in Heaven. Mom was an excellent cook and baker and the sisters used to enjoy the fruits of this talent. When she made ice cream, joy reigned in the school. In addition, Monsignor, then Father, Gerald B. Mahoney had come from St. Charles to All Saints. It was rumored he had had some difficulty adjusting to colored folks around St. Charles. When he came to All Saints, little trace of that remained. My father had died when I was just five; Joseph, the oldest child, was nine and the youngest, my sister Pat, was just three. From as far back as I can remember, Monsignor Mahoney, now retired pastor of All Saints, was the nearest thing to a father we had. Especially when things were going wrong or help was needed, it was simply taken for granted that this excellent priest would be there. He was a young assistant then but neither he nor Sister Theresa could prevail on the system. I could not come to All Saints.

Father Joseph Cherry, the pastor at the time, was in many ways a good and saintly man. He was simply a product and a victim of the system. He knew it was wrong, but he was trained to put things in their proper place, and all values and principles in the Church follow after money—way after. I was nearly six and can still recall the tears in my mother's eyes; it was one of the few times I ever saw her cry. She was sitting in one of the rectory offices listening to one of the chief supporters of the parish—which was still in good shape financially—threatening the pastor to withdraw her children and stop contributing if he took in "that colored kid." He told her she was wrong but assured her he would

not, that year. I could not understand that "that colored kid" was me. I started school in P.S. 39 and went
there for two years.

All Saints was predominantly an Irish parish.
Under Monsignor James Powers, its founder and first
pastor, who came from Ireland, it was built and maintained by the hard-earned money of hard-working and
hard-fighting, and sometimes hard-stealing Catholics.
And Irish Catholics look upon their Irish Church and
its related institutions, like the Irish Catholic school, as
they do upon their automobile: "We paid for it—it's
ours." And as with their automobile, they will let no
"lazy loafer" like a six-year-old colored boy break into
their Church and their Catholic school. And they call
this Church Jesus Christ. He belongs to whoever
pays for Him, like the automobile.

And those were not the days when a five-year-old
Bridget Sweat could tell a saleswoman, "I don't want
that white doll, it doesn't look like me." There was only
one thing in those days a six-year-old colored boy who
had his mind set on going to All Saints School could feel
when told he could not go because he wasn't white: "I
wish I *was* white." As the exodus of white Catholics
began to leave All Saints with empty places, it accepted
white non-Catholics for two years. I began to feel it
then and felt it for many years to come. I wished I were
white. I didn't like being colored. I wanted to run away
from it as any six-year-old would flee something bad
and harmful.

One might think my mother would have said "to
hell with the whole thing." But like most black Christians, she really had the faith. She believed what the
Jesuits had taught her. She thought there was more to
Catholicism than the white people who had certificates
and wore the name "Catholic." She succeeded, when I

was about to start third grade, in getting all the boys into St. Mark's, an eleven-block walk from where we lived.

St. Mark's was run by the Sisters of the Blessed Sacrament for the Indians and Colored People. One might expect that under these circumstances—an all-colored school with nuns dedicated to the colored work—my ego would be restored. This was not the case. The colored kids were kids yearning to be white because they already knew it was better to be white. The sisters were white and were part of the system that reinforced our belief.

In the first place, this was quite a few years before the community, dedicated to the Indians and Colored People, even considered accepting a colored candidate for the community. There were two colored lay teachers at the time, but they were well trained in the system as all of us soon would be. Besides, we kids knew the nuns were the smart ones, not only because they wore veils but because they were white. In fact, only smart people could wear veils. That's why only white ladies became nuns and there were only white priests. The janitor and cleaning woman were colored because colored people were dumb. Sisters and priests were white because white people are smart. Every day I went to that all-colored school, I learned how smart white people were and how dumb colored people were.

You may notice that I am saying little about my academic career—that is, the reading, writing and arithmetic kind of concerns. Throughout my academic life, I have always received much better than average grades. Grades were never a problem with me. What I am particularly concerned with is the psycho-social aspects of the Catholic education I received in its school system. Many people ignore this. Yet it is of equal importance and at times more important than simply learning how to read or write or add or speak or accumulate facts—things some people think education is exclusively concerned with.

The Catholic school does not exist in a vacuum. It exists in the real world, at a definite time. It is part of a social arena, a society with which it interacts consciously or unconsciously, for better or for worse. Moreover, in general the educational system of any society is constructed by those in power to prepare students to become part of and thereby defend the existing order. That is why in our present university crisis politicians and all kinds of people who couldn't care less about education suddenly become greatly concerned about our educational system. Real changes here are a threat to the society they helped to create and on which they live as parasites.

My mother had expected something else of the Catholic school system. That is why it was so important to her that we go to the parochial school in spite of the indignities she suffered in the process. She had been accustomed to indignities and double standards for quite a while. When my father died suddenly, leaving her with four small children (the eldest died as a baby), in her confusion and helplessness she turned to Catholic Charities. They informed her that she would be helped if she were willing to give up her children for adoption. She did not, of course, and turned to public welfare, which is not an extraordinary experience for black folks in this country. In the meantime, two white families on the same block were having similar problems. In one, the husband had also died, while in the other, the father had deserted his wife and children. They, too, were Catholics and both went to Catholic Charities to offer to give up their youngsters. They were cared for, one for six months and the other for nine, until one sought public aid and the other moved. They were cared for by Catholic Charities, who convinced both mothers that giving up their children should be a last resort. "It was God's plan that no one could really take the place of a mother to her children." This was the same Catholic Charities which would help my mother, provided she gave up the children she wanted all along and did not have to be persuaded to keep. Apparently the God they knew did not have the same plan for black mothers and their children as He had for white mothers and their children.

Nevertheless, in regard to school, my mother thought that things would be different. After all, the historical reasons for a separate Catholic school system —immigrant populations—no longer prevailed. Now surely its theological reason—to function in conjunction with the Church's mission of making real the message and presence of Christ to all men—could come to the fore. Instead, we found the same attitudes and behavior toward colored under a religious veneer as was rampant in the other educational systems that supported the racist society we lived in.

I remember the first fight my brother Joe was involved in at St. Mark's. Fights among schoolchildren are so unusual, of course, that it justifies making a federal case! Well, the principal and the eighth-grade teacher at the time—my brother was not in her class— called in my mother. "After all," she was told, "you're only paying half bites." The "half bites" was in reference to the reduction in tuition given my mother for the three boys. At the time, Mom was paying tuition, book rental fees and all the other little odds and ends for which some parochial schools can charge so outlandishly. In fact, if it were not for Monsignor Mahoney at

All Saints and Father Dayton Kirby, C.S.Sp., at St.
Mark's, we might not have made our first Communion,
since we were unable to buy blue serge suits, bow ties
and arm bands and, oh yes, the overpriced first Communion sets which were so necessary for us to have in
order to embrace the poverty-ridden Christ for the first
time in Holy Communion.

All of this mother was eking out of the paltry welfare check the city sent her once a month and which
went hand in hand with the poor excuse for a human
being called an "investigator." The only thing the
skinny, insulting bitch did not investigate was what
Mom left behind her in the toilet. Mother was "happy"
on welfare. Black people are delighted to be on public
aid. They simply thrive on the insults and indignities
involved in preventing their children from starving to
death before their eyes. That's why so many of them
are on it. Miriam Lucas was just another one of those
"lazy, good-for-nothing prostitutes begetting illegiti-
mate children by the dozen and expecting the Welfare
Department to take care of them." They will be very
moral, of course, when they can afford nice, clean, respectable and expensive abortions.

Well, Mom fed us well—extremely well when I
look back—and clothed us well. Then she squandered
what she saved through positively brilliant budgeting
on our education. She could do no better than "half
bites." So she was reminded of this by a religious when
my eleven-year-old brother got in a fight. She took the
hint. She knew how Catholic schools take care of
"problem children," especially colored ones, from six to
thirteen. In too many cases, they still do so today. They
don't try to understand them or attempt to solve the
difficulty. They simply throw the brat out, right into the
public school. Catholic schools have no problems; they

are proud of their "discipline." Mom talked to us hard
and long. And we toed the line.

The school was already playing a major socio-
religious role. The mere fact of the tuition, book ren-
tals and other fees meant that it would be serving primarily the better-off even among the poor. Since it was
the only Catholic school that took colored kids—St.
Thomas had accepted a few of the elite—it could really
be choosey. In addition, it was a gold mine for conver-
sions. A Catholic baptismal certificate was the price of
entrance. This is true in many places today. I can still
look back and chuckle at some of the families I know
where the mother and father drew lots to see who
would go through the ridiculous and childish course of
instructions, "have the water poured," and then receive
the certificate which enabled them to have the kids baptized, thus allowing them to get into Catholic school
and stay out of the ghetto public school. Such things as
Sunday Mass attendance—sometimes obligatory even
for the non-Catholic partner—and contributions to
Sunday collection were necessary to keep the kids in the
school. Some of the more zealous and practical pastors
developed techniques whereby if parents could not get
to Mass on a given Sunday, the "contribution" was still
extracted.

At St. Mark's I did not experience the blatant
racism that some do even today. (There is a nun at the
all-black Blessed Sacrament School in Newark, New
Jersey, who warns the kids "not to act their color"
when they misbehave. At the same place, Father William Gibbons—with the approval and consent of the
pastor—was forbidden from entering the school because he was talking to the children about Black
Power.)

But nothing told us more eloquently as kids how, if

you can't be white then the closer the better, than the honors system. Apart from the few darker kids of the "prominent parents," the criteria for being chosen to be the sweet young lady who crowned the statue of Our Lady in the May procession, or one of the boys who monitored or one who "gave signs of special promise," were increasingly clear. There were exceptions, but the cumulative evidence left no doubt that being "light, bright and damn-near white" was a distinct advantage.

In 1942 All Saints finally broke down and accepted its first Negro child, my younger sister, Patricia. She was a sweet, petite and quiet thing then. Since she was the only Negro in the school, this six-year-old did not present a grave threat. Strange how white people attribute tremendous powers to black people. How whole communities become engulfed in confusion at the mere suggestion of bussing six- and seven-year-old black children to "their" schools. It's like white folks who invest much money and time to raise and maintain property values. Then all you need is one black face to come into that neighborhood, look at one house and, zoom, those property values go spiraling downward. It takes a nigger only a few seconds to destroy years of hard work of good white folks. Well, three years after All Saints had heroically admitted my sister, and had overcome their fears, when she hadn't burned the school down or wrecked the property value or driven away the good white Catholics with money, her three brothers plus two other Negro children came to the school. It was extremely daring to take in five at one time. Heaven knows what could have happened. (Incidentally, my sister could not have driven out any white Catholics with money, because most of them had already disappeared.) For those who remained, the Negroes were a psychological boon; they no longer had to feel they were low men on the totem pole. They could always feel superior to the niggers.

I entered All Saints as a sixth-grader. My sister was in the fourth grade and had had, in general, a better than livable experience with her classmates and teachers. The teachers ran from Mrs. Alice Mullaley, who warned that name-calling would require parental explanation to Miss Edna Burke, who allowed a scrawny little kid to tell the class, "Last Saturday he jumped into the tub like a big black nigger." Miss Burke smiled and remarked on how cute he was. Needless to say, he wasn't that cute to the only Negro child in the class.

By this time the Lucas family was well known in the parish. In fact, we had become favorites of many of the remaining whites. It was the era when Negroes were proud to be in the company of whites, to visit the homes of whites and, above all, to show off to blacks when white friends would condescend to come to their houses. We went through the whole bit understanding each other but without saying these things. The whiteness of the Negro's companion, acquaintance or friend was far more important than his genuine friendship or character. In the white school the implications of our acceptance of inferiority came out. As more Negroes came into the school, it is interesting to recall how Negroes avoided other Negroes. The children reflected their parents beautifully. White playmates were preferable. When little white girls played with little Negro boys and even whispered or told their classmates, "I like so and so," that was about as close to Heaven as the Negro could hope. I was not the least popular of the Negro kids. The white kids used to tell me what they did not like about the other Negro kids. I had always been a rather friendly and outgoing type of person. In those days, of course, the goal was to be accepted by whites: my friendly nature and this ambition made a great combination. By the sixth grade, I was smart enough to know that if I dressed right, spoke correctly, did not smell, and watched my manners with whites, they would welcome me with open arms. The more they praised and liked me, the more I responded and the more I succeeded.

My classmates' parents and the adults in the parish loved me, too, and generally were very kind to me. It was years before I could realize or even care that they had different feelings than I thought toward colored people, or that they were making an exception for cute little Lawrence then. They were particularly fond of me at the weekly worship service—Monday night Bingo. Father Cherry, who had died in 1942, was replaced by Father John Cuneen, who proved to be a financial genius. Bingo was part of the operation; in fact, from the interest and concern, some felt it was *the* operation of the parish. I used to sell the refreshments at Bingo. The players liked to rub my hair for luck and would give me a nickel or dime. It had to be a black head for luck.

One fact became clear at All Saints. While all my white friends would say with pride, I'm Irish or German or Italian or Polish, I would keep my mouth shut. What I could not or must not say, unless it was with much apology, was: I'm colored or Negro. There was something wrong with that.

St. Patrick's Night—Irish Night would be a more accurate title—was something else. The school kids would put on a show before their parents got stoned in honor of the saint. I remember how cute everybody thought I was when I got out on the stage with my classmates singing my fool head off about being proud of all the Irish that was in me. And you know, after a while I did begin to be proud of all the Irish that was in me, or all that I would have liked to have been in me.

Things have not changed much today. In my own archdiocese, since St. Patrick is the patron saint, there is some justification for black grade- and high-school youngsters marching in the St. Patrick's Day Parade. In Newark and other dioceses where Patrick is not the patron, black schoolchildren (like Italians and others) were still marching in 1969. Of course, this shows how "integrated" we are.

This is no disrespect to the great St. Patrick, nor is it any suggestion that honor to the saints must be given only along racial lines. On the other hand, let's be honest. It would take a great deal of imagination to say that in most of the March 17 parades it is St. Patrick who is being honored rather than the Irish. Just look at the colors, the badges and buttons, the slogans, the banners, the radio and television commentaries, the "how great to be Irish" talk and the inebriation connected with a March 17 in New York and ask yourself whose day it really is. At best, St. Patrick gets a few honorable mentions during the course of the afternoon.

I am not suggesting that the Irish should not have a parade on March 17 or any other day. I am saying that we should be honest enough to say whether it is a religious event or a racial or national one—unless, of course, there is no distinction between Irish and religious and Catholic.

I was a hit on the stage in All Saints on Irish Night. And I was proud of the attention. This little darkie with his green tie and green hat and green carnation singing with all his might, "I'm proud of all the Irish that is in me," was quite a success. There was no problem in those days, but there are Catholic high schools and grade schools and colleges today in New York, Indiana, Louisiana, New Jersey, Pennsylvania, you name it, where black students may not wear symbols that proclaim that they are proud of all the blackness that is in them. There are all-black schools taught by Sisters of the Blessed Sacrament, Josephites, and some administered by whitened Negro communities where the dashiki and the Afro, or natural, hair style are forbidden by good white nuns and priests and frowned upon by whitened Negro nuns and priests.

The following year I asked my mother if I had to take part in Irish Night—not because I was seeing things clearly then but just out of plain embarrassment. All Mom said was "I'm glad you asked me. I don't think it's a necessary part of going to school." That was my last star performance as the cutest little Negro Irishman or Irish Negro in All Saints history.

It was at this period that the Good Lord arranged to have Father Edward Bergin sent to All Saints. He was ordained in 1944 and All Saints was his first assignment. Father Mahoney took him under his wing and it wasn't long before he became a close friend of the Lucas family. Here was a man who was about as rough as anyone I've known and who was still loved by the kids. He'd beat the daylights out of you and as soon as the punishment was over, he'd forget the offense. In addition, he was fair and would literally do anything for anybody as long as you played it square.

In many ways, Father Bergin was ahead of his times. Had he lived, he would have been interesting in these days of "radicals." One of the big days in my life was serving Mass for the first time. With the excellent instruction of Father Kirby at St. Mark's and my mother, who tutored me in the Latin she had learned during her convent-school experience in Jamaica, I was ready in a short time. By the end of the third grade

Father Kirby was able to assign me to serve. I'll never forget my mother's pride when she came with me every day that week while I was serving the 8:15 Mass.

When I got to All Saints, I had simply assumed that I would be an altar boy. But they were not just ready; a colored altar boy was unheard of in All Saints parish. Friends tried to ease the pain, as did the sisters who simply did not talk about it. Most spoke about that shadowy, unenlightened "they" who would not approve. And as usual, when white people talk about the unenlightened, prejudiced, misunderstanding, etc., white people, it is always the "good," "understanding," "patient" Negro who must restrain himself and hold back. These virtues apparently are no good for white folks. So the unenlightened, misunderstanding and prejudiced whites have their bigoted way.

Well, Edward Bergin had a different approach. The pastor, Father John Cuneen, who was rocking all kinds of boats in the raising of money, wasn't going to rock any boat when it came to putting Negro kids on the altar. So Father Bergin, without saying a word to anyone, simply asked me if I wanted to and if I knew how. When I answered yes, he gave me a test and found I was way ahead of most of the older white children. He told me the day for the altar boys' meeting and told me to "be there" and that was that. So I was the first Negro altar boy in All Saints. There was some hostility, but the major reaction was shock, then acceptance of the inevitable, and finally I became the darling and devout altar boy whom everybody knew and loved.

At the end of my seventh grade, the Sisters of Charity pulled out of All Saints, the last grade school they had in Central Harlem where at one time they had run most of the parochial schools. But by now, while All Saints School was still predominantly white, especially in the four upper grades, the neighborhood for all practical purposes was completely Negro.

We had become rather attached to the Sisters of Charity. It was, therefore, difficult for us to believe that they, too, were fleeing because Negroes had over-run the once "good" neighborhood. They were very kind about it, though. Maybe they were not exception-ally honest, but they were good enough to say their leaving was due to condemnation of the private house in which they were living on 126th Street and Madison Avenue. And since they could find no other place to live in all of Harlem, they had to leave.

By coincidence, two weeks after the Sisters of Char-ity abandoned their convent, it became a church with a much larger membership than its former occupants. A year later it became a residence once again as it still is today. Thus entered the Sisters of the Blessed Sacrament for Indians and Colored People. By now, with the exception of two schools, these nuns operated all the parochial schools in Central Harlem. I was go-ing into my last year. The coming of the Sisters of the Blessed Sacrament was the infallible sign that All Saints School, like the rest of Harlem, was to be con-demned to the Negroes.

My final year in All Saints with the Sisters of the Blessed Sacrament was not too eventful. The old atti-tudes first encountered at St. Mark's were still present. Being older, I was more attuned to them and their effect. Nothing brought this out more than the "you people" approach. What it said was that our white teachers, their religious garb notwithstanding, were more white than religious. This fact is one of the main reasons why the Catholic school system has failed to play a relevant role in the social aspect of the education of black children, and the reason why much of its effort is vitiated. It is the reason why community control of the schools—public, private or parochial—in the black communities is such a vital and important issue. There is no identification between the white administration and teachers and the black children and their parents. The expression "you people" is a manifestation of a deeply held belief that "you" are something other and inferior. This is why the Catholic schools as they are now administered and staffed cannot provide for black children what they provided for white children, Irish, Italian, German or Polish. Their teachers and principals and administrators referred to them (not in a patronizing or condescending way) as "our children" and talked to their parents as "we."

Not too long ago, when integration of schools was of high priority in this country, I had many discussions with my own archdiocesan officials on integrating our schools. The public schools had already started some bussing programs. Catholics, as usual, were still providing leadership from behind—way behind. Thus the parochial schools were becoming havens for segregationist whites who feared the public schools might take integration seriously. They did not, of course, as it turned out.

Our archdiocesan officials gave the usual arguments against bussing. I pointed out that in most of our suburban areas the bussing of school children had long been an accepted way of life. There were some schools in the city where for prestige or snob value children of all ages were bussed or driven in from more than eight miles. It would seem that bussing was all right for many things. However, when the aim was integration, bussing immediately became a bad word. The entire matter was concluded when one of our distinguished monsignors in charge of education and one of our more distinguished bishops told me, "As for bringing Negro kids into white neighborhoods, we will leave it to individual pastors to decide. We cannot ask our white parents to run the risk of sending our children into Negro neighborhoods."

His conclusion said a great deal. His "our" versus "Negro kids" said more.

My big event in the eighth grade was when I told Father Bergin that I would like to go to Cathedral College, the minor seminary for the Archdiocese of New York. Edward Bergin had already gone through the ordeal, in regard to my oldest brother, of convincing seminary authorities of the exceptional Negro of exceptional character, intelligence and stability of whom whites could be proud. Joe had gone to Cathedral College and remained there a year.

The lack of continuing contact with the Holy Ghost Fathers after I had left St. Mark's, the fact that the Jesuits were not taking colored candidates, and an unpleasant experience my brother Alvin had with the Franciscans discouraged me from considering a religious order. Alvin, who was two years older than I, had begun writing the Franciscans about entering their order when he was in the seventh grade. Perhaps the vocational director didn't recognize his address as a Harlem one, but the correspondence became ever more serious. A Father Daniels came to visit the house. It took three more visits of leading Alvin on before he got enough courage to tell my mother, "I must lay my cards on the table. We don't take colored." In any case, I wanted to stay at home and to be of some help to Mom. These reasons led me to decide on the diocesan priesthood.

The priesthood had not always been on my mind, although later on I was to find out that Mother suspected and was hoping and praying for it. Like many youngsters, I was fascinated by firemen and at one time even wanted to be a cop. Thus, when the word got out, the process of due praise and the enshrinement of this "exceptional" Negro was begun. My intensive orientation was also begun. You can imagine the advice and lectures concerning my grave responsibilities at the tender age of twelve or thirteen. How all eyes would be on me; how extra careful I would have to be as a Negro since the fate of many others to come would depend on me, etc. Fortunately for me, I was not to be the first or the only one. Eugene Hicks, who was to be the first Negro priest ordained for the New York archdiocese, had graduated from Cathedral in 1946. Harold Salmon and William Johnson were going into their fifth year (equivalent to freshman in college), Samuel Brown was going into his second, and my brother had spent a year and left. My brother's leaving was my only concern. White boys departed left and right, but when a Negro did, it was said that "it might make it more difficult for other Negroes to come in."

I took the entrance exam for Cathedral and passed. The nuns seemed shocked, not that I passed, but that I took it. High-school examinations were different then; each school gave its own, rather than the one-test system with choices of school now in vogue. The nuns announced the date of each exam and naturally we took all the ones that fell on school days in order to get out of class. The reason I mention this is the wee bit of fun I had with Rice High School. Being white first, the nuns were permitted a little deceit when dealing with blacks.

Rice High School is a Catholic high school located on 124th Street and Lenox Avenue. It is the only high school—public, private or parochial—in Central Harlem, where about forty thousand pupils attend elementary and junior high school. It was in Harlem as much as anything could be, yet in 1947 Rice was still not taking colored. In fact, it was almost twelve years later before it began to take a few. The school is only a block from the subway. Thus, in the morning and afternoon white kids need only dash a block to safety and a block back to the subway that will take them out of the jungle and back to civilization.

The sisters did not tell me. They did not want to hurt my feelings, so they simply didn't mention that exam to me. Since it was on a class day, I inquired about it. "You would not want to go there," they told me. (They didn't say "that Catholic school is no Catholic school, they are prejudiced and discriminate against you because you are black and they are white and that makes them feel better than you." They told me, "You would not want to go there.")

I graduated from All Saints School in June 1947, receiving the general excellence medal for studies, along with a lovely white girl. Everybody thought it was so wonderful. In September 1947 I entered Cathedral College, where I would do my high school and first two years of college study in preparation for the priesthood for the New York archdiocese.

When I entered Cathedral there were three Negroes there. Eugene Hicks had graduated the year before and was in the major seminary at Dunwoodie. Of the three, only Harold Salmon was to be ordained; one left the following year and the other after completing college in Dunwoodie. A real surprise was the appearance of another Negro who came that September, James Violenus from St. Paul's in Harlem. We were in the same year but different sections. Thus, for the next twelve years in the Catholic educational system—high school, college and seminary—I was the only pea in the pot of rice integrating my class.

In many ways, if the Violenus and Lucas families and Jim and I had not become good friends, things might have been much different. The first reaction of my whitened bowels on seeing him was disappointment. After all, nowhere in our society or in the Catholic system were Negroes encouraged to think in terms of identity with other Negroes, to seek them out, to associate with them as desirable and worthwhile. Moreover, there was the threat of having to share the prestige and honors of being the only Negro for three whole years and the problem of sharing the attention, affection and friendship of white folks. Under ordinary circumstances, Violenus and I would have avoided each other, made sure we didn't "congregate" or appear too sensitive or self-conscious about Negroes. Meanwhile, the Italian and Irish kids were forming all kinds of cliques in the classrooms, lunchroom and wherever the hell they went. And if you wanted to see sensitivity and self-consciousness about being Irish from faculty down to secretarial and building help, you should have been around any March 17.

Today, of course, you walk into a room or situation, look for another black face and head for that direction in a hurry. With the other you feel safe and expect to find someone with whom you can discuss shared experiences and feel a certain unity in understanding, goals and values. True, you may be wrong; you may have headed for a black face that is *only* a black face.

During this time, I developed some strong and lasting friendships. This was somewhat remarkable when you realize that many of the white kids had really never

been within two feet of a Negro. Some of them knew a
"great deal about Negroes," just as most white people
today know so much about those with whom they care-
fully avoid any kind of meaningful contact. Mostly
their knowledge comes from stereotypes handed down
for generations and from stories in the white press.
There were those who were fortunate enough to have
policemen as members of their families. And who could
possibly know more about Negroes than white police
officers?

Unlike my brother Joseph, who one time came to
blows with one of his schoolmates at Cathedral, I can
say that I did not experience any of the blatant antago-
nism that most people limit racism to. The nearest it
came was when my name was mentioned for a class
office in my second year. I overheard one of the gents,
with whom I later became good friends, say, "We can't
have him."

The questions they would ask were something else.
Like, "Does your skin cut?" or "Why do you need a
comb or soap?" One would imagine I had been a visitor
from another planet. They were nice and polite and all
the rest, but they unconsciously looked upon me as a
foreigner to the human race. Most of the questions
were introduced with, What or how do Negroes think
about this or that? Whites disagree among themselves
left and right. To get a consensus from them on most
issues is impossible. Yet, for some reason all Negroes
were expected and assumed to think alike, feel, smell,
walk and talk alike. Therefore, all you need is one representative and he can tell you how every Negro reacts
to every imaginable situation.

Perhaps the greatest indication of the system's
competence was my own successful adjustment. I remember the evening our class team was going to play

basketball against a parish team just outside of Harlem. Mike McCarthy, one of my classmates, called and suggested that we all meet and go together, since we had to pass through a "dangerous neighborhood." Dangerous neighborhood, of course, meant a Negro neighborhood. I responded somewhat ironically that I felt no particular concern, especially if I went alone and met the others at the place. "Hell, Lukie," McCarthy rejoined, "you're one of us." How accurate McCarthy's words were then, and how well he understood what he had said are in doubt. I do know that a few years before I would have rejoiced in those words. After all, wasn't that what integration was all about, Negroes making themselves acceptable to whites in return for certain "white privileges"? Instead, I spent a few days thinking about Mike's words. Something was going wrong somewhere. Today, I see those words: You're one of us, in terms of Brother Malcolm: What the hell is wrong with you, man; that whole system is geared to integrate you, to integrate, to integrate!

A few years ago I visited Mike, now Father McCarthy, at his house. It was a few weeks after the funeral of his father, who died while I was in Indianapolis. We had a few Scotches, which has a good way of loosening the tongue, although Michael never required much help in telling me what was on his mind. Commenting on my present position and recalling the past, McCarthy began attacking me for "fooling the class." "Why hadn't I let on to them the way I actually felt?" After a little more of it, I asked, "Aren't you going to leave me room for change and growth?" In a sense, I did fool you. You never understood my looking into restaurants for another black face before I went in, or the queer feelings I got from the odd looks of people when I visited some of you in your segregated neighborhoods. The whole system, and all of you, made me fool you as well as myself. I had to in order to survive. The goals, the means to those goals, your overemphasizing my individuality, made me fool you. And, if I had ever spoken in the seminary as I now speak, how long would I have lasted? And if I had been dismissed, who in the class would have raised even a faint voice of protest? Those who would not have applauded the departure of a troublemaker would at best have regretted that Lukie went off the deep end.

I graduated from Cathedral College in June 1953, having completed high school and the first two years of college. By this time I had picked up the reputation of being fresh. Having for some time concluded that exams there, as is true in many institutions of learning, were tests more of memory than of ability to think, I took a cynical attitude toward marks and the emphasis placed upon them. Moreover, I was curious to see the reaction that would follow if my marks dropped from the category of super-Negro. I did a tremendous amount of unassigned reading (I have always been a voracious reader). And my horizons widened, while my marks declined, but never near the failing point. It was while one of my professors was commenting on this decline and my being a Negro that I cut him off with the remark that I was not a test case for Negroes. This observation began my reputation of being fresh. I was never questioned by any member of the faculty about why I had said it. The reputation stuck. It wasn't until just before graduation that I found out about it and learned that at one point Monsignor Charles Giblin, the president of the College, and several others had had to do some real battling to keep me from being dropped.

My sister, Patricia, also graduated in June 1953

from Cathedral High School, a girls' school run by the Sisters of Charity. She had been talking for over a year about entering the convent, but now it was definite. My mother, brothers and I tried to persuade her to begin college first and to work for a few years before entering. Here again, she faced the same limitations of choice that my brother Alvin had come up against years earlier when he tried to enter the Franciscans. Patrica Lucas began getting the same runaround, evasions and dishonesty that black girls before her had gotten from white communities. Ultimately she entered the Franciscan Handmaids of the Most Pure Heart of Mary, one of the three Negro religious communities of women in the American Church.

In September 1953 I entered the major seminary of St. Joseph at Dunwoodie in Yonkers, New York. Eugene Hicks had been ordained in 1952. Harold Salmon and William Johnson were three years ahead and James Violenus came in the year after. Four was the largest number of blacks that had ever been there at one time and after Johnson left, it was never more than one in a class. Many times we used to joke about not getting together lest we be called cliquish.

The seminary was pretty much the same as Cathedral College except on a more complex level. We learned all about beautiful principles applied to experiences that differed from our own back home. People did not talk differences, while constantly living them. It was at Dunwoodie that I became more conscious of the fact that I lived in two different cultures—one black and the other white. The faculty and students, even in trying to be nice, did not really take me as I was but as they saw me in their white minds. In this structured white society which is the Church, the psychological adjustment expected of me was not to religion or the priesthood but to whiteness. This was not due to individual overt acts of prejudice or bigotry. The worse incident I recall is when my subdeaconate was deferred because the chant professor deliberately lied in saying that I *alone* had wilfully absented myself from a session without reason. He forgot to mention at the faculty meeting that more than two-thirds of the class was missing and he didn't even bother to ask them why. This, however, was not so much racial as it was personal dislike.

It was at this time in my life that my outlook changed. To assimilate myself and imitate whites was without value. In addition, I did not see myself at Dunwoodie as proving anything to white people. I had gone just as the others to prepare for the priesthood. As human beings, my schoolmates and the faculty mattered. As white people, they did not. Certainly, they did not mean anything more than my people back home. If there was no need to prove to black people that I was human, there was even less need to prove it to whites. Any white who needed proof, I felt, was incapable of receiving it. That is why as the time for ordination got closer, my close friends and relatives were more surprised each fall when I returned to the seminary.

I was ordained on May 30, 1959, by Cardinal Francis Spellman in St. Patrick's Cathedral. It was a grand occasion that included my first Mass in All Saints Church the day after. Many of the former parishioners, including some who had run from my mother and brothers and sister and me when I was a kid, came back for the occasion. They were all so proud of me and happy for my mother (who had died the previous summer). At that time I was all but completely adopted into some of my classmates' families. In fact, I had always gotten along well with most of their families and in some cases all our families have maintained very close relationships.

Ten days after ordination the new priests received their first assignments in the "gold room" at the chancery office from Spellman himself. I was assigned to St. Joseph's Church in Croton Falls, New York, in upper Westchester County. The intention of assigning me there was good in terms of the times. The idea was not to segregate Negro priests in Harlem. They were priests first, not colored priests, and should be able to be assigned anywhere in the archdiocese. It was the time of the I-am-a-priest-who-happens-to-be-Negro bit. Emphasizing their role enabled many men to avoid the dreadful fact that they were black. My own realization that I am a black man who serves as a priest was to come a little later.

In Croton Falls, the people were exceptionally wonderful. They did not hate or run from the Negro priest nor did they overdo it. They just remained themselves. Nonetheless, I lasted only three months. There was a white Catholic gentleman with money. He owned a place in Peach Lake which served as a mission chapel for St. Joseph's in the summer. But Negroes were not permitted. Peach Lake was out of bounds for niggers.

I have never laid eyes on William Peach nor do I know if he ever laid eyes on me. But to the white man, a nigger is a nigger. So a Catholic priest who was a Negro—that's the way we saw it in those days—could not officiate at a place where white Catholics celebrated Mass with Jesus.

In September of the same year, I was moved from Croton Falls and rewarded with St. Peter's on Barclay Street, where the income and living were fine.

2

Basically, Lord, It's All Racism

On January 8, 1969, the Roman Catholic Archdiocese of Newark, New Jersey, was rocked by a public statement made by twenty priests who work in inner-city parishes in Newark. "It is the considered, convinced opinion of the twenty undersigned Roman Catholic priests that the official Church of the Archdiocese of Newark, administered by the Most Reverend Archbishop Thomas A. Boland, S.T.D., L.L.D., has made no significant contribution to relieving the deplorable agony of the 500,000 black people in the inner-cities of the Archdiocese. For a decade, the drama and urgency of desperate need of the inner-city has been ignored by the official Church in Newark. The official Church is apathetic. It is racist." Of the twenty priests who signed the statement, nineteen were white and one black. They had done it with the knowledge and support of black people, Catholics and non-Catholics, in Newark and some outside of Newark.

"Twenty Priests in New Jersey Accuse Newark Archbishop of Racism" was the headline in *The New York Times* the next day. The priests had gone on to add, "The official Church is contributing actively and passively to the delinquency of justice in New Jersey. Isolation from the powerless, rather than the involved love of compassionate brotherhood, is the official Church policy. The passion of our priesthood demands a positive decision of allegiance to the ideal of peace through love." They listed seven demands. These called for the formation of an advisory committee for inner-city affairs, a better method of screening priests in black areas, and the transfer of some pastors who have "not proven a predisposition for justice by their performance."

They had also demanded the replacement of the pastor system with team ministries, the opening of Church-owned recreation facilities to all persons, and an increase in experimentation and in the support of priests who "set out to fight city hall." Finally, they asked for a discontinuance of a recently established human relations office, referring to it as a "cheap, deceptive Madison Avenue public relations trick to explain why we do nothing in the inner-city."

The priests promised to explain their charges at a press conference the next day. The statement concluded: "The first additional priest we invite to join our dedication to the inner-city is Archbishop Boland. He can stimulate our movement with his involvement, and by giving our seven demands his immediate and sincere approval. Until then, we withdraw ourselves, not from the Church, but from his attitude." The dedication, for organization purposes, was named "Inner-City Priests United for Christian Action."

This was not the first time anybody had ever called the Catholic Church racist. The Kerner Commission Report of 1968 charged American society and its institutions with being infested with white racism. This is true whether we consider "institutions" as formally organized and structured groups, large or small, or as widely accepted, relatively stable ways in which we cope with basic human needs. As an institution in both senses, the Catholic Church is as vulnerable to the charge as the rest of American society.

Within the Church itself, some individuals and groups, both black and white, had already faced up to the fact that it is infested with white racism. In 1968 Matthew Ahmann, then executive director of the National Catholic Conference for Interracial Justice, wrote: "Any observation on the role of the Church in the urban racial crisis must recognize the guilt the Church shares for the way racial minorities have been exploited in our society. . . . It is not difficult to document the extent to which the institutions, leadership and people of the Church not only made an accommodation but provided structures that undergirded and strengthened the rise of racism. . . . But far worse than the remaining segregated social structures in the Church is the extent to which racism permeates the beliefs and behavior of the 'People of God.' "*

The first meeting of the National Black Catholic Clergy Caucus in 1968 opened its statement with these words: "The Catholic Church in the United States is

* From "The Church and the Urban Negro," *America,* Feb. 10, 1968.

primarily a white racist institution, has addressed itself primarily to white society and is definitely a part of that society." The sentiments and statements of the National Conference of Black Nuns and the many black lay groups springing up in the Church are no less incisive.

The reaction to the assertion of the twenty Newark priests from the top down was expectable and indicative. Archbishop Boland, the seventy-three-year-old ordinary of Newark, emphatically denied the charge of racism. The day after the charges were made, he issued his own statement, which was supposed to dispel the "false charges immediately." "I have been overwhelmed and greatly consoled," he said, "by the literal avalanche of expressions of support of my efforts and the acclaim of my leadership." He did not indicate whether this "avalanche" was black or white.

"I must also point out to these priests," said the archbishop, "that there is a more suitable and befitting method—admittedly less dramatic—to ventilate their complaints than to hold a press conference and charge the archbishop with white racism and indifference to the needs of minority groups who are disadvantaged. . . . To make a public allegation not only embarrasses the archbishop but all other priests of the archdiocese who are dedicatedly and zealously working through unified effort to accomplish successfully the goals of the spiritual and the social programs of the archdiocese." He seemed incapable of realizing that they had resorted to public protest not simply to ventilate their complaints but to try to get some meaningful action. Father Francis E. Schiller, one of the twenty, had said: "We have talked, pleaded, made plans and received promises that something would happen. But nothing has happened, and this is the only course left."

The embarrassment felt by the archbishop and his other priests seems to have outweighed in their eyes the conditions the priests described. The archdiocese's inept response to human desperation and human needs should have been far more embarrassing to the archbishop and his dedicated priests than a public discussion. If their thinking was that nobody had noticed the state of affairs until the twenty priests spoke out, it would have had to be assumed that everyone in Newark is blind. The bishop then, a little late, stated what seems to be the classic introduction of most bishops when they discuss these matters. "The Church cannot do everything," he said. "The Church does not have unlimited resources and we cannot simply neglect all other programs to help the inner-city along. While we are concerned with the inner-city, we must also be concerned with the entire archdiocese."

Now, on face value, who can quarrel with that? It's the phony assumptions behind that remark and the phony conclusions to which it leads that make most of the subsequent discussions irrelevant. The first assumption is that the archdiocese or the Church, though it cannot do everything, is doing all that it can. The second is that the Church keeps in perspective what is more important and what is less, and has separated out the necessities from the luxuries. A final assumption is that it possesses criteria for determining priorities. As assumptions they give way before the facts.

The archbishop then went on to discuss, in happy confusion, the federal, state, city and Church programs, and to list all the wonderful things the archdiocese of Newark was doing for minorities and the poor. "These programs," he said, "could hardly have been created, stimulated, developed and supported by a white racist." He went on to point out, "We have listened to the people of these communities and have attempted to involve them in the actual planning and implementation of the projects." That statement indicates that Archbishop Boland has no idea of who the people of these communities are, or that he has a strange notion of what "listening to" and "involving" is all about. He ended by alluding to the relative youth and lack of "experience" of the twenty priests who signed the statement, and closed with the words, "Finally, I should like to remind these priests that they cannot operate legitimately within the Church independently of the authority of the ordinary to whom they have promised reverence and obedience at their ordination."

The archbishop had said: "These programs could hardly have been created, stimulated, developed and supported by a white racist." The question is, Why not? This is not the place to review the Newark archdiocese's social programs, or to ask what are the realities as opposed to the statements of these programs, or to wonder how many of these programs were initiated with an eye to obtaining federal and state funds, or to ask what percentage of diocesan money is actually spent for the poor and what percentage comes from the poor, or even to ask who from these communities was consulted and involved and on what level.

Racists can run programs for black people and do things for them just as easily as non-racists. The racist can do good for black people as well as evil. It's a question of white supremacy and black inferiority, the "doing together for all of us what is the right thing to do," the attitude of the lover versus the attitude of the patron. The patron requires an inferior, the lover demands an equal. The dependent is merely a statistic out there somewhere whom one might help, but superficially. The beloved must be known, understood, sympathized with, and appreciated for the person he is. The racist can be a great patron, or a poor one. He cannot be a lover. The white racist may delude himself into thinking he loves black people, all of them, out there somewhere. He may care a great deal for a limited and very special few good Negroes or white folks with dark pigmentation. These are "exceptions," of course, "not like the rest of them."

And the white racist cannot in fact love any black person without much psychological torture. He is unable to put himself in a position where he can really get to know black people. That is why segregation is so crucial to white people. Real integration would crush their myth of superiority. True, the white racist can have an association that is congenial enough, that might look like love. To love a black man, he convinces himself that this black complexion is only an illusion. The man is really white, "he is just like one of us." He may love a black man only by conceiving of him as white; it is absolutely necessary for his psychological well-being. Thus, the white racist can at best love the one or two Negroes he allows himself to know better than the others, and whom he conceives as white. This, of course, requires of the Negroes in question an ability and willingness, even a pride, in being perceived as a white by whites. But the heart of the matter is that while the white racist cannot love many black people, he can patronize many, many black people or black people in general. Then he confuses patronage with love.

That is why Archbishop Boland's statement that "these programs could hardly have been created, stimulated, developed and supported by a white racist" is significant. It is a belief he shares with so many of the American hierarchy as well as with other white Americans. It is a kind of ignorance that leads one to say,

"With the exception of the government, there is hardly another single agency in our country which is attempting to solve the problems of all the people—black and white, Catholic and non-Catholic—as is the Church," and then launch into praise for Catholic Charities and the Mount Carmel Guild. A little more diocesan money, much more federal, state and city money, more offices, more meetings, and expanded staffs and all under the tight control of white decision-makers to "help the poor" is accepted as the supreme proof that white racism does not exist. Archbishop Boland, like so many others, denies the charge of racism but he doesn't know what racism is about. Like many others, he is a sincere man. He sincerely believes he is not a racist and that under his leadership, the Archdiocese of Newark is combating racism. So natural is racism to white Americans that they cannot even recognize its existence.

The Reverend John J. Ansbro, vicar general of the archdiocese, was even less astute and more self-incriminating. He, too, found the charges "basically unfounded and unwarranted." "This is a completely unofficial group," he said, referring to the twenty priests, "and we feel that their statement as we have heard it is untrue." I wasn't sure what he meant by "completely unofficial." Perhaps the thinking is that unless we say *officially* that we are racist, the charge cannot be true.

When he met with one of the twenty, Father William Gibbons, then assistant at Blessed Sacrament parish in Newark, the vicar general had this pressing concern: "What about all the people who have been scandalized?" Gibbons: "What people?" Ansbro: "The white people." Gibbons: "I think that if a person were Christian, he would not be scandalized. And did you ever think of asking the black people of the parish what they think?" Ansbro: "They have nothing to do with it." Gibbons: "What do you mean they have nothing to do with it? They are the parish." Ansbro: "Oh no, the parish doesn't belong to them. It wasn't established by them or built by them."

If you are beginning to get the idea that many people who react so emotionally and so strongly against a charge of racism do not really understand what they are reacting about, you are reading me well. This phenomenon is not limited to the ignorant and unintelligent; it is also prevalent among intelligent and educated people. An example of the latter is Jeffrey Hart.

Mr. Hart used to write a weekly column for the *National Catholic Reporter* until he resigned in protest over its "radical" editorial policies. The prestigious N.C.R., in spite of its occasional melodrama, is one of the few Catholic newspapers that deserves to be read. Hart wrote an article entitled "Racist, Racist, Racist," which appeared in the January 29, 1969, issue. He was responding with some surprise to the charge of racism, leveled against him by a Jesuit priest the previous week in N.C.R. "Perhaps I shouldn't have been so surprised, for the word 'racist' has virtually been emptied of meaning in the process of becoming a kind of universal term of abuse in our political vocabulary. It's become, in fact, the current analogue of the older brickbat, 'fascist' (1930–1964). . . . But now it seems 'racist' has taken over. The late lamented Kerner Report helped: 'We are,' it said meaninglessly, 'all racists.' "

The Kerner Report did not say, of course, that we are all racists. Moreover, with its hundreds of pages of documentation, it is an odd mind that would describe its analysis of racism in America as meaningless. Hart plunged on: "I, for my part, had nothing to do with it," he said, "and I don't know anybody who did. . . . I must say that I don't know anyone who hates Negroes or wishes them ill." It would not be difficult to conclude that Mr. Hart is living in a dream world, but it's clear why he is surprised at the charge of racism. One of the reasons is that he obviously does not understand what racism is. He thinks it involves abuse or insult, and that it means hating Negroes or wishing them ill. Racism is not insult or abuse. In this country, it is white supremacy in practice. Anyone who believes that he doesn't know anyone who wishes Negroes ill, must be divorced from reality, or is confused and ignorant about what is going on around him. Hart doesn't understand what racism is, so it was easy for him to conclude, "Now it is not metaphysically impossible that he [Archbishop Boland] is in fact a racist, though it is very unlikely. . . . Notice how certain perfectly plausible human failings —indifference, indolence and sloth; the age-old faults of almost everyone—are suddenly transformed into the very fashionable political sins: racism, bigotry, prejudice."

A lot of people are in the same boat. They react emotionally to accusations of racism against themselves or their friends or the people they respect, like their bishops or other good people. They think racism means hating blacks and wishing them ill. This is not true of themselves, they believe, or of their friends or acquaintances. Maybe it's true of a few "misguided" people, who are a small minority. Thus, the description of our society in the Kerner Report is "meaningless." Of course, the victims of racism do not see it as meaningless. Many people would have no difficulty agreeing with Mr. Hart's final assessment of the Newark twenty: "Judging by the violence of their attack, and their rhetorical modes, these priests aren't acting in the interest of justice, much less of charity. They are bidding for political power, power on their own terms." And that is why this chapter and this book are all about racism. Throughout the book we will see its relation to integration, separation and desegregation, to love and justice and freedom.

On January 19, 1969, the first of several rallies in support of the twenty priests was held in Newark, New Jersey, and I was invited to give the keynote address. The rally commenced with a concelebrated Mass at Our Lady Queen of Angels parish in Newark, followed by an outdoor gathering in which there were several speeches and the singing of songs about the black revolution. Apart from two interruptions from fire trucks noisily rushing to a fire nowhere in the vicinity, the day went by rather smoothly. There was a large proportion of whites from many of the suburban parishes outside of Newark.

In my speech I did not single out Archbishop Boland and the Newark archdiocese. Boland and Newark were simply representative of the hierarchy and people of the Catholic Church. The news media were there and, as often happens, *The New York Times* bombed. Having had experience with the *Times,* I was not surprised to see that in its story, it concentrated excessively on my preliminary remarks, rather than on the message itself, and it missed the point even there. "The Rev. Lawrence E. Lucas," it said, "a Negro priest from St. Joseph's Church in Harlem, said that although the dissident priests had criticized Archbishop Thomas J. Boland of the Newark Archdiocese for the failure of the church to concern itself with Negro problems, the criticism was really aimed at white Catholics, whose 'bigotry' was reflected in 'indifference' to Negroes."

The two words they put quotes around were words I had not used all afternoon, namely, "bigotry" and "indifference." I certainly did not say that Archbishop Boland was not a racist, and that the Archdiocese of Newark was not a racist institution. Nor did I imply that this public charge was a mere technique to call attention to white Catholics "whose bigotry was reflected in indifference to Negroes." What I said was that Archbishop Boland's racism was not limited only to him but typical of most of our bishops. In this sense the priests' statement was not a personal attack.

My main point was to clarify what we were all about. There are some basic misunderstandings that white people, white Catholics, have concerning this racial thing in America. I thought it extremely important that the people present understand what they were about in condemning racism and in committing themselves to working against it. "There is great danger," I said, "that while using the same word or words, we are not necessarily saying the same thing."

It is necessary that the white man understand racism, because it is basically his problem. He is racism's chief victim and he suffers from it. It has turned him into a neurotic beast. It is necessary, too, that the black man understand racism. He is victim number one in another way. It has confused his mind, though he is coming out of it; it has caused him to hate himself, his parents and his community and to act and behave in strange ways, ways that are foreign to him. It was of paramount importance to clear up the confusion about racism in Newark. It is of supreme importance to clear up the confusion all over this land. Many people are using the word and don't even know what it's all about. A great deal of the problem is ignorance.

Most people would readily agree that the following

letter I received from a Catholic woman is an example of racism. More recently, since the television program I produced in Indianapolis in 1967–68 and the syndicated column I started in August 1968, I have been getting such letters from Catholics across the country. Some of them I will share with you.

Well, this lady dropped me a line about some of the things I had said on the Barry Farber radio program. Father Daniel Lyons, S.J., editor of *Twin Circles*, an ultra-conservative national Catholic publication, had provided the opposition on the program.

She addressed me as Lucas—an odd form for a good Irish Catholic. She accused me of being a nigger first and priest second who was only out to destroy the Church. She ended by hoping that if God doesn't stop me somebody will, and by any means. The lady signed her name but it is not relevant. She is probably an advocate of law and order. Still she is not willing to let a black man even talk if he upsets her. And if he does, she calls on God—a white and racist God she has fashioned for herself—to stop him. But if that God doesn't, then this loving, Christian, nonviolent lady calls on any human being by whatever means necessary. Clearly, she doesn't even trust the white God she has made.

Still, I think it is safe to say that most Catholics would not write such things. And it is precisely because of that, that they find it hard to hear themselves described as racist. They have confused racism with name-calling, prejudice, segregation, hatred, ill will. Racism may involve any one or all those things. The racist may be a segregationist or he may not be; he may despise Negroes, or feel kindly toward them. He may be a great fighter for integration and sincerely want to help all Negroes, and at the same time he may be very, very racist. It is precisely the inability to understand this that has led Archbishop Boland, and a lot of other bishops, to be quick to respond to charges of racism by pointing to programs and gimmicks that mask symptoms without treating the illness. It is the same ignorance that led Jeffrey Hart to conclude that "racist" is a meaningless term of abuse of the new political vocabulary because, "I, for my part, had nothing to do with it; and I don't know anybody who did."

A number of people had gathered at the rally at Queen of Angels in Newark that Sunday afternoon. The newspapers estimated them at about one thousand. A large percentage of them were white and from the suburbs. They were there in support of the twenty priests, and to protest against discrimination, prejudice, indifference, bigotry, in the archdiocese. More importantly, they were pledging themselves to do something about it. Mrs. Zil Groux and Tom Buck, two of the leaders, and others had assured me of that. It was not to be another demonstration followed by absolutely nothing. This was all to the good. What concerned me was that all of them were speaking about "racism," the term used by the Newark twenty. This concerned me because I was convinced that many of them were unwitting racists. I had seen that before. People who had sincerely believed there was not a racist bone in their bodies, when faced with the reality of racism, were shocked to find it infested not only all their bones, but their muscles and marrow and blood and nerves. Moreover, they had no idea how it got there. For many, the shock of recognizing its presence was all they could bear. Others were not even prepared or ready to acknowledge its presence, much less try to treat it. And so they blamed me and others like me for exposing them to themselves. We are racists, radicals and militants who alienate our white liberal friends who desperately want to help.

By racism, I was not primarily speaking about indifference or of the archdiocese's not really being involved with housing or schooling for the poor, or its apathy in integrating its high schools or other facilities, or even the committing of paltry amounts of its own money to the inner city. I was telling whites and blacks that what we are about is an all-embracing change of attitude and behavior. We were telling people in Newark and in the United States that we are out to change the relation between black and white in the Catholic Church as well as all other American institutions. The point is not primarily whether the master is good, bad or indifferent: the point is that as long as the master is *master,* he must go. In the Church to be white is to be master.

The purpose, then, of my talking this way is that you take stock of what this racism is all about. It's quite possible that some of you, I told them, when you find out what the program is, may not want to support us. You might as well understand now so that when you go home you can make important decisions that are based on reality rather than on self-delusion. It is important that one ask himself if he is ready for this kind of thing. Each must answer honestly, or the final stage of the person's development could be worse than the first.

When a belief in group superiority and the right to rule is joined to a sense of duty to control the supposedly less endowed group and to rule them for their own good, it does not matter how much one does for the other, he is still a racist. A person may love Negroes dearly and work harder than Martin Luther King, Jr. did. But if in his dealings with black people, he finds he always and easily assumes that he is automatically better qualified to lead and make decisions while the black man follows and obeys orders; that he must always speak for or at least approve of what the black man may say; that he must always be doing *for* the black man and never working with him for both; that it's impossible for him to work under a black man: then, in spite of any good he may do, he is racist. And when a majority of individuals believes and acts that way, like white Americans and white Catholics, the society is racist.

Since definitions only go so far, let us consider the following questions. They might help in determining to what extent one is or is not a victim of racism. How many white Americans really have good friends who are black? I do not mean simply the "nice guy" with whom I went to school or with whom I work or the really "exceptional girl" in the office. Nor do I mean the extraordinary occasions when I might invite a Negro to my home with some fanfare, or that I might even return the visit. What I am asking is, How many whites can distinguish between the relationship characterized by the statement "some of my best friends are Negroes" and the one characterized by the same comfortable and unremarked companionship they have with white friends?

Do you find mystifying and completely inexplicable the cycle of naming from "colored" to "Negro" to "black" or "Afro-American"? Is this a sign to you of the black man's schizophrenia? Are you outraged by Black Power or fearful of any organization with "black" in its title? What is your source of information about Black Power? Are you upset by natural hair or frightened by black symbols or derisive of Muhammad Ali's change of name in spite of the fact that the change is legal and that some of our most estimable Americans have changed their names? Are you quick to point out that "Negroes are getting ahead," meaning Sidney Poitier, Ralph Bunche, Bill Cosby and some of the other exceptions, while you ignore the overall situation of black people in America? Do you view the "high crime rate" in black communities as indicative of the inferiority, lawlessness or natural criminality of blacks? What of history, or is history to be ignored? Have centuries of systematic exclusion from "upright, law-abiding" society nothing to do with high crime rates? Are you seriously threatened by the least sign that black people intend to assume equal status? Do you justify your negative or cool response to this search with comfortable beliefs that communists, Black Power extremists, radicals, militants and criminals are responsible for this self-assertion?

Behind some answers to these questions lurks the assumption that is basic to racism: black people do not share a common humanity with whites. Few people today would outrightly deny that black people are human beings. Yet so many assume somewhere in the backs of their minds that black people possess a somewhat lesser grade of humanity than white people. They see varying degrees of being human among blacks, but even that "exceptional Negro" whom they love, respect and admire so much still lacks something. "He just cannot measure up completely." And this belief justifies the limitations whites put on even "the best of them."

This assumption is essentially what lies behind the inability of whites to understand what black people are thinking, what they want, and above all, why they want it. Consider how many whites betray themselves with the question, What do Negroes really want? White people do not understand that what black people want is simply the ability, the power, to be and to become themselves. The black man also seeks self-fulfillment to become what God wants him to be. Black people want to enter into American and Church life—political, social and economic; *but not as this life is now, but as it should be*. And they want to share in the revolution. They desire to enter society as black individuals, as a black people, and not as inferior carbon copies of what God never intended them to be. Unlike white America, they have no interest in dominating and exploiting other groups. What they are interested in is an effective share in the total power and the resources of the society.

The "promises" explanation of black people's current dissatisfaction makes a convenient theory to explain away or to place blame for the rising up in black communities all over America in the sixties. It goes: "Many liberals, do-gooders, nuts and, of course, expedient politicians have been stirring up black people by making ridiculous promises which they cannot deliver. When these aroused expectations are unfulfilled, it leads to frustration and anger, causing riots and the like. Moreover, exaggerated promises have resulted in restlessness in the black communities and the even greater demands being made by blacks." Some of the "liberals" responsible for these promises would include people like the Kennedys, the former Johnson-Humphrey team, senators like Charles Percy, governors like Nelson Rockefeller, and mayors like John Lindsay. President Nixon in his campaign echoed the same sentiment. Many people who should know better have fallen in line. Walter Lippmann in a *Newsweek* column* put it this way: "The reaction of the

---

* Walter Lippmann, "Too Great Expectations," *Newsweek*, Jan. 13, 1969.

preponderant mass is against the excessive promises made since a liberal majority came into being in the first part of this century. The critical point was passed when the liberal reformers promised not only the redress of specific grievances but universal and utopian glories." In fairness, Lippmann did not limit this to the black phenomenon.

Of course, it is true that unfulfilled promises can lead to harmful frustrations. However, the position easily becomes dangerous nonsense. Too often, the conclusion is: Do not make excessive promises and they (the blacks) will be satisfied and peaceful with their lot. One is a racist down deep when one assumes that a desire for human dignity, freedom and the ability to pursue happiness arises in black people only when white liberals promise these things to them. To that mind, the black man's longing to be recognized and treated as a man, his desire to have a meaningful part in the society in which he lives, is a result of excessive liberal promises. We have no difficulty understanding these aspirations in white people, but for black people these natural desires must be aroused.

It is crucial that we understand that black people are revolting not against broken promises but a life experience that is damnable. They are demanding change and fighting for change in their life style in America. It is not the promises that are causing the revolution, but the living realities.

3

My Lord, What Have They Done to You?

When Jesus Christ told His disciples, "As the Father sent me, so am I sending you," or, "As you sent me into the world, I have sent them into the world" (John 17:18), He was not just sending them out; He was sending them precisely as the Father had sent Him. So close an identification in spirit and mission between Himself and them did He hope for that He told them, "Anyone who welcomes you, welcomes Me; and those who welcome Me welcome the one who sent Me." When Christ uttered those words, He was not speaking just to those men or for the limited time that He would be with them. This responsibility was to redound in different ways to every individual Christian and to all Christian bodies throughout the ages until His Second Coming. If this is true, then in terms of present realities, this responsibility has been ignored.

When we look at the New Testament, we see a prayerful Christ but one who did not use prayer, solitude, meditation, worship, as excuses for avoiding contact with the real world. We see a Jesus Who cared eminently for human beings, not only with regard to how often and when they prayed or said sweet things, but how they lived, how they treated each other, how they were clothed, where they slept, what and how often they ate—their physical as well as their spiritual health. Moreover, He is conscious and concerned about the conditions of life, what we would call the system, or the institutions that operated in that society. Priority is given to the poor and outcast of that society. He doesn't patronize them but loves them.

He knows when to speak mildly and consolingly, like to Mary Magdalene: ". . . then neither will I condemn you." But, He also speaks openly, harshly and strongly: "Alas for you, Scribes and Pharisees, you hypocrites! You who are like whitewashed tombs that look handsome on the outside, but inside are full of dead men's bones and every kind of corruption. In the same way you appear to people from the outside like good honest men, but inside you are full of hypocrisy and lawlessness." He talks of peace and of forgiveness many times over. But He is also able to say, "Do not suppose that I have come to bring peace to the earth; it is not peace I have come to bring but a sword. For I have come to set a man against his father, a daughter against her mother, a daughter-in-law against her mother-in-law. A man's enemies will be those of his own household."

This Jesus is little bothered about stirring controversy or seeking friendship and popularity with the establishment or people of influence and power. On the
contrary, controversy raged all around Him and about
Him almost from the moment of birth. The establishment and the Romans, and the Scribes and Pharisees, the
Jewish Uncle Toms, hated Him to death. They were
able to stir up His own oppressed people to nail Him to
a cross because they were not ready to run the risks or
pay the price of freedom. He does not have a magic po-
tion that will accomplish His mission overnight without
sacrifice, pain, sweat and blood. His primary concern is
not how high are His taxes or what's happening to His
property values or His interests on investments. His
primary concern is people and their entire well being,
and especially His poor.

His few possessions are a means to ends. He is willing to give all that He has and all that He is, including
His life. He does not limit himself to inane statements
long after issues are decided and events have confirmed
them. He is in the thick of things, consistent with His
principles and statements of belief, letting the chips fall
where they will. This same resurrected and glorified
Jesus has called us individually and collectively to identify with Him so that He can continue this life and mission in our day through us. This is why people today,
Christians and non-Christians, legitimately judge
Christ and Christianity by the individuals and institutions that claim to be Christian.

The poor and the outcast of our American society
are also making that judgment. And they are not neg-
lecting to include the Catholic Church in that judgment.
Black people who represent such a large proportion of
America's poor and outcast are looking at this Catholic
Church. They are doing so with much clearer vision

than they ever had before. They are trying to see whether this Church, in spite of or because of its claims, can be identified with the Jesus of the Gospels, Who now strives to live. They are not concerned primarily with the theology and philosophy of this Church or with the statements of individual Catholics, clerical or lay. Nor are they concerned about the collective statements of the American Catholic bishops of the last twenty or more years. What they are concerned about is the attitudes and behavior of Catholic individuals and how the Catholic Church, as an institution, acts.

The fact is that, by and large, black people, when they look at the Catholic Church, do not see the Jesus of the New Testament. What they see is a white Jesus, who can identify only with white interests and white concerns and activities; a white Jesus who can justify and identify with whatever white people are doing, and who can only condemn what black people are about. They are seeing it this way whether or not white people agree with them, whether white people think they should see it this way or not; whether white people think they are justified or not; and whether white people like it or not.

You know what I mean about this white Christ. From the first moment I entered the Catholic school system, even when it was a Negro Catholic school, every picture we saw of Christ was preeminently white. The only black face in any of our texts was a slave. Our examples came from white America and we applied our principles according to the white experience in America. The very manner of presenting certain doctrines did little for the blacks' self-esteem. Take the doctrine of grace. If you remove it from the context of racism and an environment that says eloquently, "to be black is to be bad and inferior," it might seem childish. Put it in context and you will understand why it did not help as a child to be informed that "sin and evil make our souls *black* while grace makes it *white* and thus pleasing to God." Venial sin puts "little *black* marks on the soul and spoils its *whiteness*. The good child strives to make his soul as *white* as possible." There were many of us who wanted to make our bodies as white as possible so they, too, could be pleasing to God.

In churches full of black faces, every picture, every statue, every stained-glass window, depicted an oh-so-white Christ. And every priest, "Christ living with us," was very white, just as were the white "brides of Christ," the sisters we met daily in the classrooms. The pictures on those ugly Christmas cards which Catholics like to send out, with a priest holding the Eucharist in his hands, are all white. You'd have to look some to find white people in the Catholic Church who have had that experience in reverse.

Then there is the public worship of that white Christ —the liturgy of the Church. It is not only ancient— which is not necessarily a crime—but it is very white. Even with the changes begun as far back as Pius IX and reaching a high point with the advances of Vatican II, the American Church's liturgy is rooted in white culture. It has not been able to identify and take seriously the possibility, much less existence, of a unique, black religious culture. From the responses of both Cardinal John Cody of Chicago and Archbishop Boland of Newark to symbolic offertory dances that took place in their respective dioceses, one would have thought that a desecration had occurred. What the Church shows is that it is at a loss in a black culture. Like Christianity, Catholicism in this country has been, and is, white— culture-white white churches, and white-culture Negro churches. Yet an authentic Christianity, an authentic

Catholicism, would be at home in all cultures, including the black one.

Some of the elements of black religious culture that should be able to find a place in our official liturgy are in the area of Church music. The so-called gospels have largely replaced the Negro spiritual in the "lower-class" black churches. In these churches the spiritual is thought of as from another era. In middle-class black churches, as in some of the daring white churches, the spirituals are pretty much it. Middle-class church people may enjoy Mahalia Jackson or the Ward Singers outside of worship but the thought of using this type of music in the official liturgy is something else. The gospel, an exclusively black religious expression, is evidently unacceptable by middle-class, respectable white Christianity.

Again, the spontaneous response at worship so embedded in black religious culture—the "Amen," the shouts, the "Tell it, brother"—would justify calling the cops in any given Catholic Church on a Sunday. "You'd have to be drunk" to depart from the studied, controlled and signaled responses that mark our liturgy. I know a priest who literally blew up on the pulpit when some lady "answered him back" from the pews.

The rhythmic preaching style so much a part of black religious culture would probably become a major crisis in most Catholic churches; especially in the Negro ones. Yet what Dr. Henry Mitchell, in an article entitled "Black Power and The Christian Church," said is true: "Black preaching proceeds from radically different presuppositions about worship, the gospel and the congregation. It draws on a radically different proportion of such ingredients as poetic imagination, creative telling of folk stories, expression of emotion, personal testimony, and timing considerations or climactic utterance."

The words of Father John Shocklee of St. Louis concerning church architecture are equally true of our liturgy: "The day of hand-me-down churches and hand-me-down religion is over. The black man does not particularly appreciate the Irish architecture of St. Malachy's or the Polish Renaissance architecture of St. Stanislaus. He wants something distinctly his own, not castoffs from fleeing Irish, Polish, Italians or Germans." Our white liturgy also must begin to show that whatever can be identified as black is not necessarily bad or "inferior" or to be tolerated to appease "those people."

This will not be an easy task. If it is now extremely difficult to get Catholic whites just to entertain the notion that the adjective "black" before anybody or anything is not a signal for fright, it may be almost impossible to do so for the great majority of Negro Catholics. Most of them look upon some of the basic elements of black religious culture as distinctly "Protestant" and as contaminating "pure Catholicism."

Recently I officiated at the funeral of a well-known undertaker who had served the Harlem community for years. Her husband asked me to say the Mass at a church near the one I am assigned to. She was a Catholic from the early 1920's and so I knew what types of people the relatives and distinguished friends attending that funeral would be.

You know the price Negroes had to pay for Catholicism in those days. Many of them, and they form the bulk of Negro Catholics today, have not even recognized it and are still happily paying. The price of their Catholicism was to become a reincarnation of a white middle-class American. Not that they would be expected to share the white man's schools, jobs, homes, communities, etc. No, they had to share the white man's view both about himself and Negroes, accept the white man's understanding of the proper relationship between black and white, and participate in a limited way in the white man's culture and white-culture worship.

Once the Negro Catholic could understand this he was forgiven for having black skin and "integrated" into the church. There he would be speaking, singing and thinking white middle-class culture, and confusing it with Christianity. And to make palatable his adoption of a foreign culture, the Negro Catholic called black culture Protestantism and white culture Catholicism.

At that funeral some of the relatives and friends of the deceased got upset with me. After the gospel, I spoke personally about the deceased. One of the wife's cousins began gesturing wildly, trying to shut me up. It wasn't what I was saying: it was the very fact of my speaking. "Catholics do not have sermons at funerals," she explained to a friend of mine later. I was introducing Protestantism into Catholicism.

The point is that Catholicism has so bleached Negro Catholics that many of them today are whiter than white Catholics. It is quite possible that some of the fiercest opposition to a black religious culture in the Catholic Church may come from Negro Catholics that the Church has produced, nourished and promoted.

Everything that black people use belongs to the white Christ and this white Christ doesn't let you forget it. It is this white Christ presented by white Catholics who for centuries has been able to speak to Negroes in terms of our people and your people, our schools and your schools, our churches and your churches, our community and your community.

Most of the churches, schools and hospitals with the word "Catholic" on the outside that are used or occupied by Negroes today were built by white Catholics for white Catholics. Then, when blacks appeared on the scene, the white Christ, after fighting like hell to keep them out, fled and abandoned their buildings to the niggers as one step better than blowing them up. In the cities the abandoned edifices of this white Jesus' love are allowed to die a slow death from lack of upkeep and support.

This was the thing about Archbishop Boland's denial of the undeniable. Like so many bishops, Boland was proud that "Catholics stayed in the inner city of Newark." This can only mean that when the white Christ ran away from the invading niggers, he did not put his buildings—churches, schools, hospitals—in his pocket or put a match to them. No, he was in such a hurry he just left them behind and appointed some "heroic" white lieutenants to keep the niggers from utterly destroying his investments while feigning a response to their needs.

Praising the Church for not fleeing the ghetto can be compared to the praise James E. Vann gave the San Francisco cops for their behavior at a "Free Huey P. Newton" rally. ". . . when the police perform an *outstanding* job, the effort should be acknowledged and the police be given due recognition. One such worthy occasion was the 'Free Huey Newton' rally . . . Though speaker after speaker sprinkled his remarks with uncommon words and bitter condemnations of the system, the uniformed police, though visible, maintained a reasonable distance and confined their peace-keeping func-

tions to directing traffic away from the peaceful rally—
a truly legitimate and useful function of the police in
serving the people."

What is frightening here is that what Mr. Vann
said is true. We have progressed so rapidly that it is
now considered outstanding behavior on the part of our
police that at a peaceful rally, when people criticized
the police and the American system, the police did not
go berserk. On that occasion in San Francisco the police
did not crack any skulls, fire mace at people's faces or
blast tear gas into the crowd. Because the police did not
behave like animals, they were praised for performing
an outstanding job.

So, too, with the archbishop. Because the white
Christ fleeing black people did not take (though part
of the reason is that it is uneconomical) or destroy his
buildings, he is to be praised. The man was pointing
with pride when he should have been crying with self-
disgust.

Getting back to this white Christ, as soon as he gets
to a safe neighborhood, that is, devoid of black people,
he begins again to build buildings with white money for
white people. Then he turns around and says, "Why
should we slave and build our schools and let niggers
into them?" Or in a more generous mood, this Jesus
will tell black folks, in the words of Professor Vincent
Harding of Atlanta University, "Of course some of
your most spiritual (and quiet) people may come to
our churches, and your wealthiest (and cleanest) people
may move into our communities, and your brightest
children may come to our schools. But never forget: I
expect regular hymns of gratitude for our condescension. Always remember that these communities,
schools, churches, whatever they might be, belong to
white people."

When he gets extremely generous, this white Christ will send a few pennies back to the ghetto from which he fled to keep his abandoned buildings in existence and one-quarter functioning. This will enable him to speak about all that he is doing for black people. Moreover, it will let him feel he owes no apology for his relationship with black people and allow him to get up in public to remind the people of the inner city that "other areas of his archdiocese also have needs." Not only is this Jesus white in appearance, in his worship and in his possessions, but his theology is also white. Thus, he has little difficulty in justifying whatever white people are doing or constraining black people to do for them. On the other hand, his white theology cannot understand what black people are doing. More often, if it doesn't remain silent, it can only condemn whatever black people are about so long as it's not initiated, directed and controlled by white people.

I spoke not long ago on the subject of black theology. Of course, as soon as you put black before anything that is not already taken as bad, like "black sheep" or "blackmail," it is immediately suspect, if not rejected. My remarks had scarcely ended when a priest told me that he had a "great deal of difficulty even listening to me." "The title alone," he said, " 'black theology,' was a misnomer." Then he went on to say that "theology is only one and there is no such thing as black or white theology."

No one seems to get too excited about such expressions as French theology, German theology, Spanish theology, etc., and the real differences they represent. But put "black" in front of anything and one loses perspective, training and everything else, including one's mind. We have been dealing with white theology all our lives, but we are simply not honest enough to admit that fact, so we call our white theology, simply, "theology." The situation is comparable to our using a euphemism for white history or white distortion of history. We call it American History, and many people take the name seriously. But as soon as black students start talking about the need for "black history," folks yell, "shame," and "separatist nonsense." In the meantime, from grade school to the universities we go on teaching white history and calling it American History.

This priest, I assume, had sense and education enough to realize that theology is not something static, handed down from on high completely and uniformly, to remain forever the same. Christian theology is always evolving precisely because it involves understanding and appreciation of the Christian message in the light of and through the experiences of people. All theology arises from individuals and especially communal experience with God. In the light of this exclusive preoccupation of Catholic theology with the white communal experience—hopefully with God—a black theology is necessary. At this moment in time, we need a theology that speaks in language understandable to black people and not couched in terms formed by and biased in favor of the white experience. There is need of a theology that arises out of the black communal experience with God and the expression of that experience. And it must be expressed in language that speaks relevantly to and of the contemporary mood and acts of black people. This is what "Black Theology" is all about.

I stirred up a hornets' nest the night I spoke of the need of a black theology that will explain what black people are presently engaged in. "Not just the good, national Negro leaders white people have made, nor the safe moderate and responsible Negro organizations white people support and control," I said, "but a theology that can justify what the Black Panthers are doing and all those black extremists, radicals and militants, whom white folks so generously identify for us." Not that a theology would justify them, I pointed out. Rather, it would explain and expose the justification by which they were already justified, rather than the policeman who could shoot and kill a fourteen-year-old "looter" in the back while he was running away. Or rather than the judge who would impose a hundred-thousand-dollar bail that would hold twenty-one members of the Black Panther party under circumstances that violated most of their constitutional rights, and even the requirements of international agreement for the treatment of prisoners of war, because of an alleged plot to blow up department stores for which little evidence has yet come forth. Rather than a police officer who could be held in five hundred dollars bail for killing a black girl.

Well, nuns, priests, lay people, all began to object. They spoke about "objectivity" and "impartiality." "How can a theology that seeks to justify anything from the start be impartial; and if it is not impartial, how can it be objective and true to its name?" one priest asked. I pointed out the distinction I had made earlier between justifying and exposing a justification. Then, I started to laugh. It was only a week after the New York archdiocese, of which I am a member, had issued its response to the *Black Manifesto*. They knew in advance they were going to condemn it, refuse to give any money, and deny James Forman permission to see the cardinal. Having made those decisions on the basis of other priorities, they went seeking after theological and philosophical reasons to support them. It was a good example of white theologizing in practice. It took a long time that evening before it began to dawn on some people that the kind of impartial theology we have actually been dealing with was the sort that had adjusted Catholic consciences to the expediency of the slave system by arguing, "The Christianizing influence that slavery afforded was sufficient justification for Negro enslavement." No doubt, the "Christianizing influence" was the joy of being brutalized and enslaved by white Christians rather than by white pagans.

It was an impartial theology which justified the Jesuits' keeping of slaves because they were "nice to them." It was an impartial theology which "questioned" or denied outright that Negroes had souls. This enabled white Christians, including priests, to treat blacks as subhuman, so that Cardinal Herbert Vaughan in 1876 remarked in amazement after touring Memphis, "Negroes are regarded even by priests as so many dogs." It was an impartial theology that could look upon the massacre and plunder of the American Indians as "advancing the frontier of civilization" and defended it. Today, it is that same impartial theology that allows Cardinal Terence Cooke, as military vicar of the United States, to go to Vietnam and praise and shake hands with some of the cream of America's young black manhood for killing and destroying men, women and children and homes and even that most sacred of things known to Catholics—private property— "on behalf of freedom and liberty and justice," and then return home to allow St. Patrick's Cathedral to be filled with New York's nonviolent cops lest anyone from the Black Economic Development Conference interrupt a "religious" service.

Nothing brings out better the impartiality and objectivity of this white Catholic theology today than our reaction to the Johnny-come-lately phenomenon of black violence in our cities. It partially explains why American Catholic prelates and bishops and priests can counsel love and forgiveness for white oppressors and enslavers of black people here and at the same time approve or counsel flaming death for the North Vietnamese. It explains the inappropriateness of the majority of American Catholic responses to violence—supporting it in Vietnam, and condemning it in America when used by blacks.

In a talk in Indianapolis one evening, I spoke, as I have done many times, on what I called "responsible Christian violence." A nun stood up and said what I have heard from inner-city priests in Indianapolis and from Catholic audiences all over: "I am very sympathetic with those goals," she said, "but I just can't see this violence. It is so un-Christian and accomplishes nothing. It just bothers me."

Violence, of course, may bother her but it has really never bothered the majority of Catholics any more than it has other Christians. Like our Old Testament forebears, we have always been engaged in violence. White Catholics participated in, and their religious leaders defended and reaped the benefits of, the "lawlessness," "criminality" and violence of the American Revolution. Catholics were among the American Christians who bought and abducted blacks from Africa, brought them here by violent means and maintained them in inhuman slavery by violence. It took a violent Civil War to break the back of this one kind of slavery in some sections of our country. And the Church accommodated itself nicely to the violence of the post–Civil War enslavement of black people. The Church in America, as in other countries, has consistently refused to come to terms with social revolution—except where its own people are concerned—and has sided often with the violence of the oppressors in the name of law and order, thus losing in the process its authority to proclaim the Gospel for large segments of the nation.

That is why white Catholics can defend and be a part of America's response to the social conditions that are detailed in the Kerner Report; in the elections of Nixon and Agnew, Reagan and Yorty and Stenvig. That is why they can support the building of more sophisticated weapons of destruction with which to arm more policemen and more national guardsmen. That is why they can rush through more laws to give their "defenders of law and order" the right to violate more human rights of black folks in order to keep them in their place. That is why Mr. Nixon can "reform" the Supreme Court and we can stand for it; that is why we put up with J. Edgar Hoover's particular uses of the nation's largest law enforcement agency, which is powerless to defend blacks against the outrages and killings of white policemen but is great at busting up Black Panther groups and was good at bugging the telephones of Martin Luther King, Jr.

Irish Catholics who have been among the most violent people to hit our shores are interesting in this regard. Now that present generations are in a position to reap the rewards of their parents' and grandparents' violence, they've suddenly become very nonviolent. That is, they are nonviolent, except when Irish policemen are dealing with nigger lawbreakers, or some of them are defending their neighborhoods in Yonkers, New York, or Detroit, Michigan, or stoning radical Father James Groppi in Milwaukee or writing "love notes" to myself and to Father George Clements of Chicago when he was made a pastor.

When the plight of the Catholics in Northern Ireland became unbearable and bloody rioting took place in Ulster recently, American Irish Catholics here showed great flexibility. "Of course, the situation there is much different from the black/white situation in America," they told me. What that difference was they never explained. All I learned was that the years of quite open discrimination against six to seven hundred thousand Irish Roman Catholics in Ulster in housing, employment, cultural, political and civic affairs, justified bloody rebellion that involved looting, destruction, attacks on the police, and fire bombing. But for some reason, hundreds of years of oppression, lynchings, the worst kind of slavery man has known, injustice in the courts, and continued repression along with stiffening white resistance to change—all of these do not justify the black man in America for taking other than his traditional peaceful measures.

Irish Catholics well understood the appeal of Cardinal William Conway of Armagh to the Ulster government "not to make the mistake of seeing recent happenings in purely political terms. . . . The immediate causes of these outbreaks," he stressed, "were social; they had grown out of the frustration of ordinary people who wanted housing, jobs and fair representation." Yet it's very difficult for the American hierarchy and American Irish Catholics to stomach the Kerner Report or Eldridge Cleaver when he says the same things about black Americans.

When white Catholics say they cannot understand black violence, they are right, of course. For over two hundred years black people have been the most nonviolent group this country has ever known. Moreover, they have always been on the receiving end of violence. For most of them that's the way it's been and is supposed to be. When it comes to it, white Catholics cannot support black violence. They have always been able to support black violence when white people have organized, legitimatized, controlled and directed it for their own interests. That is why white folks make killers and destroyers out of black boys, dress them in uniforms, give them a flag and say, "Go thousands of miles away from home and fight and kill and destroy for freedom." "We'll be proud of you," they say. "We will give you medals and call you heroes. It may not get you and your children better living conditions, better education, better jobs and respect back home, but, then, you have to be patient and—above all—nonviolent. We will tell you when you are going too fast and when we think you may aspire to attain the recognition of your human dignity.

"And remember, nigger, if you try any of this stuff back home or use any of the techniques we've taught you, and put any confidence in the bombs and gases and bullets in which we place our ultimate hope, in order to emancipate yourselves from our oppression, we will crush you. It is for white folks to tell black folks when they are to be emancipated. And if you forget it, we will destroy you. In the name of law and order and peace."

That is why my archbishop is in Vietnam at Christmas. He shakes hands with all those black men trained to be killers by white folks *for* white folks. After all, they are represented in our armed forces—except the home forces like police and sheriffs and national guardsmen—way out of proportion. They are dying in Vietnam out of proportion. That's where white people want our young black manhood—in Vietnam getting maimed and killed for white security and white power and white wealth. In fact, white people still do not believe there are enough black folks getting killed. The army is in the midst of a drive for more. They will make two or three more black generals with soft or public relations jobs and no commands, promote some more Negroes to minor positions, and hope this will bring black boys running to be killed.

I question any black man in service who does not have to be there. I am wondering why more have not chosen to sit in jails rather than to be shot in the mud. You tell me that many of these black men are in service because they want to be. Opportunities for advancement and conditions of life are better for black people in service than they are back home. You point out that they can achieve some measure of self-respect and recognition of their dignity and worth.

Apart from the opportunities to be wounded or killed, to be confronted with the reality of human brutality at its worst, conditions are generally considered better for blacks in service. This belief is very questionable considering the April 1969 report of an ad hoc committee set up to investigate the treatment of black marines at Camp Lejeune in North Carolina. "Many white officers and non-commissioned officers," it said in part, "retain prejudices and deliberately practice them. The most numerous manifestations lie in the racial stories, jokes, and references to and about blacks and black marines. The result is obvious when made within the hearing of black marines." The committee made particular note of the behavior of the military police toward blacks at the marine camp. Three months later a bloody battle broke out at Camp Lejeune involving blacks and Puerto Ricans against whites in which one white marine was killed. Men I know returning from Vietnam tell me racial conflicts among our troops are taking place there far more frequently than reported.

Even if conditions in service are generally better

for blacks than they are at home, blacks must realize that it is the man who creates and sustains the situation that makes it "better" for them in service. By his oppression of them at home and the conditions under which they are forced to exist in America, and by his draft boards run until recently by General Hershey who in his law-abiding way refused to implement the law of the land, the man forces or cajoles black men into the service. Some may think they are volunteering, but it's the man who is dragging and pushing them right up there in front of those bullets.

Cardinal Cooke, representing not only the military, but so many American bishops and lay Catholics and nuns and priests "who cannot understand this violence bit," is in Vietnam shaking hands with all those black men and boys. For killing every Communist oppressor in sight, for destroying everything they can, including women, children, homes and entire villages, they were heroes. He told them they were fighting for freedom and "we are proud of them." As expected, no one told them whose freedom they were fighting for. The cardinal came home and talked about law and order, and no need for confrontation, and about brotherhood and love and peace. The former heroes in Vietnam fighting for human liberty and freedom at home suddenly became militants, extremists, criminals and hoodlums and irresponsible. And as the white folks' nonviolent army, and national guard, police and deputized game wardens and red necks of all description come out to crush those criminals, you can be certain they will have the full support of masses of Catholics.

Talking at Essex Catholic High School in New Jersey, I reminded the audience that we did have theological and philosophical principles in the light of which we might consider the moral implications of violence. I pointed out the principles we all learned in theology concerning the moral guilt of acts done under the influence of violent passion and how this guilt is to be judged primarily in terms of the causes that lead to passionate outburst. It would be interesting to see these principles rather than just our emotions applied to the outrage, anger and frustration that has erupted into violence in our cities. Apply them in the light of the conditions described in the Kerner Report and see to what conclusions they lead concerning where the greater responsibility and guilt for this type of black violence lie.

As to deliberate, planned, voluntary acts of violence, Catholic theological and philosophical tradition has for centuries taught and developed the concepts of the "just war" and legitimate self-defense.* The Church has been slow to apply this concept to social revolution. It would certainly be more honest and fruitful to judge black violence in the light of these principles than in the context of white emotions and interests. They are not mentioned when one is dealing with the

---

* By just-war doctrine, I am referring to that body of norms produced by Christian philosophers and theologians over the course of about a thousand years, from Saint Augustine in the fourth century to Francisco de Vitoria, a Dominican theologian at the University of Salamanca, in the sixteenth century. It was designed not to promote warfare and violence among men, which is as old as man himself, but to confine and control warfare among Christian peoples.

It states that all these conditions must be verified before warfare can be morally engaged in: (1) war must be declared by legitimate public authority; (2) a real injury must have been suffered and the damage likely to be incurred by the war should not exceed that injury; (3) all possible peaceful settlements must have failed; (4) there must be reasonable hope of success; (5) only moral means may be employed in prosecuting the war; (6) innocent life may not be taken directly and intentionally.

The principle of legitimate self-defense can be stated: The innocent party confronting an unjust aggressor is possessed of the prior right morally. He is permitted to make use of all appropriate, necessary, and proportionate means in order to defend himself and those who rightly depend on him for protection and to ward off any grave damage.

long and continuing history of white violence especially against black people. If it's white, it's right.

This is one of the realities of our life that Americans have yet to face. No nation with our history of violence can escape the consequences of how it was conceived, was born and grew. Whatever stood in the way of wealth and power had to be removed; it was, and is, as violent as conditions demand. At the present time, whatever seems to threaten the power and wealth of the white majority is dealt with as the need demands.

But whatever America does, no matter how brutal, it is assumed to be responsible and moral. If this nation does it, it's moral; if white people do it, it's moral. In the past these assumptions worked beautifully. The vicious robbery, then extermination, of the American Indian was called "extending the frontier of civilization," or Manifest Destiny. Today the brutal and fascist suppression of legitimately sought rights under the guise of "law and order" is justified. And in all this, we can be certain of the support of the Church and the churches or, at least, their silence.

When I asked white Catholics to judge black violence in terms of their religious principles, one administrator of a Catholic high school (in which a large majority of the student and faculty voted for George Wallace in a mock election prior to the last presidential election) accused me of "condoning violence." On another occasion, a man charged me with "encouraging criminals on the streets." One person, in reference to one of my articles on the same subject, asked me, why not a theology of rape, of incest, of murder and of robbery?

There has always been a minority view in Catholic and Christian theology that condemns all violence. Early Christian writers such as Origen, Tertullian, and

Lactantius questioned the validity of the just-war doctrine and asserted unconditional pacifism was the only proper Christian stance. This view has always been a minority opinion. The weight of the Christian (and Catholic) tradition has been a conscientious attempt to reconcile the Christian imperative of love and forbearance with recurring violent conflict. The Old Testament is filled with violent incidents in which people believed not only that they acted according to God's will but that God played a positive role in behalf of His people. In the New Testament, Christ does not forbid us to resist unjust attack in due measure, still less does He forbid us to strive to eliminate injustice from the world. He forbids us to resist injustice by returning evil for evil in the manner of the Jewish law of talion (an eye for an eye, a tooth for a tooth). Christ Himself spoke approvingly of violence, as in Matthew 10:34, and acted in a violent way on at least two recorded occasions: the cursing of the fig tree and His rage over the money changers in the temple. In fact, it may be argued that Jesus' pacific behavior (and that of the immediate post-Resurrection church) rested on the fact that He expected God to be violent *soon*, hence there was no need for Jesus to be.

When I advocated a theology of responsible violence, I meant continuing the process of applying and developing theology in terms of the exigencies of the black situation and social revolution. The divine or theoretical equality of all men—which we preach—is a revolutionary concept. "The spirit of rebellion," Albert Camus wrote, "exists only in a society where theoretical equality conceals great factual inequalities." There is a need for Christians, who have been among the world's most violent groups of people, to be violent more reasonably and with integrity. We do not have to ask questions like "What would Jesus do?" or "What would we have done if we had been Jesus?" Rather we should be asking, What does Christ want us to do here and now?

Therefore, when I ask white Catholics to look at black violence in terms of their theological and philosophical principles, I am asking them to stop turning theology into a vehicle of support for white exploitation and oppression. This is why any white person, including Catholic nuns, bishops, priests and lay people talking to black people about nonviolence, makes me sick. They should be upset about violence, but particularly about white violence. They have a whole lot of teaching to do about nonviolence, and it should be directed to white people. They have already misled too many Negroes on that score. One of their major tasks is to teach, exhort, and motivate white people to stop making the use of violence necessary for black people. In America, the Word of God has been ignored, distorted and adapted until it has been made into a crutch to support a racism that sees Negroes as a race accursed, destined until the end of time to be the servants of their white masters. A theology that has allowed white people to demean and dehumanize black people has also allowed whites to demean and dehumanize themselves even more.

From my earliest experiences in the Catholic Church, the virtues drummed into me in school, convert classes, etc., were nonviolence, obedience, humility, love, patience, forgiveness of enemies, long-suffering and hope in a future reward, but not in this life. Rarely did I hear about the other virtues of self-esteem, pride, gratitude to God for what we are (rather than gratitude for the ability to become, if not white, then gray or colored), legitimate self-defense, just anger, liberty and freedom, the right to share in Our Father's earthly goods in this life.

It became clear that the humility, obedience, love and forgiveness that black people were supposed to practice were to be geared primarily toward white people. Moreover, the white man gave no indication that he felt these black virtues—nonviolence, patience, long-suffering, humility—were equally applicable to himself. In the white Catholic churches, there is no insinuation that white Catholics are bound to test these virtues in their relationship with black people. It is no wonder today that black people see white theology as a way of manipulating black men in the name of Christian truth. The black man has watched the white Catholic missionary come into his land or his ghetto, Bible in hand, preaching the virtues of humility, obedience, etc. After him came the white Christian, and often Catholic, conqueror, gun in hand, to take his land and exploit his labor and demean his person.

The Church, therefore, must have black theology if it is to provide a faith capable of giving meaning and guidance to black life. It must explain the mysteries of black life not in terms of slavery, inequality and patronization, but in terms of freedom, equality and dignity. In the face of white oppression this theology has got to be a theology of black liberation. It must see the black condition in the light of God's revelation in Jesus Christ so that the black community will be able to see that the gospel is at home with black humanity, and that it can help the white community to see it too. This theology must help whites to see how they have demeaned and dehumanized themselves in demeaning and dehumanizing blacks, and encourage them to live by the beautiful ideals they mouth. In helping to emancipate black people from white racism, black theology will provide authentic freedom for both black and white.

It is not hard to gather from the New Testament that Jesus Christ gave special priority to the poor, to those who were looked upon as weak and perhaps whom some would consider bothersome. He shocked the "deeply religious" by allowing Himself to be touched and handled by an adultress and was openly criticized for consorting and dining with sinners. The only recorded instance of His being in the governor's house was not by invitation, or to cover corruption with the mantle of religion, but when He was brought there for trial. Jesus would not have been caught dead with the establishment. He was at home with those whom the establishment despised.

The Christ or proxy for Christ that we find in the American Catholic Church seems to be something else. Its religious leaders would not be found dead with the people He spent time with. The poor get a quick look at their spiritual leader in their own neighborhoods only on special occasions and accompanied by newspaper and television reporters. How many ordinaries, bishops or cardinals have ever walked through a poor neighborhood, especially a black "ghetto," much less have been familiar with its inhabitants? Our bishops will never have to fear the "better" people accusing them of consorting with and dining with sinners. They are just too respectable and above that. They are rarely on the outs with the establishment; in fact, they are among its chief supporters.

Basically, Lord, this white Catholic Church has switched Your priorities. Its priorities lie in a different direction from where we found Yours in the New Testament. That is a problem and a serious one.

Black people realize that when, for example, President Nixon makes important decisions, he may look at all the angles, all the factors and all the varying interests. Yet, when the decision must be made, the interest that takes precedence over all others is that of white, affluent people. Other interests are only secondary and only God knows where the interests of black people would figure in. When black people look at the American Catholic Church they see the same set of priorities —the interests of white people with money. By and large our bishops are not leaders (and certainly not religious leaders). They reflect their constituency. This constituency is overwhelmingly white and predominantly conservative and middle class. Moreover, since they surround themselves with secretaries and advisors whose priorities are "protect the bishop"—meaning keep bad or disturbing news from him no matter how true or urgent—and "let nothing be said or done which embarrasses the bishop," the problem is compounded.

Wealthy people, members of religious communities and especially pastors, have always realized where the priorities are. Take the New York archdiocese as a typical example. For years, pastors and any priest who aspired to the glorious title of monsignor knew all they had to do was build something. The catch was that in the long run it could not cost the archdiocese anything. In fact, a good chance to make "Right Reverend Monsignor," the higher degree of monsignor at that time, was that the archdiocese make money from the investment. So pastors, especially, and even non-pastors built. They built cathedrals in parishes that needed chapels. And, since money was the key, most of the buildings were in areas that could afford to be taxed. There were

exceptions to the general rule, like the St. Charles Borromeo School in Harlem. After eleven years of bussing
the children of that parish to a dilapidated second
building at St. Joseph's parish, the late Monsignor Cor-
nelius Drew collected what he could from the poor and
from better-off personal friends, and the archdiocese
made a significant contribution to the school.

The general rule, however, was building not where
the need was the greatest but where the money was the
mostest. More affluent parishes sharing their abundance
with poorer parishes is not yet a widespread practice.
The wealthier parishes want to build up bank interest
for a rainy day. Meanwhile, it's raining like hell outside.
Pastors and non-pastors built like crazy for people who
could pay, i.e., for white people. And monsignors of all
ranks, depending on what they built, were a dime a
dozen. The Archbishop of Indianapolis once greeted a
delegation of Catholics from the Catholic Interracial
Council with these words: "There you go, always devi-
sing ways of spending other people's money. You
should be out making converts." They had come to ask
him to review archdiocesan building policy on the basis
of need.

Our present school system—or whatever will soon
be left of it—is another good example of our priority
system. I remember speaking to a monsignor friend of
mine, a professor of moral theology at New York's
major seminary. I had suggested on a radio program
that one of the real contributions the Church could
make to black people is in the area in which it has had
some experience and success—education. I said that the
only place where our separate school system would be
justified today is in poor neighborhoods, especially in
black ghettos, where the public *school* is school in name
only.

The monsignor thought it was impractical of me to say that the parochial schools in Harlem should be opened to all in the community regardless of religious affiliation, that more should be built in those areas and there is where our greatest resources should be directed. "The Archdiocese," he said, "is already subsidizing most of those schools and we simply cannot afford it." He went on to tell me about the struggle his brother-in-law had to keep his children in parochial schools. The family is making that sacrifice because they think the spiritual training to be found in the parochial schools is extremely important. "If it were only the secular education," he said, "the kids would do better in the public schools, where what is available through federal and state support cannot be had in the Catholic schools. Therefore," he asked, "how would my brother-in-law feel if we closed his kids' school and asked him to pay to provide for children in Harlem what his own are denied? After all, his primary responsibility is toward *his* children."

His thoughts were certainly more intelligently stated than those of a lady who recently wrote me: "Why should we let the niggers into our [Catholic] schools when all of us cannot get in?" The monsignor's argument makes very good sense if one accepts the assumptions and priorities behind it. In the first place, it was assumed that what was being suggested was to close a school here and there and send the money saved to the slums. In fact, I was suggesting that the Church get out of at least grade schools completely, *except* in the poor areas. That the Church should commit herself to the running of the finest schools for the neglected poor.

A second assumption is that the parochial school system as we know it is desirable and necessary today.

This is at the least open to question. Certainly the historical reason for a separate school system, the bigotry of Protestant America, has not been a major factor for some time. And it is not evident that the theological reason that the school would share in the overall mission of the Church to bring the knowledge and love of our Father through Christ to all men is understood, desired or achieved. The monsignor's position assumes that the parochial school is the only way or the best way or even a good way of providing for the spiritual, moral and religious upbringing of children. This is questionable. For one thing, it is not very evident that our schools have been inculcating the Christian values as we so readily assume they are doing. It is not clearly evident that these schools have been helping children to form Christian consciences or to mature in the process. I am still running into cases where a child's ability to think and to ask serious or difficult questions frequently brands him as a "troublemaker."

When we consider the attitudes of our products of Catholic education on such matters as poverty and race, we have reason to wonder about what we really are doing. Studies like "The Notre Dame Study of Catholic Elementary and Secondary Schools in the United States" and plain experience have indicated that on these questions, the attitudes of Catholics do not differ from their fellow Americans. The adaptation has been perfect. Catholics are one-hundred-percent American. In fact, many times in the inner cities and largely Catholic surburban areas, the behavior and attitudes of Catholics are worse than those of other Americans. Even if our educational system were imparting these Christian values, there is no reason to assume that we must also be teaching English, arithmetic and spelling in order to do so.

Moreover, preoccupation with the parish school, tied to a restricted understanding of what the parish is, has had negative effects. The first is the almost complete neglect of the religious education of children and teenagers who do not attend the Catholic schools. This fact is better focused when we realize that the great majority of Catholic children are in the public school system. A second effect of this preoccupation is an almost total lack, in most dioceses, of adult religious education. At the present time we are paying the price in so many ways of sending forth generations of Catholics to live mature adult religious lives with a grade-school-level, or less, understanding of religion. When we consider how quick these schools are to throw out "troublemakers" and how anxious we are to make sin impossible rather than to prepare the child to make rational Christian choices, it becomes clear that we have sent out many without any Christian perception.

Our present parochial school system predominantly serves middle-class white Catholics and, as a side line, some of the better-off Negro Catholics. We may question whether the system is answering real needs even in regard to secular education, not to speak of religious ones. It is doubtful whether middle-class whites, who are carrying a disproportionate share of our tax burden but who also contribute greatly to the circumstances that drain them, can or will continue to afford the luxury of the Catholic school.

A ludicrous example of our priorities was in the dual action of the United States Catholic bishops in 1968. At the same time they were allocating forty-two thousand dollars for a National Urban Task Force to deal with urban social problems, they were earmarking one million dollars for the important study on rhythm by Washington, D.C.'s Cardinal O'Boyle.

In my own personal experience, I have to admit painfully that institutional Catholicism has been more concerned with not offending bigoted white Catholics than serving the religious, or any other, needs of black people, Catholic or non-Catholic. When bigoted white Catholics have money, black folks don't stand a chance. Whenever white bigotry challenges our ideals, our words or values in terms of the black man, it is always the black man who must be "patient and understanding" and who must be sacrificed before the altar of white bigotry. That is why my brothers and I were not able to start in the parochial school across the street from where we lived in Harlem. That may be why my brother Alvin is not a priest today; they were not taking colored. That is why I had to leave a parish at Croton Falls; they did not admit blacks at one of the missions. That is why never more than sixteen Catholic papers carried *The Black Voice* and why *The Clarion Herald*, Portland's *Catholic Sentinel*, and Buffalo's *The Magnificat* canceled it in less than a year. That is what held up any real integration of the Catholic school system when that was relevant. That is why bishops like Cooke of New York and Cody of Chicago make appointments of black people, even for black people, on the basis of how they please white people. The overriding, inbred assumption is that the white man, even when a bigot, and especially when he has money, must be satisfied or at least not displeased at any cost.

Sometimes we may even sacrifice our God—money —to achieve that end. Take the case of the gym and community center building at Blessed Sacrament, a black parish in New Orleans. Clarence Broux, a black contractor, drew up plans with other men who were professionals in the business. They estimated a cost of thirty thousand dollars since they were going to contribute the labor gratis.

John Cody, now Cardinal of Chicago, then Archbishop of New Orleans, said no. Archdiocesan contractors—white of course—had to do the job. They estimated fifty thousand dollars. The job, now referred to by the parishioners as a white elephant, actually cost one hundred and sixteen thousand dollars.

One of the best examples of how the Church's priorities work out is the Negro Catholic. By the time he has satisfied the man and been given a "responsible" position, he has learned his lesson well. I know several of the most "objective" people in the world. Man, do they look on all sides of any black/white issue. Looking at all sides is fine. What they don't realize is that after seeing all sides, all sides do not have equal value or force. Black interests are way down the line. In some cases, things are so bad that Negro Catholics are ashamed to even come together by themselves. Everything they say, everything they do, becomes valid or legitimate in terms of how their white friends will feel, what they will think and how they will react. Concerns like how relevant is this or that to black people, or how will black people feel or what will they think or how will they react, do not enter into their minds. When they do, they are not very high on the scale.

Yes, Lord, white Catholics have not only twisted Your priorities, they have trained Negro Catholics to go and do likewise. They have made You completely white in Your appearance, Your thinking, Your interests and Your concerns.

4

My Lord, What Have They Done to Themselves?

Part of the problem lies in the historical inability and lack of desire on the part of the Church to identify with black people in the context of the American environment. It has always been inclined to use the psycho-social reality of race relations in this country, especially in the South, to justify its lack of leadership in attempting to change the system. At best, the Church as a whole accommodates itself to the American racist system, taking some token steps within it, but always within and part of it.

In this country Catholicism is the product of immigrant groups who had been Catholics for centuries.

Following the French, there were the waves of Irish, German, Italian and Polish immigrations. When these groups arrived they brought their Church and their priests, as part of their baggage. When the Irish were wrecking the French ecclesiastical structure in America, when they were fighting, demanding and favoring their own kind—as they still do—their priests, who in rural Ireland consolidated a national consciousness which obliterated any distinction between church and country, provided the leadership of the American Church. When the Irish were tearing up the cities in America, their Irish priests were not preaching patience, law and order, and nonviolence.

As Irishmen they understood oppression and the need to throw it off. The same was true to some extent of other groups. The Catholic Church in America could be Irish, German, Polish, Italian, but never black. When these groups were oppressed and were trying to redress their grievances, real or imagined, their clergy and their Church never distinguished between "them" and "us." It was not "theology" that determined the Church's involvement but the historical, cultural, sociological and, especially, ethnic factors involved. The black man in the Catholic Church has never had these things going for him. Whereas, for example, the Irish and the Church relationship was simply, "we," with the black man it has always been "us" and "them."

A great deal of the American Church's problem lies with its Irishness. It is often difficult if not impossible in the Church to distinguish between what is to be "Catholic" and what is to be "Irish." One need but look at the American Catholic hierarchy to see a fairly good ethnic picture of the American Catholic Church. Wakin and Scheuer in their book *The De-Romanization of the American Catholic Church* wrote:

Cardinal Spellman is a child of the American Church, whose sons brought their dreams and their faith to the new world and watched many of the dreams come true and the faith flourish. It was a faith that they transplanted in their distinctive style, mixing nationality and religion. Each did this: The English, French, Irish, Germans, Italians, Spanish, Scandinavians, Polish, Czechoslovaks, Bulgarians, Lithuanians, Lebanese, Greeks, and many more. But it was the Irish who imposed the dominant ethnic brand. More than anything else this side of eternity, American Catholicism comprises a Church of immigrants, with its lingering accent a brogue . . .

The point is that many of the attitudes that I am discussing here are very strong among Irish Americans, who have pressed their image on the American Catholic Church, and among other ethnic groups that are normally Catholic. In certain areas these attitudes connected with ethnic groups traditionally Catholic can be devastating.

The police departments in many large Northern cities, for example, are often heavily peopled by Irish and other Catholics. Many city riots have been sparked by the behavior of Catholic police. Instead of challenging and condemning such attitudes and actions, the Church supports and reinforces them by its silence or encouragement.

In the areas of education and communication, the Church supports racism. This is very important because modern oppressive societies have found in their police and military forces, the communication media and educational system, some of their primary mechanisms for control. Police, media, and educational system play an important role in our society's oppression of black people. The Church's own communication and educational systems and its supportive role of our police and military forces are strong testimony of its attitude.

In one of the numerous "crackdowns on dope pushers," the police had arrested several "junkies" in the inner city. After which I suggested at a meeting that I could take society's concern more seriously if along with police activity there was an effort to change conditions that prompt people to seek an "out" through narcotics. Moreover, I considered law enforcement procedure which consists of arresting a few "junkies" in Harlem, or the Martindale section of Indianapolis, as a cruel joke. It would be far more to the point to crack down on those responsible for producing and bringing in the stuff. These are usually respected and wealthy inhabitants of much different and very segregated neighborhoods who can pay off the right people to remain in operation.

Well, I was saying this when up jumped a gentleman who later identified himself as a policeman. To much applause he informed me that talk like that was simply providing excuses for criminals and encouraging them. "These people," he proceeded to tell me, "are preying on your people." He was right about who are the chief victims of inner-city crimes. What he could not and did not want to see was that worse criminals living outside the black communities are preying on poor people, especially poor black people, and are responsible for the criminals who live in these areas.

A white, Irish Catholic police officer related to a close friend of mine was home for a family affair a while ago. They got around to the race issue. This side of the family seldom discusses it in my presence. Good Irish Catholics do not hurt the feelings of priests nor do they insult them except when absolutely necessary. Well, my friend got upset over some of the policeman's attitudes and challenged him. The policeman insisted that he agreed with the goals of black people but was dismayed by the "criminality of black people." He then backed up his position with quotes and half-quotes from the crime statistics published frequently by the F.B.I. Quoting from the head of the federal bureau, he spoke about the "high rate of crime in the Negro ghettos," crime on the subways and in the streets, all attributed to blacks. He talked about what "these criminals needed," "and how they should be handled." He could hardly wait to meet one of them on the subway. "Their goals, even though just, simply do not justify all this ignoring of law and criminal activity."

This is a young, Irish Catholic policeman in New York City speaking. In this there is a great deal of irony. The man does not suspect that the only reason an Irish Catholic is on the police force in New York today is because of the "criminality" of his grandfather and great-grandfather. It was less than one hundred years ago that New York City streets, like those of many other cities, were the arena of daily battles. There were bloody battles between Irish Catholics and the New York City police. Black people, in their wildest episodes, haven't even begun to approach the kind of thing that was typical of the fighting Irish. It is only now that the Irish have taken over the New York City Police Department that they can forget the past.

In any case, this whole thing about crime and criminality is a very tricky business, because a great deal depends on who is defining the terms and applying the labels. In August 1968, when David Dellinger was a leader of the demonstration in Chicago during the Democratic Convention, the media frequently referred to him as a "left-wing agitator and aging hippie." However, a year later when he was negotiating the release of American fliers held by Hanoi, the same media referred to him as a "prominent American peace worker" and a "leading U.S. pacifist." Our definition and understanding of criminality has a tendency to shift somewhat, depending on what side of the fence we are on. People who are fighting to throw off oppression cannot possibly see the same situation in the same light as their oppressors. When we were doing things to escape the oppression of England, the British were talking a lot about "criminals," and "crimes against the society" and "law and order." We were talking about the same people and things in terms of "patriots," of "blows for freedom and liberty" and "order of justice and right to be created."

In the beginning of the workers' struggle, for example, nearly everything that was done was "criminal." In fact, criminal activity is not completely absent in labor disputes today. The labor people were, from their point of view, engaging in a battle for just wages and humane working conditions. The Irish when they fought pitched battles with the police and other agencies were labeled criminal, lazy, and opposers of law and order. They ignored the oppressors' labels and conceived themselves as heroes in the struggle against oppression. These groups won their struggles. Often what makes the difference between criminal and noncriminal acts is the fact of winning or losing. White Catholic people, including Irish Catholic cops, must begin to accept that those who participate in the black man's freedom struggle are no more criminals than their white ancestors who fought for their own freedom. Sensible black people already understand that any attempt by the powerless to take power—especially if the endeavor seems capable of success—will be called criminal. They know that those in power write the laws to suit their wants and that they define what is and is not criminal. Obviously, anything that attacks the man's power is criminal. Like the Irish, like labor, like the revolutionaries before them, black people today cannot afford to give a damn about what labels their oppressors are going to pin on them.

Nine out of ten times, at the end of any lecture I give that even remotely touches on the racial question, someone armed with some section or other of the F.B.I.'s crime report will challenge me on the rate of crime in "Negro ghettos." Anger rises when I retort by demanding the sources of the figures, and who has gathered them? What about the method used and the honesty and accuracy in police reporting? Do these figures refer to arrests or convictions? What do they mean? Do they truly reflect increase in the number of crimes committed or increase in the number reported or increase in police activity, misactivity or harassment of the poor? What are the assumptions that underlay the techniques and the survey? A priest attacked me recently when I suggested such considerations. "That kind of talk," he said, "simply encourages the criminals who are harming your people mostly." Another important question is, Who defines and decides what crimes will be surveyed? If a survey is limited to certain types of crimes, e.g., those generally associated with poverty, you will get one kind of picture. Black people are far and away overly represented in the poverty group. On the other hand, if you include crimes generally engaged in by people of some respectability and social status, the picture changes somewhat.

Also apropos is the bias involved in the administration of criminal justice which applies exclusively to the professions and business and involves only the upper socio-economic bracket. Fraud, swindling, tax evasion, price fixing, are crimes which do not involve arrest by uniformed policemen, which are not often tried in criminal courts, and which are frequently not punished by prison sentences. Murder, assault, burglary, robbery, small-time drug pushing, are crimes which are dealt with by the police, involve juvenile and criminal courts, and jail sentences. The first class of violations of law or crimes are often not included in criminal statistics. They do not come in under the gaze of young Irish Catholic cops.

One day in 1968 headlines blazed the arrests of two Black Panthers by the F.B.I. and New York City Police at Kennedy Airport in New York. The men were Tyrone Smith and Jourdan Major Ford, described respectively as Minister of Defense of the Black Panthers and the party's East Coast leader. They were said to have been attempting to board a plane to California while armed. This was in violation of federal law. Both were on their way to Oakland to attend the funeral of Alprentice Carter, a West Coast Panther leader who was shot to death the previous week on the campus of the University of California at Los Angeles. The forces of law and order have made it known that they keep tabs on *alleged* Black Panthers. I say "alleged" because in New York and many other cities these days, when any black man is arrested he is a "suspected Black Panther," or "the police [have] found Black Panther literature in his car." The man is out to get the Black Panthers in this country—there can be no more doubt about that—killing them everywhere, from Los Angeles to New York, and throwing any survivors in jail after going through farces in so-called courts of justice. This criminal-fighting is a funny thing. The federal government does not prosecute for murder since murder doesn't come under its jurisdiction. Thus, even when a murderer of civil-rights workers wears an official badge, all the federal government may do is to prosecute for the violation of civil rights. The F.B.I. sees no need to tail gun-toting Ku Klux Klansmen and Minutemen.

In January 1969, a little brown notebook was accidentally dropped in a New York City courthouse. Subsequently it was found to belong to a policeman and proved to be a treasure chest of information about ambulance-chasing lawyers, about police steering "criminals," sometimes with threats of woe or promises of leniency, to certain lawyers on whose payrolls the cops are, and about gift-chasing cops. This kind of thing does not appear on Hoover's list of selected crimes.

The ring of federal narcotics agents, treasury agents and members of the narcotics squad of the New York Police Department selling drugs does not make that list. We go after the little junkie, the victim-tool who is himself an addict, in the Harlems, the Bedford-Stuyvesants, the Wattses, and the Houghs of our nation. These people, who make life so miserable for the inhabitants of our black ghettos, could be put out of business tomorrow if we went after their employers and protectors.

The majority of white people in our black ghettos today are police. Businessmen, Roman Catholic priests, nuns and other white clergy who are moving in now that it has become the fad for those who want to be "involved," are poor seconds. In many of these cities, the police are of ethnic backgrounds traditionally identified with Roman Catholicism. It is important that we understand this. This is why what young, Irish cops believe, say and act upon is so crucial. In so many ways they are saying to black people, "this is what Roman Catholicism is all about." Perhaps the whole area of the

Church/police relationship demonstrates how well the Church can live in a racist and oppressive society without lifting a finger for change.

In New York, the Irish are so strong in the police establishment, as they are in the Church establishment, that the department's top brass has long been known as the Irish Mafia. At the time of this writing, for example, the top echelon of the New York City Police Department reads: Leary, Dodds (Negro), McManus, Taylor, Lusson (German), Cone, McGovern. Of the four hundred and fifty top officials, only seven are black and three were added only in the last five years. The rank of captain must be achieved before further advancement and there are four blacks out of two hundred and seventy-eight captains. The top brass in the New York archdiocese reads Cooke, Maguire, O'Brien, Byrne, Heneghan, Murphy and Mahoney.

Few priests in New York or Chicago do not have members of the immediate family or some relation through marriage or some school friends involved in some kind of police work. In a white parish, one would have to apologize to the congregation for suggesting anything that might seem derogatory to the police, no matter how true it might be. Correspondingly, the police have been known for kindness to the clergy and especially to Catholic priests and religious. Of course, some exceptions are made for "radical troublemakers" who do not realize that the job of the priest or religious is simply to mouth pious phrases which nobody takes seriously in real life, and talking about anything but the present realities one day a week at Mass.

One of the factors the Kerner Report found—it was not the first nor will it be the last time we have been told this—was that underlying much of the difficulty in our cities is the poor relationship existing between the police and the poor communities, especially black and Puerto Rican communities. The vast majority of white Catholics I know simply refuse to believe this and do not want to hear it. Since relatively few live in the black communities, they delude themselves into thinking that police-community relations in their neighborhood are the same as in the black community; that law officers are just as responsive and respectful in dealing with the poor in certain "ghetto" environments as they are toward the "good people" in better neighborhoods.

These are delusions, of course, because while with but three exceptions my own personal relations with police departments have been better than adequate, the opinions just mentioned are simply not borne out. The police, as I have mentioned, are generally nice to priests. Many close friends are members of the New York City Police Department. To presume that policemen deal with me typically in the Harlem community, where I've spent my life, is ludicrous. By clinging to such illusions white people can convince themselves that only criminals or communists or dupes criticize the "defenders of law and order." Thus, they can continue to support their local police and attack those favoring the criminals without any qualms of conscience.

When I said some of these things at a Catholic college, where one would expect a somewhat more sophisticated audience, a priest accused me and "people like me" of being more responsible for crime than the criminals. I suggested that this made me a criminal too.

Remember the silence from Church leaders in heavily Catholic-populated Chicago when the Walker Report came out on the behavior of Daley's police during the Chicago Democratic Party convention? A priest friend of mine from the Chicago archdiocese told me he practically was asked to apologize for just mentioning the "Walker Report" in a sermon.

Recall back in 1965 when Bull Connor's defenders of law and order brutally attacked the nonviolent demonstrators in Selma, Alabama. A month later William F. Buckley, Jr., editor of the *National Review* and a vocal Catholic, addressed the New York Police Department Holy Name Society at their annual communion breakfast. In what he described as an attack on the "world of the newspaper creation," Buckley blasted the press coverage of Selma. He complained that while criticizing the excesses of the policemen, the news media failed to criticize the excesses of "those who provoked them beyond the endurance we tend to think of as human." Those who would defend police violence on the grounds of their being pushed beyond "human endurance" or their being jeered at and taunted in Chicago are the first to say that no amount of intimidation or brutal treatment done to the Afro-American for centuries justifies his resort to force or violence.

Referring to the murder of Mrs. Viola Liuzzo, a white woman who had come to Selma, he chided the press: "Why, one wonders, was this a story that occupied the front pages from one end to another, if indeed newspapers are concerned with the unusual, the unexpected? Didn't the killing merely confirm precisely what everyone had been saying about certain elements of the South?" He concluded his remarks with a comparison between the demonstrators in Selma and the Ku Klux Klan. "If the grand wizard of the Ku Klux Klan," he said, "were to announce that he and a band of his fellow cretins were coming up to Harlem to demonstrate against the voting rights bill, would we not warn them of the dangers of any such affront, and would we be surprised if fewer Ku Kluxers left Harlem than arrived there?" The six thousand members at the police communion breakfast cheered wildly.

When the report of Mr. Buckley's talk hit the papers, I got a copy of the text and made a detailed response. After the intervention of the late Cardinal Spellman, the *Catholic News,* the New York archdiocesan newspaper, printed my response alongside the complete text of the Buckley speech.

The following week, Monsignor Joseph Dunne, Catholic Chaplain of the New York City Police Department, had this letter submitted to the *Catholic News.* (Of course, he did not require the Cardinal's help to get it printed.)

To the Editor:
I can appreciate your sense of fairness in printing both Mr. William Buckley's talk and Father Lucas' criticism in the *Catholic News.* I do not care for this type of rebuttal, however, wherein one contender can go off into flights of fancy and "wondering" with little or no relevance to the basic subject.

Father Lucas was not present to hear Mr. Buckley, and I sent him a copy of the speech. How he is able to construe this text as an attack on civil rights, is in itself a "wonder."

Anyone who is close to the realities of the civil rights struggle can see that serious mistakes have been made on both sides, North and South, black and white, demonstrators and police. Thank God more and more leaders are now working harder in the areas of communication. Here we can make progress in bringing about mutual understanding, trust and confidence in the sincerity of the "good people" involved.

Who does not regret the cruel injustices, the senseless delays and the culpable complacency of the white majority? Who will not reject the excesses of demonstrators, taunting police and defying laws which at times had no relevance to the rights being sought?

I hope that the demonstrations have sufficiently shocked our country into a realization that prompt action must be taken in behalf of citizens who are denied basic rights. By the same token, I hope that minority groups will also realize that police must enforce the law for all concerned, equally and without prejudice. Police are not to be identified with the status quo, as though they are protecting the injustices under discussion.

Communication requires us to listen to the other party and gain understanding of his position. Father Lucas would do well to re-read Mr. Buckley and reduce the size of the stereotyped image he has of ultra-rightist, hate-rouser and un-Christian Catholic. Mr. Buckley is none of these.

Rt. Rev. Msgr. J. A. Dunne
Catholic Chaplain, N.Y.C.P.D.

Notice the approach of the chaplain's letter and his great anxiety to defend the police from my attack. He mentioned irrelevantly that I was not present to hear Mr. Buckley, though he acknowledged that the complete text of the talk had been available to me. Moreover, he forgot to mention the many people who were there, including himself, with whom I had spoken.

Monsignor Dunne accused me of "going off in flights of fancy." What I had done was to make a detailed criticism of the speech around six points. And Mr. Buckley's entire speech was printed so that readers could judge for themselves. Dunne took issue with what I had said by completely ignoring what I did say. Rather, he made some general remarks about the "civil rights" movement and about his being surprised how I "was able to construe the text as an attack on civil rights." He concluded by admonishing me to change my "stereotyped image about Mr. Buckley" (as if one Mr. Buckley were not enough).

Then there was the case of a black community leader in Indianapolis. He is director of a radical action project there and like other black leaders, he has been under constant harassment by the Indianapolis Police Department. He is a "bad guy" because he is trying to open the eyes of the Indianapolis blacks. Father Lawrence Pushor, a teacher at Selina High School, had planned to invite him to discuss some aspects of the racial situation with the students. As soon as the word got out, the police department, through their chaplain, informed Father Pushor's superiors of their shock inasmuch as the man has a record, was involved in a riot, and is a dope peddler and a pimp. Father Pushor was discreetly informed that he could not be asked.

I wrote a letter to the *Criterion,* the paper of the Archdiocese of Indianapolis, which they did not publish. In it, I noted that this kind of business gave the lie to their clichés about their desire for more communication among the races. Anyone, I said, who has experienced or is familiar with living in the white-created black ghetto knows that the probability is that its inhabitants have police records. Using this to justify excluding black people who make them uncomfortable was hypocritical. If the other charges mentioned are true enough to be whispered, then one might say they should be true enough to warrant an arrest.

This man has been allowed since then to come and speak to a class. The police chaplain hasn't spoken to me since. The important thing is that, like their counterpart in New York, some chaplains think their role is to defend the police under the garb of religion, no matter what.

Then there was the case, again in Indianapolis, involving Father Boniface Hardin, O.S.B. Father Hardin has been stationed for several years at Holy Angels, a black parish in Indianapolis. He had been interested and involved in social and civic affairs while I was there. One of his concerns was in the area of police/community relations. His honesty and straightforwardness soon began to annoy some of the police brass. Thus, a certain police captain—since promoted to deputy inspector—had the job of informing the archbishop that

Father Hardin was "embarrassing the police department."

I was there when the department went through the farce of a hearing involving two policemen who had been accused of manhandling a young black minister. What took place to the delight of the Birchers and Ku Klux Klansmen who had jammed the room was a smearing of the minister by bringing up all his past arrests—without any mention of how many were followed by convictions and for what. The accuser became the defendant. The investigation was handled by the department's high-ranking Negro officer. Handle it he did! He has a reputation for being a good investigator and he is. He did not miss a single run-in with the "law" that the minister had since the age of five. The only trouble was that he should have been using those skills to find out what had really taken place. The two officers were acquitted, to the great delight of most of those present. These are the same persons who tell black people, "Why don't you use the legal process and legitimate means to right your wrongs?"—while making a mockery of the same processes.

A department that should be either disbanded and/or completely retrained and reorganized complains about being embarrassed! If they are right and that is all the priest was doing, they should be rejoicing. Father Boniface and others should be doing a lot more toward changing the Indianapolis Police Department than simply embarrassing them. But all the police had to do was tell the archbishop, a known and trusted ally, that a black priest was embarrassing them and the process for his removal was underway. There was no need for even the pretext of a hearing. Oh, yes, they threw in a few other things. "Father Boniface," they said, "was hanging around the Panthers." You know how the police love Panthers. In New York, for example, police in civilian clothes attacked a group of Panthers in a Brooklyn court shouting, "me tiger; tiger kill black panther." They also said that "Father Hardin was trying to incite a riot." Now that should go down as one of the better punch lines of the decade. The Indianapolis Police Department thinks that black people who live in West Side Indianapolis, or the Martindale section, for example, need a priest to incite them to riot. What is more amusing is that they are talking about riot among Indianapolis Negroes. In Indianapolis when I lived there from 1966 to 1968, you couldn't get ten black mice to riot against one ten-day-old white kitten if you gave them all the cheese in the world. By and large, Indianapolis Negroes must bear the shame of being the least progressive, most apathetic, most indifferent and least organized of any group of Negroes living in a city of comparable size in these United States. And the Indianapolis Police Department thought Father Boniface was trying to "incite to riot."

Some people did become upset when they heard rumblings of a plan to transfer Father Boniface on the basis of such nonsense. People calling themselves "Concerned Christians" walked out of Saints Peter and Paul Cathedral as Archbishop Schulte was about to begin his homily at the 11 A.M. Mass. Spearheaded by the Catholic Interracial Council led by Amanda Strong, her sister Doris Parker, Charles Williams and Joseph Smith, they did so as a sign of protest and disgust over the whole affair. In lieu of money, the group offered letters of discontent and concern in the collection baskets. The archbishop's only comment was that he knew something was up. Monsignor Raymond Bosler, Fathers Bernard Strange and Albert Ajamie, all three distinguished and interested priests of the archdiocese, went down to discuss the matter with Archbishop Schulte. A kind of a promise was elicited that Father Boniface would not be transferred if he got out of civic affairs.

This was less than a year after April 1968, when a meeting of the National Conference of Catholic Bishops had made this statement: "We strongly urge Catholics of every color and ethnic group to ally themselves with these religious and civic programs as the most convincing way of demonstrating the love of neighbor which is the proof of love of God." There is the issue. In a white institution a black man, in order to avoid being dispatched to a useless assignment, would have to stop being a black man relevant to black people. In other words, the criterion for what he does is that it doesn't embarrass white people or as in this case, the police department. At the present time, if a black man is not "embarrassing" white people and their legal enforcers department, alias the police, it is a good sign that he is not black and is not doing a damn thing for black people. In the Catholic Church, as in all other white racist institutions of our white racist society, it is almost impossible to be a black man working for black people. You can be a good little Negro. You can be a front and rewards might even come to you for that.

Black people realize that law-abiding, respectable, middle- and upper-class white America, which has been acting criminally toward black people for centuries, does not want to get its hands dirty and so it has turned over to its police departments the dirty job of keeping the chains of slavery around black people and keeping the lids on the garbage cans, or the ghettos white people have created for black people. Black people do not resent the policeman because he represents justice, honest law enforcement and the anti-criminal. They resent the policeman in the black community because consciously or unconsciously he represents the enforcing agency of an oppressive society, disguised. Many police departments are aware of this and are revolting against this burden. Others are completely unaware of it. The former head of the Patrolmen's Benevolent Association of New York City issued instructions that policemen are to strictly enforce the law "regardless of what orders we may get from any superior officer." Black people know exactly what that means. Other policemen and departments seem to relish the role. One policeman friend of mine was visibly shook when he heard his six-year-old son pipe up one day, "I want to be a cop so I can shoot Negroes."

The Church must remember that police will act in exactly the way their superiors seriously demand that they act. Police superiors, on the other hand, are not going to demand good performance until our churches and other so-called responsible institutions insist on it. In many large cities, moreover, so many police and their superiors belong to our Church. When black people see the way the Church has behaved in the area of police/black community relationships in such cities as Chicago, Indianapolis, New York and Los Angeles, they can draw one of two conclusions: either the Church is ignorant, and such ignorance would be inexcusable, or the Church doesn't give a damn.

Another racist attitude prevalent among white Catholics refuses to admit that black people have criminality, extremism, imperfection, stupidity, ignorance, weakness, disagreement, etc., in their midst. As soon as it appears whites and some silly Negroes are shocked, unable to relate, ashamed for and sympathetic toward all black people. But they can meet the same things every day in white society and not feel that all white folks are expected to go under or stop existing because

of it. This attitude can hardly be squared with a consistent belief in white supremacy, but racism is not the
most logical of human phenomena. What this attitude
really does is to demand a superiority from the alleged
inferiors. Black folks are expected to be educated while
they are denied admission to our educational facilities
or are condemned to the typical ghetto school systems;
they are expected to be trained for jobs while appren-
ticeship programs and unions refuse to accept them,
and so on. What it does for the racist society is to
allow it to make room for *some* of the special or
exceptionally gifted Negroes while the masses go to
hell. At the same time it can quite readily find places
for white folks ranging from geniuses to damn near
idiots.

Whites are unable to deal with black disagreement.
This incapacity prevented the U.S. bishops from dealing with the Black Clergy Caucus, just as it has ob-
structed many of my discussions with chancery officials,
and in fact has blocked most black/white efforts. When
they talk to black folks, white people get hung up
over black "unanimity." White layfolks can disagree
and still act; white priests and religious disagree among
themselves and can move; white bishops fight like hell
with one another and still make statements and allocate
funds for projects. But when they talk with blacks, the
first question is, "Do all of you, every single one of you,
agree on this?" And as soon as they find one dissenting
voice, all action immediately comes to a halt.

The so-called Negro churches in the black ghettos
are almost always pastored by white persons who depend to a large extent on white financial help, usually
from the chancery office, for their existence and their

meaningless programs. The vast majority of the plants in the large inner cities were built many years ago by and for white Catholics, who were much larger in numbers and far more affluent than the blacks and Puerto Ricans who live near them now. When the blacks came into the neighborhoods the whites fled, leaving their churches and schools behind them. Some white people are still wondering why black Catholics in these areas, who have little or no money, don't support the mammoth religious edifices as they did?

The only Catholic diocese with a Negro bishop is New Orleans. But there, Bishop Harold Perry is an auxiliary bishop. This means he has little or no power of decision. At this time, he is not even a pastor of a church and so doesn't even have the power of a pastor. Negro Catholics and others fool themselves into thinking that being a bishop is equivalent to having power in the Church, and so they are quite proud when the man "gives them a bishop."

There are about ten or fifteen black pastors in the entire American Catholic Church. Most of them are in the South. Pastors have power. Thus, in the South, the racist system appoints a black man over a little Negro enclave in the district of a white parish where it is assumed the white man is really the boss. In the North, the racist system uses all kinds of excuses not to appoint them.

I was speaking in this vein at Manhattan College in New York when one professor suggested that the black man's position in the Church was like that of the laity in relation to the clergy. Of course, there is a real difference. Black people have no influence or power because they are black. When white lay folks have no power or influence, it is because they are poor. A few better-off Negroes, where they are available, are invited for post factum "consultation" and agreement on what has already been decided. And wealthy white folks may not exercise all the power and influence they want, though some individuals and some groups exercise considerable power. More importantly, it is the priorities and the concerns of the affluent whites that bishops try to be attuned to, and try to serve.

Not only does no black person or group of black people exercise real power in the Catholic Church, but white Catholics are intent on keeping the situation that way. An event in Chicago that involved Cardinal John Cody, Fathers Rollins Lambert and George Clements and St. Dorothy's Parish is a good example. As in many other places, there had been some agitation in Chicago for a black pastor to be appointed. On March 7, 1968, Cardinal Cody appointed Father Rollins Lambert, a black priest and then Newman Chaplain at the University of Chicago, as pastor of St. James Parish on Wabash Avenue in Chicago. St. James is a middle-class parish in a neighborhood almost evenly Negro and white. Of course, many might suspect that when you are dealing with a middle-class, fifty-fifty Negro and white situation, you really have a ninety-percent white situation, skin color being the only difference between Negro and white.

Well anyway, Father Lambert was made pastor of St. James. Father Lambert was senior to Father Clements, also a black man, in ordination. Yet, he had extremely little parish experience, having spent most of his career in university work. Father Clements, on the other hand, a man of thirty-seven, had spent all of his priesthood in parish work. He certainly would have seemed to be a more likely choice to pastor a parish. But Father Lambert was considered "safe." Father Clements was "militant" and associated with "black militants." And so, as in any white racist structure, the Negro who is good and safe for you because of his quietness and safeness, real or imagined, is rewarded and allowed to serve the oppressors, and the "uppity," "noisy," "bad nigger" whom you cannot use to continue to oppress black people is passed over. Cardinal Cody has no monopoly on this kind of behavior. Most of the bishops are experts at it. Father Lambert, therefore, was appointed to St. James.

Things would have gone on and Negro Catholics would have believed that the white man on top had really done something for them had not things started happening at St. Dorothy's, a middle-class parish which is almost entirely black in its parishioners. Word got out that the cardinal had intended to accept the request for retirement of the incumbent pastor, Father Gerald P. Scanlon. He was getting on in age. It was also strongly hinted that he was allowing Father Clements, who was an assistant there, to do pretty much as he pleased. Several months earlier a white assistant priest and five nuns had asked out because "it was impossible to live with Father Clements." They could not live comfortably with a real black man.

There was a sentiment in the parish that this was the time for a black pastor in St. Dorothy's and that none would be more fitting for the job than George Clements. The four black priests belonging to the archdiocese, including Father Lambert, went down to discuss the subject with Cardinal Cody. He refused to talk to them as a group, sent home three, and discourteously chewed out Father Clements, telling him he would stay at St. Dorothy's under any administrator he, Cody, would choose. The folks were having none of that.

Luckily, the matter was not left exclusively in the hands of Catholic Negroes, who are programmed to be safe. All kinds of groups got into the act. What Cody and others like him had to realize is that black people are determined to control all institutions that operate in the black communities. The Church is no exception. In the face of the uproar that followed, including a threatened walkout by the four black priests, Cody pulled a typical last resort. In order to satisfy the demand for a black pastor at St. Dorothy's, he persuaded Father Lambert to take the assignment.

Catholics know how almost irremovable pastors are in the Catholic Church. They know that when given a church, Catholic pastors usually find there a lasting city to which they are wedded until death and/or retirement do them part. So adamant was Cody in denying a pastorate to Clements that in spite of the fact that Father Lambert had been appointed to St. James less than ten months before, he was now moved to St. Dorothy's. Moreover, the cardinal was evidently willing to pass this off as a favor to black folks. You see how funny white folks are. They can be crucifying black folks, but they will do it with a smile and while doing it, they will try to make you think they are doing you a big favor.

Well, black people in Chicago were not falling for it this time. They did not see it as a victory for black people, but a victory for racism. What Cody had done was to try to use a black man to disarm the protest of black people and their white supporters. The move would keep Father Clements in his same position, keep the number of black pastors in the archdiocese to one, and concentrate half of the archdiocese's black priests in one parish. Encouraged by the black brothers and sisters, Father Lambert saw the light. In a dramatic press conference he accused the cardinal of simply making a "political" move and said that he was guilty of "unconscious racism." He threatened to leave St. Dorothy's immediately if Clements wasn't given a church of his own. These events led to the celebration of January 12.

On Sunday, January 12, 1969, black people came together at St. Dorothy's Church for a celebration. This, after all, is what Mass is supposed to be—a celebration. (I've offered thousands of masses as a layman before ordination. I've offered thousands of masses as a priest since ordination. But there was never anything like this.)

Black Catholics had come together for a cause, a cause worthy of celebration. They came to tell Cardinal Cody and the entire American Catholic Church that they disagreed that the Church in Chicago had no room in it for a relevant black man in a position of authority. Moreover, they were disgusted with his attempt to use another black man to knock down George Clements and insult black people. This latter point was particularly insulting to the Black Clergy Caucus. If a racist was able to use Lambert, who was the chairman of the Caucus, in this manner, how could the Caucus ever hope to aid black people and wake up Negro Catholics?

It was for these issues that black people came together. Black Catholics, black people, all came together to say, "No more, you can't do this." Somewhere along the way black Catholics, like all black people, will have to unite to tell white Catholics, including bishops and all white people, "You can't continue to use one of us to shoot another down; you can't continue to misuse and abuse black people; you can't continue to make Uncle Toms of black folks."

Mind you, it was not only black Catholics celebrating. There were Protestants and there were Jews. There were Muslims and unchurched people. There were whites in supportive roles. Then there were those lovely Black Panthers strung out all over the sanctuary. Cardinal Cody would have been especially proud of them if he had been there. But he wasn't. Organizations participated, like the Afro-American Youth Organization, Black Consortium, Afro-American Patrolmen's League, Afro-American Firefighter's League, Concerned Transit Workers, Catholic Interracial Council, and many others. There were even members of the Chicago Police Department in the sanctuary.

All the black priests from Chicago and outlying areas were there. Father Harold Salmon, vicar-delegate for Harlem, and I flew in from New York. Father Gus Taylor came from Steubenville, Ohio. There were many ministers of many denominations, including that wonderful black man, Jesse Jackson, right there in the sanctuary.

The main attraction was Fathers Lambert and Clements. Father Lambert spoke from the mind and the heart. He told it like it was. He did not speak of his promise to resign. Clearly it was in the background as he spoke of the need for self-determination and the unity required in the struggle. The crowd roared and it applauded him and Father Clements. Clements was definitely the man of the hour. The issue had now resolved itself upon him. Would he be quiet and remain at St. Dorothy's as assistant, or would he, with the support of black people, stand up and oppose racism in the Archdiocese of Chicago and the very conscious racism of Cardinal Cody?

There was no recognition on the part of the archbishop of anything that took place then. *The New World,* the archdiocesan newspaper, did have some comments. Originally the issue was an appeal to the cardinal to appoint a black pastor to a black parish. Then, with its white eyes a little wider open it saw that "the strategy has now shifted to an attack on the authority of Cardinal Cody to make pastoral appointments." The editorial went on to state that "some wild and reckless charges have been leveled at the Catholic Church and the cardinal" and cited various "militant organizations which have gotten into the foray and found a platform for their ideas." The "reckless charges" were perhaps racism in high and low places. Official Catholic diocesan newspapers do have strong feelings against "reckless charges," "attacks on authority," and any person or group that does not recognize the obvious perfection of the institutional church and its leaders. Thus, not only was *The New World* against the black militants involved, and their tactics, but it wasn't too happy with the white priests involved either. "This is one time," it stated, "where we strongly urge white priests to go home. Then the parishioners of St. Dorothy's could rally around their new pastor . . . to give him the support he so earnestly desires." That editorial was published before the statement of Father Lambert about resigning. *The New World* had no difficulty with Cody's behavior and his attempt to misuse Lambert. It called for parishioners' support and for "outsiders" to leave. A few days later Lambert expressed other ideas and priorities.

There was, however, a follow-up. In the January 22, 1969, issue of the *National Catholic Reporter*, Francis Ward wrote: "A source close to the chancery office of the Chicago Archdiocese said Thursday that Cardinal John Cody plans to name Father George H. Clements as pastor of a predominantly or all-black parish. The move, to come within the next two or three weeks, said the source, would be a major break in the near-stalemate that has developed between Cardinal Cody and Chicago's black Catholic community."

The *National Catholic Reporter* knew that Cardinal Cody had made such a promise to Fathers Lambert and Clements. What it did not know was that the archbishop had indicated that Clements would be made a pastor if Clements and the others went home, kept quiet and kept the thing out of the newspapers. This would take the pressure off Cody, who could not allow himself to appear to be bowing to pressure.

But that was precisely the problem. Too many bishops have this hangup about bowing to pressure and demands as an affront to their authority. It was not really a question of pressure at all. Pressure as such was not what disturbed the cardinal and what is disturbing his other episcopal confreres. The question is pressure from whom? The bishops have not become accustomed to, nor do they desire the experience of, bowing to black pressure. They find no difficulty in bowing to white pressure, especially white economic pressure. Cardinal Cody himself had informed both Fathers Lambert and Clements of the letters, phone calls and telegrams he had received from fellow bishops and "good Catholics" telling him not to kowtow to this pressure. He just could not disappoint them, he could not let down these people, he said. In the next breath he was talking about how, if he bowed to this kind of pressure from the black community, it would weaken his authority.

The cardinal was right. He simply did not specify that "this kind of pressure" meant black pressure or pressures from black people. Bowing to the pressure of black people would be an acknowledgment of and a concession to the power of black people. And no racist can acknowledge and concede to a shift in the relationship of power between white and black.

Father Lambert in a news conference had described

Cardinal Cody as an "unconscious racist." That was a grave mistake. Cody realized better than anyone that there was much more at stake than simply making Father George Clements a pastor in the Chicago archdiocese. At stake was a shift, ever so slightly but still a shift, in the power relationship between black and white in the Archdiocese of Chicago. Other bishops quickly realized that if Cody bowed to black pressure in Chicago, they would soon be making concessions to the same pressures in New York, Philadelphia, Detroit, Indianapolis, Los Angeles, Baton Rouge and all over this land. So they, with other "responsible" white Catholics, pressured him. That is why the cardinal promised to make George Clements a pastor in Chicago if he and his supporters would remain quiet for a while. They had to take the pressure off him. It was the price to be paid for becoming a pastor.

This was precisely the price that could not be paid. At that time the significance of the pastorate was far more important than just a pastorate for George Clements. (So urged Clarence Lockridge and Jesse Jackson and others in Chicago. I urged this at a meeting held in New York with Fathers Kenneth Brigham, Richard Weathley [two black priests of the Chicago archdiocese], Clements and Salmon.) One thing had to be clear. Clements was not to be made a pastor at Cardinal Cody's price. His becoming a pastor was not to be a reward for going home and behaving himself for a while like a good nigger should. This would entail no shift in power. But it could not be another episode in the long history of the great white Father rewarding the good or contrite Negro for behaving himself. The all-important consideration was that Clements' being made a pastor be seen as a concession to the legitimate demands and aspirations of black people.

At the meeting we had in New York, some of the priests began to suggest that the blacks should compromise. The Catholic Church has produced a flock of Negroes who are excellent compromisers. The Church encourages them and loves them. She benignly refers to them as "cool," "diplomatic," and "able to compromise." Most white people love the compromising Negro. When the Negro compromises with the white man, it invariably means the Negro backs down on his demands and the white man maintains his position.

These priests "understood" the position of the cardinal: "We had to give a little to get Cody off the hook."

The whitewashed black man did not understand at all. Only a black man that is duped could have spoken of compromise in these circumstances. He is duped because, first, he doesn't understand what the white man really means by "compromise." Second, he could not see that what he really was saying is, "Look, fellas, we can't stand pat without moving back. Racism is here to stay."

From January to June 1969, things remained the same. Father Clements went on an extended vacation during which he lectured widely on the situation in Chicago and the black/white situation in the Church. Father Lambert remained at St. Dorothy's parish. The surface, at least, was quiet.

All during this time individual groups had been meeting and discussing what to do about the situation. Tempers and patience were wearing thin. Then, in the middle of June, I got a call from George Clements. Cardinal Cody had appointed him pastor of Holy Angels parish in Chicago. In addition, two other black priests were made pastors: Father Kenneth M. Brigham for Our Lady of Perpetual Help, and Father Dominic Carmon for St. Elizabeth. They were having a second Mass of Black Unity for their installation. Would I be willing to preach?

This Mass, like the first, had its wonderfully moving and relevant liturgy including music, African sculpture, African-style vestments. Besides Fathers Clements, Brigham and Carmon, who were the main celebrants, twelve other black priests from various parts of the country concelebrated the Mass. I was one of them. It was truly a black thing, with many whites supporting it.

One of the highlights was the oath of office the three priests took to their respective black communities and to the black community in general. Taking seriously the role of the priest as servant of the community, they pledged themselves to resign if and when the black community decided they were no longer acting in its behalf. As Clements explained: "We are not defying the Church, but we want to dramatize the plight of the blacks within the Catholic Church. In our communities, the Church is seen as a white man's Church and is losing ground rapidly."

In my sermon I recalled the events leading up to the appointment of the new pastors. The day was a climax and a victory for the unity of Chicago's black community. It was the beginning of a greater opportunity for three men to be more fully black Christs forming a black nation through which salvation might come to the entire Church. They would have to follow in the footsteps that led to Resurrection only after suffering and death. I said: There will be some very definite signs that will follow you if you are on the right path. You will be despised by the powers that be and feared and distrusted by your own, whom you will make uncomfortable. The poor, the lazy whores and loafers on welfare whom white, hard-working Catholics identify so readily, and the outcast of society will seek you out. The wildest-looking black men, the "radicals and militants," the Black Panthers and all those whom the establishment abhors and with whom good people, like Catholic bishops, would not be seen dead, will approach your doors. And when these things begin or continue to happen, you will know that you are about your Father's business.

In a sense, the work was just beginning. We could not stay too long at the celebration. The Chicago archdiocese became the first large Northern diocese to have most of its black priests pastoring black congregations. The manner in which it came about showed there was a great deal that remained to be done. This was at best a small beginning of a long, long journey.

I learned my lesson early about what the white man thinks of black people and about their willingness to be the tools of those who enslave their brothers. When a black man rears his ugly head and seriously demands freedom for his people, the white man assumes he can find a Negro willing and ready to be used to slap his brother down. When I was in the sixth grade of All Saints School, there was one other Negro—that was the term then—in my class, a fellow named Marvin Hansen. Well, one day the Sister got angry with him over some childish trifle. She screamed out loud and clear in front of the whole class, "You black nigger."

Curiously enough, white people used the word "black" then, in spite of the fact that they are so terribly afraid of it now. Maybe it's not the word that frightens them, but who uses it and how and why.

Well, Marvin went home and told his parents, and his mother raised hell. That was the kind of thing Negroes raised hell about in those days. Only later we woke up to the fact that we had a great deal more to raise hell about and that we had better start raising it.

The principal and staff were embarrassed. The Sister, of course, was anxious. She did what white people do when they are scared or get in trouble with black folks. She called me up to her desk the next morning. Smiling, as white people do before they kill you, she told me what a lovely mother I had. That, believe me, was true, but my mother was the furthest thing from her mind that morning. She told me that she did not mean what she said yesterday and she knew how understanding I was. I was eleven. "If they ask you whether I called Marvin a nigger," she said, "please say no."

She smiled at me, praised my mother, praised me, and told me, "Nigger, I want you to let me use you to crush another nigger." There were twenty-six other children in that class, all white. She did not ask any of them to lie for her, to say that Marvin was lying.

The situation never arose. Only God knows what an eleven-year-old Negro in a lily-white school would have done in a showdown. After all, wasn't it white Jesus speaking to me? If He told me to lie, it must be all right. Perhaps my mother would have stopped me from obeying this nun. She used to tell me, "Not everyone is what they claim to be." Anyhow, Marvin's mother took him out of the school and I've never seen him since. He left me there alone, a black kid to be taught by white Christians and white religious. The question I wasn't sophisticated enough to ask was, "What am I being taught?"

The appointment of the first black pastor in the New York archdiocese is an interesting example of the attitude of the white Church toward black leaders. It took place in August 1968. As early as the 1940's, far-sighted black Catholics and non-Catholics had been talking about the possibility and desirability of a Negro Catholic pastor in Harlem. But we had no black priests in the archdiocese. The archdiocesan major seminary at Dunwoodie did not begin to accept blacks till 1945. The first black priest was not ordained for the archdiocese till 1952. In the middle 1950's, with three men in the major seminary and one ordained there was a lot of talk in certain quarters about having a black pastor. Father Harold Salmon had been ordained in 1956, I followed in 1959, and James Violenus in 1960. By 1961, the year I was assigned to Resurrection in Harlem from St. Peter's on Barclay Street, the rumbling about a black pastor had grown to an audible roar.

Cardinal Spellman had long before adopted the seniority system as the basis for choosing pastors. Exceptions had been made in the past, however, and certainly by 1964 many exceptions for special reasons could be counted. The cardinal, following the recommendations of his advisors, insisted that none of the black priests were old enough, "old enough," that is, in the seniority system or years ordained. We were all grown men. The white pastors in Harlem, when queried, took the position that a Negro pastor would have the effect of lessening their own prestige and influence. Lessening the prestige and influence of white people in relation to black people is, of course, unthinkable. No white man's position should be threatened in a black community. It was much too early to consider consulting even safe Negro Catholics. It wasn't certain that their minds had been "properly formed" on the matter.

During the period from May 1961 to September 1966, except for Father Violenus, who spent a year at All Saints Parish in 1962, I was the only black priest in Harlem of the five black priests in the archdiocese. Father Eugene Hicks had spent two years at St. Charles in the mid-fifties.

In September 1966, I was granted a leave of absence to accept a grant to study sociology and broadcasting in Indianapolis. During the previous four years I had been increasingly vocal, especially on racial issues, and many people therefore suspected that I was "being done in," but this was not true. Cardinal Spellman had always been perfectly honest in his dealings with me. I did not agree, obviously, with all his decisions and thinking, but when he spoke to me I knew he was telling me what was really on his mind or what he really thought. When I was invited to go to Indianapolis for two years, Spellman left the decision to me, and I accepted.

In the meantime, drawn along by the black power movement, Negro Catholics and other black people began insisting on a black priest in Harlem and a black pastor. Monsignor Gregory Mooney, then director of the Lieutenant Joseph P. Kennedy, Jr., Memorial Community Center, had been urging this for some time against fierce opposition, much of which came from the Harlem priests.

Recognizing finally the inevitable as far as a pastorate was concerned, the white priests got together and finally decided in 1967 that what Harlem needed was a black vicar. Moreover, they decided who this should be—on the basis of the one with whom they could get along better. Not even a pass was made at consulting the people whose interests they were serving. (A few months later Monsignor Joseph O'Brien, a vicar general of the archdiocese, was pointing out to me Archbishop Cooke's concern for the people in appointing a Negro pastor and vicar delegate, "as the people wanted." "What people?" I asked. "Well, that's what the Harlem priests decided," he responded. And he was right. When a group of white priests decided that they should allow Negro Catholics to have a pastor, that the Negroes in Harlem needed a vicar and who it should be, it was quite natural for Monsignor O'Brien to say, "that's what the people wanted.")

Thus, on July 3, 1968, about two months before I was scheduled to return home from Indianapolis, Archbishop Cooke announced with all the cameramen, newspapermen and fanfare that could be mustered that he was appointing Father Harold Salmon as vicar delegate for Harlem to "coordinate the overall planning and efforts of the seven Harlem parishes so that they may better serve the total community." Moreover, Cooke was naming Father Salmon as the first Negro Catholic pastor in the archdiocese. He was to be pastor of one of the largest Catholic parishes in Harlem, St. Charles Borromeo, where less than fifty years ago a white priest stood on the steps with a bullwhip to drive the Negroes away to St. Mark the Evangelist, "their church."

At the time of Father Salmon's appointment, he had had relatively little relationship with Harlem. In his thirteen years of priesthood he had never received a parish or parochial assignment. He had been rather silent on racial affairs and was generally considered moderate. The decision was made exclusively by white priests. They felt they could control him and accomplish what they wanted through him and at the same time pretend there was real black leadership. In commenting on the assertion that Monsignor Owen J. Scanlon, the former pastor of St. Charles, had stepped down for Father Salmon, *The New York Times* stated: "He is credited with having recommended, together with other white Catholic priests in the area, the selection of Father Salmon for a major role in Harlem church affairs." Adding insult to the injury involved in the reasons for the choice, many of the same white priests who as little as five years before were opposing a black pastor as being a threat to their positions began taking copious bows as being responsible for the appointment.

Whatever his personal reasons, certainly the pressures brought by white priests when he resisted simply being a tool in their hands, the pressures from some colored Catholics who thought him too militant and had resented from the start his replacing their white master, and pressures from black Catholics who wanted real black leadership did not help. On February 1, 1970, less than two years after his appointment, Salmon took a year's leave of absence from his duties. Sure enough, the people most responsible for creating the impossible situation in the first place, and who had counted on manipulating him, were the first to talk about his lack of experience and inability to fill the role.

The same procedure is followed in so many of our parishes when it comes to forming parish councils or choosing parish representatives; they are council and representatives in name only. Frequently, they are the handpicked voice of the pastor or some priest who is using them as a front. Such things are not limited to Negro parishes, to be sure. However, in terms of the psycho-historical situation in the black communities, the effects are far more detrimental here. That is why black lay Catholics, those few that remain, are beginning to organize themselves into Black Catholics in Action (B.C.A.) groups in Baltimore, Detroit, Newark, etc. —in order to confront their Church's racism more directly.

It is safe to presume that in the next several years more ordinaries will be appointing Negro auxiliary bishops. Needless to say, the same methods and the same criteria will be used. Moreover, you can rest assured they will be joining the ranks of the powerless bishops. And you Negro Catholics, and Negroes all, will be expected to rejoice and shout, "Look what the great white Father has done for us!" Yes, he will have done nothing more than he has always done: try to trick you and to use you.

Yet there are still some Negro priests who are looking to be bishops. They still talk in terms of what they can do for their people as bishops. That is, what they can do for their people under the present system. They do not realize that the only value that a powerless Negro bishop has is prestige, propaganda and show value, and all for the man.

Such Negro leadership can do nothing worthwhile for black people, and it will not be expected to. During one of Father Salmon's first interviews after his appointment, a reporter kept asking him, "What do you thing of Stokely Carmichael and Rap Brown?" What the reporter really wanted to know was whether Salmon was a "good" Negro; that is, good for white people. The best way of discovering that would be to have him repudiate a black man trying to open black people's eyes.

One of the signs of the Church's racism is the powerlessness of its black people. The entire process of choosing what Negro leadership there is is directed at keeping black people powerless. It's this process and this intention that I am talking about, not primarily the persons involved. On the other hand, the process is not infallible and sometimes it goofs. As more and more black people think in terms of black people rather than individual "advancement," as they were taught to in the past, they are refusing to let this white thing, the Cosa Blanca, work. They are either going to refuse such appointments or they will dedicate themselves to making sure that the reasons for their being chosen will be refuted.

The reception the National Black Catholic Clergy Caucus got when they first proposed a central office of Black Catholicism in the United States is an example of the controlled condition of black people in the Catholic Church, and is somewhat comical.

After the second meeting of the N.B.C.C.C., which took place from November 7 through 9, 1968, in Washington, D.C., the Caucus sent a letter through its Executive Committee to Archbishop John Dearden, the president of the National Conference of Catholic Bishops. In the letter dated December 8, 1968, we expressed our resentment and anger at the total lack of response by the bishops to the statement of our first meeting the previous April. In that statement, we had intended to sum up our experiences as black men in the American Catholic Church. "We wanted to confront the Church," we wrote, "in order to create the atmosphere for that rapid and radical change called for by our times." At the same time, we implied our strong faith in the Church's capacity to change, by making nine specific demands. We offered ourselves for consultation and volunteered to help in determining policies and directing programs to bring the Church to a fuller Christian realization. The letter concluded, "We of the Black Catholic Clergy Caucus, because of the negative reaction of the American bishops, announce our decision to intensify our work with black people, with or without the sanction of the Church. We will ignore in the future any persons, black or white, appointed to serve our needs if there is no prior and decisive consultation with us before positions are filled or programs plotted. . . ." We included a copy of the April 1968 statement in case some had missed it.

In reply to our letter of December 8, 1968, Archbishop Dearden and Cardinal Lawrence Shehan of Baltimore wrote to Father Rollins Lambert, chairman of the Caucus, expressing their wish to communicate with the Black Catholic Clergy Caucus, "since it undoubtedly could make a significant contribution to understanding the needs of the Church in the black community." Cardinal Shehan called for a meeting with the Liaison Committee of the conference of bishops—which consisted of himself as chairman, Archbishop Thomas Donnellan of Atlanta, Bishops Charles McLaughlin of St. Petersburg, Florida, Cletus O'Donnell of Madison, Wisconsin, Joseph Bernardine (executive secretary), and John May, auxiliary of Chicago—and the representatives of the Caucus. The Caucus was represented by its executive board, consisting of Fathers Rollins Lambert, chairman, Donald Clark of Detroit, Rawlin Enette of Baton Rouge, Louisiana, Brother Joseph Davis, secretary of the Caucus, and myself. The date was set for January 30, 1969, in Washington, D.C.

In view of the approaching meeting with the Liaison Committee of the Conference, and not knowing what the bishops were doing before meeting with us, the Executive Committee of the Caucus decided to meet in New York on January 10, 1969. The Executive Committee decided that the Caucus should make only one request of the Bishops' Conference—to underwrite and finance the establishment of a Secretariat for Black Catholicism. The staff of the Secretariat would be composed of about ten or twelve people, clerical, religious and lay. It would have the authority to research valid forms of liturgy for black Catholics, to formulate programs for action in the black community, and to carry out activities it considered beneficial to the black community. Obviously, the idea was in embryo form.

The committee then adopted with a few changes a twelve-page position paper, prepared by Brother Joseph Davis of Chaminade High School in Dayton, Ohio, outlining its view of the current status of the Catholic Church in the black community. This paper was to be used as the basis for the demands of the Caucus. It pointed to the inability of the Church to attract new members in the black community and the scarcity of vocations as well as the increasing frustration and alienation of black priests and religious. It called attention to the Church's failure to work realistically against racism, including its own, and its image as a white institution with blacks on the fringe, and painted a bleak picture of its future. This paper along with the demand for the Secretariat was forwarded as an agenda to the Liaison Committee prior to the scheduled meeting in Washington. Finally, it was decided to have the Caucus demand the right to send its own representative to the Bishops' Conference. This question was to loom larger later on.

The Executive Committee of the Caucus then developed the background and rationale of the proposed Secretariat and answered the bishops' questions. The atmosphere was cordial in spite of some opposition to the idea on the part of several bishops. The question of our own representative before the Bishops' Conference did not come up. The bishops indicated that they would report on the meeting to the Administrative Board of the Bishops' Conference on February 10 since they had no power. They promised to report objectively on what the Caucus had said, as well as on the questions of the bishops, and told us we would receive further directives.

At the conclusion of the meeting the bishops' Liaison Committee and our Executive Committee issued a jointly adopted statement which said in part:

> The Liaison Committee for Priests, Religious and Laity of the National Conference of Catholics met today with the Executive Committee of the Black Catholic Clergy Caucus. . . .
> This meeting was held to discuss a proposal by the Caucus for the establishment of a Secretariat for Black Catholicism by the American bishops. The Caucus proposed that such a Secretariat consist of priests, brothers, religious women and lay people with the purpose of formulating programs for action in the Black Community. . . .
> The Liaison Committee will, on the basis of today's discussion, prepare a report for the Administrative Committee of the National Conference of Catholic Bishops, which meets February 10th.
> A second report, incorporating both today's discussion and that of the Administrative Committee, will be presented to the U.S. Bishops at their spring meeting [April 15–18 in Houston]. . . .
> The participants in this meeting have agreed to continue discussions and to consult each other in the preparation of the Liaison Committee report.
> This consultation will keep the lines of communications open and will enable the bishops and the Caucus to work together in their common concern for the future of the Church in the Black Community.

The Administrative Board, on the basis of the Liaison Committee's report, established an ad hoc committee consisting of Bishops Joseph Donnelly, Peter Grety and Harold Perry, auxiliary bishops of Hartford, Connecticut, Portland, Maine, and New Orleans, respectively, to continue meeting with the Black Catholic Clergy Caucus. On March 11, 1969, the Executive Committee of the Caucus met in Detroit with the ad hoc committee of the bishops. Also present was Father Charles Burns, S.V.D., a member of the Caucus and assistant director of the Task Force on Urban Problems of the United States Catholic Conference.

The night before, we had met to put some meat on the skeleton of the original proposal. One of the first things we did was to change the name of the proposed office from Ordinariate or Secretariat to the Central Office for Black Catholicism in the U.S.A. This was to avoid canonical hangups since those words already had precise definition in Church law and did not represent what we had in mind. We had decided that the job of fitting this Central Office into the overall structure of the Church was the bishops' problem. We wanted a structure that would be as autonomous and as strong as possible. We also decided that we did not need to supply in advance minute details of how it would work, along with an absolute guarantee of its success. It was an experiment, and all the possibilities and answers could not be predetermined.

The March meeting was again cordial and friendly; it was also very frank. The bishops expressed a sincere desire to understand but they indicated by certain questions and remarks, how far out of the black world they really were. One request was for some "little examples of racism," that they could report back to the larger bishops' body. The bishops indicated that while they were amenable to the ideas we had presented, other bases would have to be touched before they made their final recommendations. Some of these bases were the "National Black Sisters' Conference," "other interested groups," and "prominent Negro laymen."

At first glance, this would seem a reasonable approach. We had no objections to consultation with the Black Sisters' Conference and "prominent Negro lay Catholics." On the other hand, the proposal had been worked out by a group to which the large majority of America's black priests belong. You must remember that most of our black priests are products of the era when only the "exceptions" went to the seminaries— the exceptionally intelligent, the exceptionally "polished," the exceptionally meek, and often the exceptionally light-complexioned. The black clergy as a group represents perhaps the most intelligent and able group of priests in America.

Nevertheless, the bishops on the ad hoc committee could not come to a decision by considering this simply as our proposal without consulting with prominent lay Negro Catholics and white folks. The other groups they had to "touch base" with included the religious orders of white priests, brothers and nuns who had been traditionally associated with the "Negro Apostolate." They would include orders like the Holy Ghost and Josephite Fathers, the Sisters of the Blessed Sacrament, etc. By coincidence, these orders were at a conference of their own in New Orleans at that time. They were discussing black folks and had dropped black Bishop Perry a note letting him know that a discussion was taking place, but not inviting him to the conference.

Now, if anyone needs help it is these people, who

have been with black folks so long and don't have the slightest idea of what black people are all about today. The reason, of course, is that they never got accustomed to dealing as equals with the people they were serving. If they had, they'd have no difficulty understanding what's going on with black people now. After the laughter subsided, I indicated tactfully that we really couldn't care less what these people thought about our proposal. In fact, instead of our consulting with these people about what we had in mind, those people, if they had any sense, should have been consulting with us. But if the bishops wanted, for the sake of courtesy, to talk to them, fine. Brother Davis was prevailed upon to fly to their meeting and present the proposal for "information."

Again, their desire to consult prominent Negro Catholic laymen was commendable. But why waste the time and energy? Do you know what prominent Negro Catholic laymen are, especially those that an American Catholic bishop would be on speaking terms with? Granted, there are exceptions. But generally speaking, they are programmed. And no one knows this better than those who have programmed them. The bishops did not have to ask them what they thought, nor did we. And sure enough, "prominent Negro Catholic laymen" were upset with what we were doing. The Caucus was becoming "too militant." Words like "we demand" disturbed them; we might lose their support.

About twenty minutes before a scheduled press conference we in the Caucus started to withdraw to draft our statement, as the bishops had done. One of the bishops sat back and said, "Before you go, what I would like to hear you say is—" He caught himself before he was interrupted, but the cat was already out of the bag. He had been about to tell us what to say. We came back with the following statement: "The consultation sounded very promising. Only time will tell how fruitful it has been. The three bishops on the committee showed a desire to understand the problems of the black community as well as some understanding of those problems. We hope the rest of the hierarchy will respond as favorably."

A final important consideration was the matter of the presentation of the proposal before the Administrative Board of the National Council of Catholic Bishops. Who would present the proposal to the board? Would it be someone who at best was sympathetic and favorable but who had little understanding of the background and meaning of the proposal and little feeling for the urgency of the moment—or would it be the Caucus' own representative?

You see, the bishops' thing is so structured that only a bishop can address the body at large or even the Administrative Board. Black folks have only one bishop. Unfortunately, however, Bishop Perry, a member of the Caucus, had allowed himself to be appointed to the very committee we were now dealing with. Thus, he could not speak freely either as a member of the Caucus or as a member of the committee. He was, in effect, neutralized.

So strongly did I feel on the issue that I proposed to the Caucus board that the information should be made public. Needless to say, the bishops on the ad hoc committee had no power to answer then, but they would check. On the other hand, they were quick to suggest that "if we were permitted to send a representative to Houston, where the next bishops' meeting was scheduled, our representative be Rollins Lambert, our chairman." Lambert was simply not the type to put a demand before the bishops for a yes or no, as the board had mandated him.

Subsequently the bishops did agree that we would make our own presentation, and Rollins went to Houston. On April 14, 1969, he spoke to the Administrative Board of N.C.C.B. on the proposal, giving its background briefly and emphasizing the urgency of establishing credibility for the Church in the black community. Once again, the bishops seemed to respond favorably, but the proposal was still not brought before the National Conference of Catholic Bishops.

Shortly after, the bishops' committee called for a meeting of all groups that had special interest in the Negro Apostolate to refine our proposal. This meeting was rejected by the Caucus at its April meeting in New Orleans. Instead, the Caucus instructed its Executive Board to go back to the bishops and get a yes-or-no answer on whether they would fund the Central Office for Black Catholicism we were proposing.

At a June 1969 meeting with the ad hoc committee and some others, the bishops were annoyed with the Caucus for having refused to meet with other interested groups. The Executive Board of the Caucus explained some minor word changes in the proposal for a Central Office of Black Catholicism. We reaffirmed our original position that the Caucus was asking the bishops simply to make it official and support it financially. They were not being asked to establish or organize or develop it. The meeting ended with a strong reminder from Father Augustus Taylor of Steubenville, Ohio, of the ridiculousness of educated black men having to come begging to white folks to be allowed to work effectively with black people. The proposal—indeed, our whole idea—was designed within the context of black leadership for black affairs, and sought to limit the options open to the bishops. It was important to eliminate the reality or even the appearance of its being one more example of black people being used to control blacks with only a pretense of black leadership. The bishops and monsignors said they understood.

So much for procedure. At their annual meeting on November 1969, the U.S. bishops "approved" the idea. So far what this means is not yet clear and the Office has not really gotten much beyond that.

It is crucial that the group in power be in full control of the media of communication within the system. Once in control, the desire, much less the possibility, of opposing opinions being expressed is remote. Control of the vehicles of communication is essential for a racist and oppressive society. Once these media are in the proper hands, the group that considers itself and behaves as if it were superior can immunize both itself and the controlled group against any ideas that might challenge the status quo. It can prevent the spread of any knowledge that may help unite the suppressed group.

In the American Catholic Church, the media of communication, press, radio, and closed-circuit television are completely white-controlled. During 1968–69 there were five national Catholic newspapers, eighty-seven diocesan newspapers published locally, thirty-nine diocesan editions of national newspapers, eleven foreign-language newspapers. They had a combined circulation of 6,786,000. There were 316 magazines in the United States with a circulation of roughly 21 million.

There is not a black publisher, editor in chief or assistant editor. There is certainly no black person on a decision-making level. Until August 1968 there was no regular column in any Catholic paper written by a black man, nor even one that dealt on a regular basis with what the bishops themselves have called "our major domestic problem." On the whole, the staff is completely white. Very often, this leads to the ridiculous when these reporters interview black people (in contrast to nice Negroes with whom they are familiar). When they see these interviews in print many black people are angered.

The Catholic press in this country has picked its audience. It is white, conservative, and runs the whole range of what we call the middle class. But, above all, it is white. The Catholic press is one of the greatest friends this audience has. It conscientiously nurtures and defends its readers against anything upsetting. It is questionable whether the Church desires communication with black people, whether it wants to allow whites the opportunity of examining themselves in the light of how blacks see them. Such an examination could prove to be extremely helpful.

In June 1968 I received a letter from John B. Kennedy, editor of Universal Press Syndicate, based in New York. I was then in Indianapolis finishing graduate work; my two-year leave from the New York archdiocese had ended and I was awaiting reassignment.

Universal Press Syndicate furnishes feature materials to the Catholic weekly press in this country. Mr. Kennedy's letter was brief. He had seen some of my writings, an article in *Ave Maria* and a statement in the *National Catholic Reporter*. He thought they showed promise for sustaining a weekly column.

I had three questions. Could I say yes? Was the Catholic press ready for me? Would I be able to be me?

The first question revolved around my estimation of my own ability and free time, the latter being secondary. Since 1962 I had written articles for various Catholic newspapers and magazines. In addition, I had done some book reviews, but I was not interested in a writing career.

Mr. Kennedy was apparently satisfied with what he had read. Friends pointed out that "I had no choice." I had already spoken out on several occasions about the absolute whiteness of the American Catholic press. More than once I had remarked that "Catholic" in regard to our press was a misnomer. Now, they said, with the football thrown to me, I had no choice but to take it and run like hell. "Never mind the fumbles," said one friend, "just catch it and run." I decided to do that, but there were the two other hurdles.

How ready were the American Catholic press and its audience for me? It was a consideration of less importance to me personally than to the success of the attempt. By 1968 I already had a reputation as a "radical" and a "militant" and all those other useless descriptions that white folks use on black folks and on some white folks whom they do not wish to hear or understand.

The people at Universal decided that this was their problem. By this time I was dealing with James F. Andrews, then managing editor of *National Catholic Reporter* and author of *The Citizen Christian*. He told me that they had considered it a gamble they were willing to take.

Would I be able to be me? It was a very personal consideration, and to me the most important. When I try to communicate with white people—which is what one does when he writes in the Catholic press—I want to be able to tell the truth about white people. There are also things I want to tell Negro Catholics about white people and about themselves, which they don't know and may not want to hear. I want to say these things as a black man. I want to say how I feel and what I think. If what I had to say were to be conditioned by how it would be received by white people, I would be merely one more black face sounding like a white person.

It was a big question. I was concerned about the Syndicate's editorial policy. Would my articles be chopped up under the name of "editing" in order to make them pleasing and acceptable to white people? Would some editor with little knowledge of black people and the black experience be anxiously mutilating and "correcting" my views of a life that is part of that experience? I told him I felt little need of anyone's editing for content. I did not believe there are too many white people around, even editors, who knew enough of the black experience to take that task upon themselves with any assurance. I was fairly well sick of white folks who simply assumed they knew everything, including the black man, so much better than any black man.

Mr. Andrews understood my fears. All he asked was that I try. I did, and I have not yet been disappointed with the editors at Universal. Unfortunately, some of the editors of the local papers have not followed Andrews' example. Some have done real jobs on many columns "to strengthen them."

We agreed on "The Black Voice" as the title. No emphasis was placed on the "the." There is no one black voice for black people any more than there is one for white people. Some people were perturbed. They have suggested the "the" should be "a." We had assumed that most people would not read in the implication that all black, colored and Negro people think the same as Lucas does. I began on August 19, 1968, with five columns entitled "Reaction to the Death of Martin Luther King," "Gun Hysteria and Race," "Another Commission, Another Report," "Color Blindness," and "Communication Between Black and White."

Seven diocesan newspapers carried the articles. Among the first were *The Magnificat,* Buffalo; *St. Cloud Visitor,* Minnesota; *Catholic Times,* Columbus; *The Advocate,* Newark; *Eastern Kansas Register,* Kansas City; *The True Voice,* Omaha; and *Denver Catholic Register,* Colorado. Over several months, the number of papers grew to twelve, and then settled around fourteen. The number has never gone above fifteen out of 126 papers.

My own experience with the column, other writings, lectures, and public sermons have led me to conclude what many other black people in and out the Church have concluded. The Catholic Church does not really desire any communication between black and white, especially on racial matters. Dialogue is encouraged with nice, safe, moderate and responsible Negroes, whom the Church nurtures and supports. The manner and content of the communication desired are the nice little "getting-to-know-you" sessions in which some Negro gets up and tells white Catholics "all about Negroes." This reinforces stereotypes about Negroes, though in a more sophisticated way. The Negro tells them about the "progress and the great strides we are making." And, above all, we are making it "with the help of you good white folks and so we must continue working together as in the past."

There are exceptions but the New York archdiocese's *Catholic News* is typical. You can get the full details, with obvious approval, of any outdated statement
that Roy Wilkins or Bayard Rustin might make.
Whenever an archbishop or a white organization
makes some contribution to a "worthy" Negro cause,
or grants a scholarship to one or two Negro children,
or says something nice about a good Negro, or dresses
up a Negro and gives him some title, or makes a Negro
president of one of the white man's Negro Catholic colleges—brother, that's *news*. If a Negro bishop praises
his boss's "Christian act" of granting full public burial
to a known racist like Perez in Louisiana, when sixty
Negro clergymen in New Orleans call on their congregation to reject the *Black Manifesto* that calls on the
Churches to make reparation to blacks, you can read it,
every word, in New York's *Catholic News*.

On the other hand, if you are interested in what
James Forman, representing the Black Economic Development Conference, actually said, what white priests
challenging their racist Church in Newark are saying,
what black priests and people are opposing and fighting
for in Chicago, you'd be hard pressed to find more than
a passing word in the *Catholic News*. "Militant" and
"radical" blacks as well as "communists and criminal-
coddling" whites who support them, whether priest, religious or layman, simply do not exist.

Those who control these papers are strongly
backed by their readers. The kinder critics see the
column as "very negative." White Catholics are not
even willing to consider the possibility that in America
and in the Church they and I live in two different
worlds. They dismiss this notion faster than a "bad
thought."

Joy is rather limited in the black man's world. One

of the purposes of "The Black Voice" is to reveal that world to white people who abhor violent revelations of it but run from nonviolent revelation of it. Violence disgusts them, they say, even though they use it all the time. My words displease, embarrass, anger and turn them off. Funny thing about white people. They get embarrassed, angered, and turned off when I speak and write about how white people think and behave toward black people. Their attitudes and behavior do not anger and disgust them. It's my talking about how they are killing black people that disturbs and disgusts them. That's why "The Black Voice" has found its way into no more than fifteen Catholic newspapers.

After several weeks, I talked about the column with some Catholic editors. Monsignor Raymond Bosler, himself a columnist and editor of Indianapolis' *Criterion* was typical. I mention him by name only because he is a friend. He had from the start wanted to take the column but was fearful—and in Indianapolis, he has reason to be—of white reaction. Bosler was not typical because after he faced the situation, the *Criterion* did accept the column.

William F. Buckley and Father Daniel Lyons, S.J., can find room in all kinds of Catholic publications. No one gives a damn about how what they say affects black people or whether or not it turns black people off.

Similar criteria are used for the lecture circuit, though there is not so much central control, as in the press. A parish in my archdiocese presents Monday evening discussions involving high-school youngsters in the area. When the topic of race came up, I was mentioned as a possible speaker. Immediately some on the steering committee had qualms. "Maybe Father Lucas will come on too strong," they said. "Maybe the kids will be turned off."

I mention this not because I had an unquenchable urge to speak to the kids of that parish, or of any other for that matter. The point is that many white Catholic groups are having this problem. They want to communicate with black people, but on their white terms. What, for example, does "too strong" mean? He doesn't pull punches? He doesn't apologize for being black? "Too strong" for whom? White people? Black people? Everybody? It would have made more sense to say, "Father Lucas is stupid," or "he is ignorant," or "he is biased on this matter." But, to make that judgment, one would have to know something about the situation. Then he would have no difficulty proving that Lucas is ignorant and biased. And what a joy for a superior white man to show up an inferior black man before a white audience! But no, "Father Lucas may be too strong." Now, I ask you, what the hell does that mean?

I suggested to a friend from that parish that there are other priests in the archdiocese, and close by, with black faces. If any of them are judged safe enough and not "too strong" for white people, why not ask one of them? And if you don't need a Roman collar for authenticity, how about Roy Wilkins? Better yet, if you're only interested in Negroes to discuss race on the basis of what whites will accept or will not "turn off," why not have Willie Mays talk on baseball?

Several years ago when Father Joseph Leonard's book *The Theology of Race Relations* came out, everybody began talking about theology and race. I gave a talk to the Maryknoll Sisters at their motherhouse in Ossining, New York, attempting to apply some principles of moral theology to events. One of the professors of moral theology from the seminary was present. During the discussion that followed the talk, he let it be known that while he agreed with what I had said "on the whole," there were a few things to which he had strong objections. Unfortunately, the professor did not want to discuss those points then, while I was there. He apparently preferred to wait till I was gone so he could refute me.

I had asked him what was being done at Maryknoll seminary in the area of theology and current racial issues. The doctor of theology informed me without hesitation that they were waiting "until they got a trained expert." This was around 1965. I received no answer to my question, "Until you get this expert from Timbuktu, how about discussing present racial problems in terms of the principles and values you now teach, and supplement this with guest lecturers?" To my knowledge, they are still waiting.

At about the same time, St. Joseph's seminary, the major seminary of the New York archdiocese, recognized that it had to make a pass at this matter and they made it in typical fashion. White priests were invited several times during the year to give lectures to the entire student body on "the Negro problem." They represented varying degrees of knowledge and understanding and some had little more to recommend them than that they had been in Harlem for a few years (with what results we may guess at). Some had spent sixteen to eighteen years in Harlem confirming the attitudes they had brought with them. Looking at black people from close quarters through racist eyes usually does nothing more than strengthen the racist eyesight.

In 1965 there were five black priests belonging to and working in the archdiocese. Two had lived in Harlem all their lives, and one of those, myself, was then assigned to a Harlem parish. Not one of them was invited to the seminary to speak for himself. Perhaps they were afraid we might have identified the Negro problem as white people.

Apart from the white control of the communication media in the Catholic Church, and their subordination to white interests and concerns, there is also the individual problem of communication that blacks and whites encounter when they try to talk to one another. It is doubtful whether they are ever doing more than speaking past each other. Communication is exchanging not words but meanings.

Social psychologists, for one, distinguish between the denotative and the connotative meaning of a word, that is, the specific definition in contrast to the wide range of ideas and emotions which are associated with a given word. The word *work,* for example, may have a different meaning for a member of the lower class than it does for a member of the middle class. For a middle-class person, *work* may symbolize the means of getting to such objectives as prestige and the realization of one's talents. For him, work may be satisfying and desirable in itself. The lower-class person, on the other hand, may think that *work* symbolizes an unpleasant but necessary means of securing food and shelter; in itself, work is neither interesting nor desirable.

People from these two classes, when discussing the subject of work, may hardly be talking about the same thing. Believing all the while they are talking about the same thing because they are using the same word, they may really be talking about very different realities. You can imagine the situation when blacks and whites, or any people with totally different experiences, discuss (with emotions added) topics such as crime, police or welfare. Since their experiences have been so very different in America, when blacks and whites communicate they often use words which convey more high-pitched emotion than mutual understanding.

I think the kind of inability of whites to understand can be seen in the following examples. The first, which is by no means an isolated one, further suggests why I sometimes feel that unwillingness to understand sometimes causes incapacity. I have already referred to the statement of the Newark priests on the subject of the Church's racism and to the establishment's reaction to that statement. I wrote an article called "Twenty Christian Men" for my column agreeing with the statement and describing their action as a very Christian one.

The following response, reprinted whole, was written by an intelligent, educated, Catholic gentleman in a responsible position of the Catholic press. The author is Joseph R. Thomas, managing editor of *The Advocate,* in which both our articles appeared. *The Advocate* is the official organ of the Archdiocese of Newark and was one of the first diocesan newspapers to subscribe to "The Black Voice."

As a Catholic as well as a newspaper man, I am dedicated to the free flow of information, criticism and ideas, even those with which I do not agree as long as they are not contrary to faith. I am convinced that the suppressed idea or ideal is the seedbed of turmoil, as current events in the Mideast, Latin America and Czechoslovakia tend to prove just as some events in Church history have proven.

Because I believe this to the depth of my being, I have put aside, after as much anguish as any decision has ever caused me, the temptation not to publish this week's column by Father Lucas.

It appears on the following page because I also believe that Archbishop Boland, as publisher of *The Advocate,* would want it there as the strongest possible affirmation that there is no lack of freedom in the Church, even if courtesy is missing, and that the Church is listening to the black man.

Further, I also believe that more harm than good would come from a decision not to publish this particular column. Father Lucas, after all, has involved himself in the Newark controversy on the side of the protesting priests and to withhold his column could result in but one more excuse to heap abuse on the archbishop.

This having been said, I would like to offer a few comments of my own on the specific content of the column because I consider it biased, sophomoric and unjust. The reference to Archbishop Boland's age, for instance, is totally irrelevant. At 73 he has a great deal more understanding than Father Lucas because he is attempting to resolve the problem, which is more than Father Lucas appears to be doing with his insults. In addition, I question the ethics of anyone who involves himself in a dispute and then undertakes comment on it. You can make your own judgment on his "objectivity."

Further, his reference to the expected reaction "from the top down" is completely false and misleading. The fact is that the archbishop is listening to the protesting priests. And he has not kept them from making known the agreements which have been reached thus far.

One suspects that Father Lucas would rather ignore this because it doesn't square with his mythological conception of Church leadership, just as his simplistic crack about whites fleeing urban areas because of black migration doesn't square with the complexities of reality.

I see precious little evidence that people who reduce the complex to the simple and then adopt a self-righteous stance based on the cultural myths of the day contribute much of anything to the solution of real problems. Rather they peddle such anti-Christian concepts as separatism (white or black) and then look for rationalizations to disguise its inherent racism.

Oh yes, some blacks as well as some whites are guilty of racism and if you can't find any evidence of it in the current offering by Father Lucas then you haven't been paying attention on those occasions when he has attempted to define it. The insulting, sarcastic stereotype of white Catholics in the Newark Archdiocese is a perfect example.

What disturbs me is not that such attitudes exist, nor even that they are held by a priest, but that they have been expressed by a priest who has indicated that one of his concerns is overcoming racism. It is a tragic indication of just how far we have to go.

It is also a commentary on the fruits of racism because no matter how much I might disagree with the particular points made by Father Lucas, or even with his general approach to racial problems, it is simply not possible to escape the fact that there are inequities in our society and the black man is the victim of them.

Perhaps the fact that he is now talking back is a necessary step in overcoming those inequities. We'll know that progress is being made when he can view return criticism as something which one gives to an equal.

Meanwhile, it might help if we who call ourselves Christians would remember that if we have anything against our brother we are to reconcile ourselves with him before offering our gifts at the altar. Archbishop Boland in this instance has shown us how. Some evidence that Father Lucas is willing to do the same would be welcome. Until then he will continue to come across as nothing more than tinkling brass.

Mr. Thomas identifies himself, and states his ideals as a newspaperman. Because he believes in his ideals "to the depths of (his) being," he resisted the temptation not to publish my column that week only "after as much anguish as any decision has ever caused me." He failed to mention the several times he did not resist the temptation, however, to edit my articles.

I had written on the New York City school strike, an article entitled "Labor Strike Myth," which suggested that the strike was not a labor problem, but simply camouflaged as such. What was involved was what the public schools in New York City, as elsewhere, had always been. Public schools have always been controlled directly or indirectly by those whose children formed the majority of their students. It had begun with white Anglo-Saxon Protestants, moved to the white Irish Catholics, and now rests, by and large, in the power of the white Jewish population. The point was that because whites have run from the inner city and because the black and Puerto Rican communities have come of age, these communities must now control their schools. Black people and Puerto Ricans must bring about a system of education that will be relevant to their children.

Like other religious leaders, the two Catholic bishops whose dioceses were involved maintained their customary irrelevancy through silence or an inconsequential whisper. A strong specific statement and involvement will come some time after the issue is resolved. In this, they are simply reflecting most Catholics. Ironically, it has always been a principle of Catholic philosophy of education that the parents have primary responsibility for the education of their children. Once again, the poor, especially the black poor, see how readily we can ignore our principles and stay aloof when becoming involved on the basis of our principles might upset the powerful and monied. We hope that other cities might choose not to impede the legitimate course of history and some Catholics might contribute to that choice.

When my article appeared in *The Advocate* this concluding paragraph had been deleted. To discuss what the bishops did and did not do simply would not appear in a paper whose managing editor and publisher wanted my column on "Twenty Christian Men" there ". . . as the strongest possible affirmation that there is not lack of freedom in the Church, even if courtesy is missing, and that the Church is listening to the black man." The same kind of editing was done to an article I wrote on the Mass of Unity that took place in Chicago, and has occurred intermittently.

Just a few months before, *The Wall Street Journal* in an article on the Catholic press quoted Mr. Thomas to the effect that the liberal and independent *National Catholic Reporter* had opened the way for editors of diocesan papers to become bolder in what they can print. Apparently "what they can print" does not involve anything that might embarrass bishops. Apparently, moreover, his own boldness lessens a great deal and his ideal of the "free flow of information, criticism and ideas, even those with which I do not agree . . ." shifts a little when a black man describes the ecclesiastical establishment for which Mr. Thomas works.

Then Mr. Thomas offers "a few comments on the specific content of the column." I had mentioned the archbishop's age. Every paper, including his own, had done so. Mr. Thomas had listed the ages of the spokesmen for the priest group and he himself had written an article giving the biographies of the priests involved. He thinks that describing whites as fleeing the inner cities is a "simplistic crack"; that Archbishop Boland by living seventy-three years knows more about it than I who have lived all my life in a white-created black ghetto, and who know ten times more black people in the Newark inner city than he and Boland put together would care to know. He questions "the ethics of anyone who involves himself in a dispute and then undertakes comment on it." By the same logic, how many "ethical" questions should he have about Pope Paul VI who is involved in the birth-control issue and comments upon it and Archbishop Boland who is involved in the Newark issue and is commenting greatly upon it? How appropriate is it that the archbishop's wishes should determine what comments of an opponent in a dispute with himself should appear in a newspaper "dedicated to the free flow of information, criticism and ideas"? Moreover, Mr. Thomas, the questioner, while expressing his views on the matter, is also managing editor of the paper of the archdiocese directly involved. No ethical questions plague his mind when he uses his privileged position as managing editor for his own advantage. He changed the original title I gave my article from "Twenty Christian Men," to "The Controversy in Newark." In the middle of my article there was a box with large type, "For Comment See The Press Box, Page 10." He interrupted my column to say to his readers, "Do not miss my objective and sensible commentary on this article on page 10."

A final "specific" was that my remark about expected reaction from the top down was "completely false and misleading," protesting that "the archbishop is listening to the protesting priests." But events bore out my expectation. The archbishop first denied the priests' chaiges, and then went on to detail all he was doing for Negroes. His listening was also as expected.

Irene Leath is a black woman who had been very involved in Newark. Mrs. Leath lives in Plainfield, New Jersey, with her husband and two grown children. Having recently admitted to herself the truth about the Catholic Church's relation to black people and now very much involved in trying to bring about change, Mrs. Leath had taken a prominent role in supportive rallies for the dissenting priests. She has no illusions about Boland's listening: "We had two meetings with Boland. He scheduled one for us with Father Joseph Stulb [whom in the midst of the uproar he appointed as vicar to serve as liaison between the chancery and black people without consulting black people]. We turned down this meeting as useless. The sessions with Boland were a waste of time. All he wanted was to make a good public impression by meeting with us. His one concern was to protect white interests and the hell with black people. In addition, he was most arrogant."

Mr. Thomas' analyses of my articles demonstrates better than I could the difficulty of communicating realistically with white Catholics on these matters. Too many whites wear blinders or have serious mental blocks. On a radio program I mentioned earlier, I was discussing the social responsibility of the Church in America with Father Daniel Lyons, S.J. As soon as we got around to the Church's behavior regarding black people, Father Lyons wanted to talk about Swedes and the Chinese. "Not too many of them are Catholics," he stated. "The Church regretfully had not gotten around to them." He wanted to talk about the Swedes and Chinese so that he wouldn't have to talk about why blacks are excluded from the Church's seminaries, religious orders, schools and other institutions. When we got to racism in the Church, Father Lyons wanted to talk about his going to school with Negroes and about "black anti-Semitism."

Black anti-Semitism was the myth propagated by Albert Shanker, president of the United Federation of Teachers, to gain support for the illegal teachers' strike, which was opposing the legitimate demands of black and Puerto Rican parents to control the schools their children were going to. In this crisis, black people faced a Jewish-dominated school establishment and U.F.T., and if opposing this school establishment in New York City is anti-Semitic, was not the Jewish challenge to an Irish establishment anti-Irish, and had not the Irish challenge to the W.A.S.P. establishment been anti-Protestant?

Dishonesty and deceit are so often a part of black/white "communication." Remember in the past how blacks communicated with whites in power. We said one thing among ourselves and as soon as the man appeared, we showed our teeth and told him what he wanted to hear. Oppressed people are geniuses at survival. Black people in this country are experts on surviving. The individual Negro realized that if he told the man what he really thought or felt, it could cost him his job, his position, his welfare check, his very existence. In order to salvage something of his pride, he called what he was doing "diplomacy" and white folks went along with the game. Remember until about ten years ago how damn diplomatic Negroes were, especially those who had any intention of "getting ahead" in whitey's world? Negroes had diplomacy down to perfection.

The white man controlled what the black man said to him directly and what he said publicly. Even privately, the black man had to be careful lest he be "turned in" by another oppressed man currying his master's favor. This is typical of what happens among oppressed peoples. Now, however, times have changed. Many black people have lost their fear. And so they are speaking out. The truth has made them free. They don't give a damn about what their ex-owners think. The more they talk, the more other black people will be encouraged to do likewise. Good and sophisticated white folks are less willing to reveal their true intentions or expose their true minds. They are expert at euphemism and nice words.

When whites say, "What can we do to help the racial problem?" they really mean, "What can we do that looks good without really making any basic changes?" "Morality" is laws, traditions and customs that justify, support and maintain white supremacy. "You can't legislate morality" means "Don't try to control my behavior until you change my attitude, which I won't let you do." "We are with you and your goals, but only by peaceful, responsible means" means "Pray, sing and march in *your* neighborhoods but don't use the means and techniques we have always used to attain our goals." "Peace" is equivalent to not disturbing the white tranquillity of mind, their homes, businesses, recreations, all nourished by racist attitudes and behavior. Justice, equality of access and opportunity, respect for the oppressed, are at best secondary considerations. "Law and order" is nigger control. "Support your local police" means back up those whom we have commissioned to keep the nigger in his place.

I do not mean that the words "law and order" are necessarily disguises for other things. If you are reaching for the exception, let me say that order does have a definite place in society and laws are necessary in relationship to order; but the two words are not synonymous. But by "order," many people are not talking about an ordering of society in which all men will be able to live with dignity and justice, in which all men will have equal opportunity to the resources and wealth of America, in which political power will serve all the people and not just some. By "law," they are not talking about just laws that will maintain, encourage and develop such an ordering of society. They are talking about preserving an order with little justice, and certainly not for black people; an order which can only be maintained by suppression. They mean enforcing on black people by whatever means necessary those laws, traditions and customs that maintain the existing system.

Let us take as our norm the words of St. Paul: "Never get tired of staying awake to pray for all the saints; and pray for me to be given an opportunity to open my mouth and speak without fear and give out the mystery of the gospel of which I am an ambassador in chains; pray that in proclaiming it I may speak as boldly as I ought to" (Ephesians 6 : 18–20).

One evening at St. Elizabeth's College in Convent Station, New Jersey, I remarked that I did not trust white people. It was only incidental to what I was saying, yet a nun arose to ask me, "Is it really true you distrust white people? After all," she added, "I trust you. Why don't you trust me?"

It took me a few moments before I was able to respond. I was simply flabbergasted. It was inconceivable to me that any white person should be surprised or upset because black people do not trust white people. I told her, "I do distrust white people. There is no reason in the world why American black folks should trust American white folks. And until they give us reason to put faith and confidence in them, the situation will remain the same."

Sister trusts me, or at least she thinks she does. She had never met me before that night. It would have been difficult for her to consider the question, Apart from me, do you trust black people? She knows very few.

White Catholics, like all whites, continue to give black people reason to distrust them. In the past they, and especially those in responsible positions in the Church, could count on black people to allow themselves to be deceived by their lies, hypocrisy and deceit.

In a chat I had once with Archbishop Cooke of New York, the subject of my column and the archdiocesan newspaper came up. I had written to the *Good News*, a Harlem inter-parochial pamphlet, noting that it was interesting that my own archdiocesan newspaper could not accept my column though it had just introduced three new white columns in an already lily-white paper. I asked, "Could it be that I was not safe enough

for whites and too relevant to blacks?" I suggested
that if this were the answer, then the time had come to
question the need and the presence of the *Catholic
News* in the Harlem community. At the time the
column was five weeks old and was being carried by
twelve diocesan papers. Many blacks and some whites
who subscribe to the *Good News* responded by writing
to Archbishop Cooke and the *Catholic News,* but to no
avail.

Well, Cooke told me how interested he was in the
column. After telling me how interested he was, Cooke
informed me that his hands were tied in the matter.
"It's an independent publication," he said, "and archdiocesan policy is not to interfere." I had simply made
mention of it in the *Good News* and had not requested
that he interfere. "But," he went on, "you can always
get it into the *Amsterdam News."*

The *Amsterdam News* is a Negro newspaper, at
least by claim, and it is the largest of those circulated in
Harlem. Now, whatever you may want to say about
Cardinal Cooke, he is nobody's fool. In the first place,
my column is syndicated in "religious," or more accu-
rately, in diocesan, newspapers. Whatever claims the
Amsterdam News has made, being a religious or diocesan newspaper was never one of them. More important, you don't have to be around too long to realize
the state of the so-called Negro press in America and
how irrelevant it is generally to black people. Many
publishers and editors of Negro newspapers and magazines have bought the white man's version of integration and acceptability for Negroes. Many with both
eyes focused steadfastly and exclusively on the cash register appeal only to the Negro bourgeoisie. Every now
and then a bone is tossed to the masses in the form of a
decent article relating to black people, an article which

is not superficial or watered down or geared to please white people. One doesn't have to be a genius to know that what pleases the Negro bourgeoisie invariably pleases the white middle class. By and large, the Negro bourgeois is a protégé of the middle-class white. In fact, the offspring sometimes outdoes his parents.

There is a growing number of exceptions. Young mavericks are springing up all over the place with publications. They are trying to speak honestly and effectively to, with and for the masses of black people. The *Amsterdam News* is not one of these exceptions. In the last twenty years I cannot remember any time when pleasing the white man for the cash register's sake was not a primary consideration. A few decent columnists more than balanced by the safe and acceptable-to-whites bulwark do not counteract the overall image and policy. A black man, except one that has committed a crime, rarely makes its pages if he is not recognized by the white community. The recognition need not be by way of approval. It may be very strong disapproval. What is important is that white society recognizes you. If the white man gives you a title, even though it's obvious tokenism or you are a Tom's Tom, you're solidly "in" in the *Amsterdam News*. Stokely Carmichael and Rap Brown were unable to get a line until the white press, the white television and radio "exposed" them. The white communications media, like white society in general, may have hated their guts, but it recognized them. That's what got them into the *Amsterdam News*.

Cooke knew all that. Let us, our white Church in a white society, freeze Lucas out and ignore him. The *Amsterdam News* won't help him poison the minds of our good and safe Negro Catholics, or to antagonize white Catholics. So I am told with a broad and disarming smile. Never mind the *Catholic News,* you can get

your column in the *Amsterdam News*. I resisted the
temptation to ask, "Who pays attention to the *Catholic
News* unless they are sick?"

The policy of noninterference was another matter.
One example of this kind of "noninterference" in which
I was personally involved comes readily to mind:
Selma, Alabama, 1963. I went down with about thirty
priests of the New York archdiocese. Incidentally, the
venture had the blessings of the late Cardinal Francis
Spellman, who helped to defray some of our expenses.
There was a different editor of the *Catholic News* then
who felt the paper should have at least a passing acquaintance with reality, including black reality. He has
since left his job and is now working for a secular newspaper in Chicago.

The editor at that time asked me to phone in a
story, which he printed unexpurgated. It was several
weeks later that William F. Buckley, Jr., addressed the
annual Holy Name Communion Breakfast of the New
York City Police Department on this matter and that I
wrote, as I mentioned previously, a detailed refutation
which I sent to the *Catholic News*. The editor at that
time would have let it through, but he ran into static
from higher-ups. I called the cardinal and insisted on
speaking to him directly. Cardinal Spellman told me he
would obtain a copy of the talk and wanted my response, and promised he would take care of the matter.
Apparently he did. Two days later the editor called me
to say my entire article would be printed and how
would I like it handled.

Now I realize that memories can be short. I realize, further, that a new man in office can change policies
rather quickly, but the Cardinal's secretary at the time
was Terence Cooke. About our chat I am inclined to
think that the diocesan policy of noninterference really

means "noninterference when it doesn't suit our interest." He simply could not come right out and tell me that there is no place for a real black man in the irrelevant and racist *Catholic News*. He could have said that they are not yet ready to communicate with and reflect militant and radical black people in their white paper. He could have told me that my column would poison the minds of good Negro Catholics and alienate their white liberal friends.

When Cardinal Cody told Father Clements he would be made a pastor in Chicago after a little more "seasoning and experience," what else could he mean but that after George had learned to be a good house nigger? He just wasn't honest enough to say it. The immediate question to be asked is, More experience and seasoning in what? Since it was a parish involved, the only logical answer would be experience in parish work.

Now let's assume that Cardinal Cody thinks that mere years of being ordained automatically gives experience for no matter what. So a man who had spent twenty years in a chancery office would have twenty years' experience toward a pastorate. Of course, if he is not supposed to be a pastor in a parish but merely a bill payer, that's another matter. And experience or putting in your time accomplishes what? Put an ass and racist in a black community for five, ten or twenty years and will he come out an experienced expert on black people, and relevant to them? Is there no possibility he will come out a bigger ass and a racier racist?

The Catholic press offers the same lies. When people in New York heard about "The Black Voice," some began to inquire why their paper didn't carry it. A black nun went down to see the editor about it. He was extremely polite. He told her he knew about the column and was very interested in it. "But," he said, "in this age of the emerging layman I feel they would rather have a Negro layman doing a column."

The *Catholic News* has nine regular columns, three written by priests, six by laymen of whom two are women. They are all white. And with six lay people out of nine columnists, the editor is so infatuated with the "emerging layman" that that is what's holding up the appearance of a black face. He could not bring himself to tell this black woman the truth. So he insulted her intelligence by telling her that the *Catholic News* was looking for a Negro lay columnist. He hasn't yet found one.

The Clarion Herald of New Orleans had begun my column in the January 2, 1969, issue. Five months later in the June 2, 1969, issue there was a piece describing a new column to be entitled "What's Your Bag?" by Father Jerome LeDoux, S.V.D. It pointed out his qualifications and knowledge of *local* affairs which would be a balance for the paper's national coverage, which is handled by Carl E. Rowan and William F. Buckley, Jr.

Five months before, *The Clarion Herald* had introduced my column under an article heading "New Column Gives Fresh Race Insight." It went on to say, "Race relations are the number 1 problem in the New Orleans Archdiocese as Archbishop Philip M. Hannan sees things, and in the United States as a whole in the view of many experts. . . . To help toward a better understanding of this joint problem, *The Clarion Herald* brings a fresh insight in a column by the Rev. Lawrence E. Lucas, who will tell it 'Like It Is' regularly on the editorial page."

Five months later, without any explanation and under the heading, "New Column Starts with This Issue," in opening words almost identical to the ones they used five months earlier, they wrote, "A sparkling new column, 'What's Your Bag?' appears this week on the editorial pages. . . ." There was one mention of "Like It Is" (the name they gave "The Black Voice" in New Orleans). "As he [Father LeDoux] is especially conversant with conditions and needs in the South, his column which replaces 'Like It Is,' by the Rev. Lawrence E. Lucas, will give a good balance to national comment by Carl E. Rowan and William F. Buckley, Jr."

The Clarion Herald chose not to say that after five months they had succumbed to the white racists of New Orleans and had to substitute a local Negro whom they felt would be more palatable. There is one lasting effect, however. For some time to come, as a result of "The Black Voice" or "Like It Is," there will be a black face appearing on a regular basis in *The Clarion Herald* of New Orleans.

The same reasons for mistrusting whites exist on all levels. The Sisters of Charity pulling out of Harlem because "their house was condemned" is a typical example. Just recently when I spoke in New Orleans to black children about loving themselves, a nun walked out. Some of the sisters were annoyed that I had been invited to speak. Just before I spoke they had been discussing the question of the schoolchildren's being forced to attend daily Mass. Anyone who has been either a victim or perpetrator of that kind of nonsense knows that it gives no glory to God but only some kind of strange satisfaction to certain pastors and school principals. They think forcing them to go to weekday Mass makes them "good" and encourages them to "love the Mass." Most of the sisters had agreed with Sister Catherine Clough, the principal, and opposed the pastor's argument that the practice should continue.

The week following my appearance the sisters changed their minds. This was their way of getting back at Sister Clough for having invited me.

A whole book could be written on the ridiculous excuses religious communities used to give and still give Negro applicants when they do not want them. Since they are too dishonest to say simply, "We do not want you; you are not good enough for white Catholics," they say instead, "You'll be lonely away from home and miss your Mommy," or "There is something wrong with your eyes." They never told you what it was nor could any doctor discover the malady. No doubt, it was that your eyes were protected by black eyelids.

The same dishonesty results because Catholics refuse to apply to themselves what they say. A few months after their 1968 Houston meeting, when the U.S. bishops issued a statement recognizing the moral right of conscientious objection to war in general as well as to specific wars, the Bishop of Minneapolis could not allow his name to be placed on the program of a four-week adult course on "Urban Challenges to the Church," which was sponsored by the Urban Affairs Commission of the Archdiocese of St. Paul and Minneapolis, because David Pence, a conscientious objector to the Vietnam War and a worker for the Twin Cities Draft Information Center, had been asked to address the group.

I remember back when Manhattanville College of the Sacred Heart in Purchase, New York, through its president and some of its students, was making all kinds of statements concerning justice and the need of the Christian education of Negroes. It took several years more before it dawned on the same institution to accept a Negro girl.

The attitude of the diocese of Brooklyn as well as

the Archdiocese of New York during Albert Shanker's illegal strike was typical. The Church's philosophy of education has always maintained that parents are the primary educators of their children and have first responsibility in this matter before Almighty God. Any school system, public, private or parochial, they have always said, functions in a secondary capacity to the parents and is responsible to the parents.

Strong opposition to blacks' sharing the power involved in policy-making and the control of a major share of the educational budget of the city, a budget which is equal to the entire budget of many cities, culminated in the U.F.T.'s three illegal strikes over a three-month period. This did not bother the law and order folks much. But the parents of the fifty-five percent black and Puerto Rican children in the New York City schools must continue to fight to bring about a system of education that will be relevant to their children.

When W.A.S.P. control of the American school system was thought unresponsive to the needs of the Church's children, the American Church organized its own school system. It did so with the aid of outside money, particularly from French Catholics, even as late as the mid-nineteenth century. Nor did the Catholics forget the public schools. In the large cities Irish Catholics particularly not only built their own schools but fought for control of the public schools. No one gave a damn about qualifications in terms of degrees following teachers' names. The Irish realized that performance not paper was what counted. And they learned quickly that performance depended primarily not upon experience or degrees but upon concern, interest, expectations, and identification of the administration and teachers with the children.

If an Irishman had talked any nonsense about qualifications, he'd have been laughed at. The Irish knew that until they got themselves into the establishment, in a position to make decisions for their children in order to meet their children's needs, they could not turn to such questions as academic qualifications and experience. They were quite properly interested in having concern and love shown to their children by people who could understand and identify with them and not see them as "those others." They understood what harm could be done to children's incentive and ability to learn by teachers who expected them to steal and lie, who assumed that they could not learn and therefore could not be expected to learn. No number of M.A.'s or Ph.D.'s could make up for such attitudes. Small expectations, or none at all, exert far more influence on kids than anything else. This is true no matter how good the school is physically or how qualified are the teachers.

That is why in the Irish or Catholic school system, as in the public schools, the basic requirement for administrator and teacher was that he be "one of us." In Catholic schools, the only academic qualification was that the teacher have a veil on her head and a crucifix on her bosom. Nuns with college degrees are a fairly recent phenomenon. But they taught their own. It was the establishment of those days who talked about "qualifications" to the peal of Irish laughter, to the clench of Irish fists, and to the crash of Irish-thrown bricks.

The white Catholic ecclesiastical leadership in the two New York City dioceses affected by the strike remained silent for two months. In spite of the Church's philosophy of education, and its history, all we got from two of the bishops, Cooke of New York and Mugavero of Brooklyn, was a statement just before the strike ended expressing the hope that it would soon be over so the children could get back to learning. When the strike did end, another equally weak statement was issued: "The people of the City of New York," it said, "are grateful that once again all of our children are back in their classrooms receiving the instruction which will open for them the door of hope for a bright future. . . ." If there's anything that black and Puerto Rican children are not getting in their classrooms, it's instruction; and if instruction does occur, it is not opening doors of hope for bright futures.

A month later the Secretary of Education, Monsignor George Kelly, issued a press release calling for Catholics to run for the local school boards that would be set up under a school decentralization program. It was more an appeal for Catholics to be in a position to make sure they get their share of federal money that might be forthcoming, recognizing the inevitability of at least some decentralization.

In the meantime the question of community control of schools was raised in the Archdiocesan Priests' Senate which has some rather interesting priorities. (In a memo of priorities, the "Negro mission in Harlem and other areas of the Archdiocese" came under category nine, "Other areas of concern." Altogether there were nine categories.) After a special and stormy session on this issue and after going through "all that the Church has done for Negroes," "the importance of qualifications," the "danger of being involved in current disputes," and a recommendation from an Irish priest that "we wait until after the passions die down," the Senate sent a statement to the cardinal for his consideration. They approved of community control of schools and mentioned some steps to be taken. A few days later the secretaries of education of the Archdiocese of New York and the diocese of Brooklyn sent out a little-publicized two-page statement to the priests. The gist was: on the basis of the record, it can be concluded that an overcentralized management of the city's school system in recent years has proved ineffective. It was pleasantly worded to please everybody.

So far, this has been the total of *official* Catholic contribution to New York City's crisis of community control of schools. It is not too difficult for blacks to notice that the Church behaves differently where its own are involved than where "those people" are concerned. Apart from the double standard, they cannot see that a properly educated black community would be a boon to the entire country.

There was once an occasion when a white Catholic lady posed this dilemma: Several black families had recently moved into the neighborhood and one of the youngsters was caught pilfering some cookies from the local grocery store. She asked me quite sincerely what was she to do. She wanted her kids to play with the Negro children but she also did not want them to acquire the habit of stealing.

"Did you know the name of the Negro kid stealing?"

"Yes."

"Had this kind of thing happened before the Negro kids came?"

"Of course."

"Did you know the names of the children involved then?"

"Yes, I did."

"What did you tell your kids then?"

"I told them not to play with those children."

"You did not tell them not to play with white kids but you called particular kids by name, right?"

"Yes."

I was not so sure of that kind of solution, I told her, but the point was obvious. When one Negro child stole, the name wasn't important. The solution was, "Don't play with the Negro kids." When white kids stole, the solution was not "Don't play with white kids," but, "Don't play with so-and-so."

The subject of stealing brings up another point. The notion of theft that we learned in the seminary from the moral aspect was that it is an unjust taking of what belongs to another against the owner's reasonable wishes. Key words are "unjust" and "reasonable." We still say we believe that. We continue to teach and explain it. Yet many businessmen in the ghettos, overcharging for inferior goods and services, have literally been stealing for years from those who can least afford it. If they make enough money, they are welcome guests at the White House and city halls and bishops' residences all over the country. On the other hand, as soon as one of their victims snatches something and runs or holds up the place at knife point (since that's the only way the man gives up anything), or a store is "looted" during a "riot," then everybody starts talking "criminals and crooks, those who want something for nothing." They shed tears over the "hard-working man who cannot make an honest living because of those people."

You see, the man was never honest and has no intention of becoming honest. And when it comes to hard work, the "looters" have more of it. They have to wait for the right time and have constantly to be on the lookout for the bullets of law and order.

I do not condone looting, armed robbery or stealing. I propose no medals for hoodlums or victims of a depraved society who prey on innocent men and women, usually the elderly and usually their own, in the streets and in their homes. What I am saying is that if we judge these things in the light of our alleged principles and beliefs rather than our emotions and prejudices, oftentimes it is the "good, hard-working businessman" who is the greater looter and crook. The titles "businessman," "shopkeeper," or broker or lawyer, or "store owner" are frequently euphemisms for respectable crooks. And those whom we are quick to condemn may be seeking redress through the only means their oppressors have left open to them.

I condemn criminals, lawbreakers and crooks as much as Vice-President Agnew, Cardinal McIntyre or Mayor Sam Yorty. Perhaps I do it more so because their chief victims are black people. Where I differ is in how to identify crooks and where an effort for change and correction should be made first and most strongly. That's also where I differ from most Catholics I know.

I know a monsignor who is pastor of a somewhat large Negro parish in a rather wealthy diocese. It took some time to persuade him that in an entirely black community the rectory help ought to be black, and I didn't mean just the cooking and cleaning jobs. Several months after he hired a black cook and a black handyman, I ran into him and he complained to me about the cook's dishonesty. He had caught her "red-handed, stealing a small ham." He just couldn't believe that "there are people who would steal from the Church," and he suggested that that's why some pastors will not hire them.

Of course, we know that some white Church help, including ushers, for example, have been in business for themselves for years. What is worse, Church administrators have been stealing for years by the salaries they pay, by the long working hours and little vacation, by the lack of benefits and all such conditions they inflict on their employees. But these pastors do this kind of thing for God and simply do not and cannot think of themselves in terms of dishonesty and stealing.

The monsignor's cook was a forty-five-year-old widow with two children. Do you know what, in 1965, she was being paid by this complaining man of God? She was making forty-five dollars a week and putting in about fifty-five hours with one afternoon off. By any standard of Catholic moral theology, the pastor was the crook and the woman was making up for a disgraceful salary to keep herself and her kids alive. The real thief was complaining about the "stealing" cook. Morally, she could have been taking every damn thing in that house, including himself. He paid the other help with equal justice. And that situation is not out of the ordinary in the Church.

Another example of the peculiarities of Catholic operation when black people are involved can be seen in the Church's reaction to the *Black Manifesto*. Basically, it is an official document of the Black Economic Development Conference. It called for $500 million from the white Christian churches and the synagogues in "reparations" for the enslavement of black people. The money would be used to "establish a Southern Land Bank; a research-skills center to deal with problems of black people; black communication centers and publishing houses; a black university and an international black fund-raising effort; a national Black Labor Strike and Defense Fund."

Much of the rhetoric of the *Manifesto* as it outlined the failure of the Church sounded like the 1958 statement of the U. S. Bishops, "Discrimination and the Christian Conscience" or their April 25, 1968, "Statement on National Race Crisis." Some of it recalled the remarks of Cardinal John Wright, then

Bishop of Pittsburgh, to the National Conference of
Catholic Bishops at their general meeting on April 16,
1969. He recalled the 1968 statement when "Within
the Catholic community we pledged to strive toward
(a) total eradication of any elements of discrimination
in our . . . institutions; (b) to use our resources *responsibly and generously* (italics mine) in view of the
urgent need of the poor. . . . But now," he went on,
"we can look back over a year of effort. In reviewing
our commitments of last April, it seems clear that in
some areas real and measurable progress has been
made. In others we are still at the starting line. In all
areas, the need far outdistances our efforts and the employment of our resources to date. The plain fact is
that the need exceeds our resources, actual and poten-
tial. But we agreed in St. Louis that this fact, while it
might explain failure to solve the problem, would not
excuse failure to act." Some of the rhetoric of the *Manifesto* did not resemble any of the bishops' statements.
A lot of it resembled the New Testament.

On May 21, 1969, the New York archdiocese issued a three-and-a-half-page "Statement on the Black
Manifesto." In rejecting the *Manifesto,* the New York
statement denounced its rhetoric as "closely joined to
political concepts which are completely contrary to the
American way of life." The statement said that Mr.
Forman's pronouncements "have caused all of us to reflect deeply upon some of the frustrations and aspirations of the black people. However, in view of the
Manifesto's rhetoric, its manner of presentation and
other substantive considerations, we do not endorse the
Black Manifesto or its demands." The notion of reparations was dismissed with the conclusion, "The concept of reparations is highly controversial."

Previously, Fathers Harold Salmon and Emerson

Moore and myself—three of the four black priests of the New York archdiocese—were requested to discuss the *Manifesto* with Monsignors Joseph O'Brien, vicar general, James Rigney, secretary to the Cardinal, Harry Byrne, chancellor and director of the Housing and Urban Renewal Office, and Gregory Mooney of the Human Relations Office. Cardinal Cooke was away at the time. The discussion was frank and calm. After we refused to talk about the Harlem vicarate, which I did not believe should be given a small sum of money in order to avoid dealing with the *Manifesto,* we got down to business. It was clear that the chancery priests were already of the opinion that James Forman should not see the cardinal, that no money should be given, and that the *Manifesto* should be rejected. Apart from one who had a "few reservations about the rhetoric," the three black priests were of opposite mind. When the statement appeared, it was hard not to suspect that once again we had been "consulted" for our agreement with what had already been decided. Our opinion had made no difference and had no influence in the final decision.

The New York statement gave every indication that conclusions had been reached on other bases—after which theological and other reasons were sought to justify them. Up to this time the archdiocese has not given a dime nor has Cardinal Cooke seen fit even to discuss the matter with Forman or any member of the Conference. To dismiss the concept of reparations as "highly controversial" is hypocrisy. The notion of reparation and vicarious suffering is an integral part of Catholic Christology and is basic to our theology of the sacrament of penance, especially where justice has been violated. Moreover, unless one makes the assumption that the present situation of black people is the result of what "our grandfathers did," then there is room for restitution for present white behavior. Finally, this same Church had no difficulty acting to make its opinion known and influential in such controversial subjects as birth control, abortion, state and federal aid to parochial schools, etc. If the Church used the same criterion about controversy, it would have to avoid Jesus with a ten-foot pole.

That nun who was disturbed because I do not trust white people should have been disturbed if I had said I did trust them.

5

My Lord, What Have They Done to Your People?

Negro Catholics have been fed a distorted religion that makes it almost impossible for them to identify with or support the black revolution. Because they refuse to see, or cannot understand, that Catholicism has become a pseudo-religious support for the white enslavement of black people, they are torn between their natural inclination to be what God made them and their desire to be what they consider Christian or Catholic. They cling to the white man's distortions as true religion and the true message and experience of Jesus Christ. Negro Catholics have become victims of a professional job of whitewashing.

One of the great monuments of the white racist system is the behavior of black priests individually or in groups in the National Black Catholic Clergy Caucus.

Black priests, I have always maintained, are on the whole the most intelligent body of men in the Church because of the high degree of selectivity used in admitting them to the seminary. Yet the good Catholic lady who accused me and all black priests of being "niggers first and Catholic priests second" was wrong. That is precisely the problem, we are not niggers first. And that is exactly what we should be. The seminary system is well geared to take stupid, mediocre, and exceptional white men and transform them into stupid, mediocre, and exceptional white priests. The same system takes only the cream of the crop of black young men and transforms them into educated, exceptional white priests with black complexions. What changes are being made are taking a lot more time than some of us feel we have to give.

Take the case of the burial of Leander Perez and the reaction of our most illustrious black priest, Bishop Harold Perry. Mr. Perez so violently defied the authority of Archbishop Joseph Rummel in his attempt to integrate the parochial school system in New Orleans in 1962 that Rummel excommunicated him. Excommunication by the Church is an official and *public* penalty for a *public* crime. Mr. Perez never publicly retracted, but at his death he was given full and public Church burial. Archbishop Philip Hannan, the Archbishop of New Orleans, justified this by disclosing that Perez had made a private retraction, which Hannan had accepted a year and a half before Perez's death, and that he had been receiving the sacraments.

I am aware of the realities of repentance and forgiveness. I am aware that no amount of Christian burials or masses can change the essential future relationship of a man with God.

Bishop Harold Perry, Hannan's auxiliary, is an intelligent black priest and a bishop. He knows all about public crime, public penalty, public repentance and Christian burial as understood and taught by the Church. Nevertheless, Perry called the burial of Perez with the Church's full rites something that "should gladden the heart of a true Christian." A white man's act of hypocrisy was described by a black man as "something that should gladden the heart of a true Christian," while six white priests were protesting the same act.

In the National Black Catholic Clergy Caucus we black priests act as a group. The Caucus is not yet three years old, having first met in April 1968. In this short period of time, it has come a long way.

It was becoming increasingly clear to black people that whenever and wherever two of them gathered together in His name (or anyone else's), they had better come together. Negro Catholics in general still have hangups about this. They are still doing their thing with interracial councils, though some encouraging signs are visible. Well, some black priests in Chicago realized for some time they had better come together. Lord knows they had all kinds of reasons in heavily Catholic Chicago to know that.

They issued a statement about the situation regarding black people in Chicago in which they said, "The position of the Catholic Church in Chicago with regard to black people has been, until recent years, one of enlightened paternalism. . . . It should be noted, too, that the Church has consistently followed, rather than led, the demand of black people for fulfillment of legitimate aspirations." After mentioning what was then being done, they offered ten proposals as minimum but immediate steps to be taken. They closed with the words, "These proposals are not exhaustive. In the light of our experience, they may be too little and too late. They are only minimal steps toward erasing the present image of the Catholic Church in the black community, the image of the white Church unrelated to the needs of the black community for identity and power." It was signed by all the black priests working in the Archdiocese of Chicago. Some of the press picked it up. The Catholic press, behaving as one has grown to expect, virtually ignored it. Then these priests realized: We cannot be unique in this racist institution, our experiences must be true of all black priests, all black Catholics everywhere. Why not get us all together and see and plan?

I was in Indianapolis when Father Clements called. We got together one night in Father Kenneth Brigham's place in Chicago. There were all the Chicago men plus Father Donald Clark from Detroit, myself and a few others. I had never met Clark before. Father Rollins Lambert was more or less the chairman of the Chicago group and later became first chairman of the Caucus.

The first Black Catholic Clergy Caucus met in Detroit on April 18, 1968. At the same time and in the same hotel, the National Catholic Conference on Interracial Justice was holding its annual meeting. The news got out in a hurry. Speculation among the whites who had gathered for the N.C.C.I.J. meeting was wild. White priests who had come to that from New York were "delighted" to see me in Detroit. They were suspicious: they wanted to know what was going on. Many hated my guts back home. I was difficult to live with. I was difficult to talk to. Well, all that is true. They had never had to live with a real black man or talk to him. Later on in Chicago one white priest and five white nuns walked out on Clements. "He is difficult to live with: he is difficult to talk to and plan with." That's no lie. George Clements is extremely difficult to live with or talk to or plan with. In fact, he is impossible if you're a white racist, and you want him to agree with your racist talk and to go along with your plans for the maintenance of white supremacy under the veil of helping black people.

But in Detroit, my white confreres from Harlem (in New York, the racial problem is basically the concern of the Harlem priest) were "delighted to see me." They were curious to find out what was happening. Unfortunately, I knew very little. They heard I had spoken, but I couldn't even remember that. Black folks are not supposed to get together and they are not supposed to keep secrets from white folks.

So they sought out the Toms. Almost before the end of each session some of our guys were on the phone calling their patrons back home, telling them all that took place. They told them who the bad niggers were and who the good niggers were. "And you know, boss," they assured their patron, "I'se with you." You can't despise them. You've got to love them. But you can't support them by letting them kill you. You've got to bring them along even if it hurts. Anyway, with something from the Toms, and more from their imaginations, there were great stories back home.

The very coming together of black priests was something remarkable. Even to have suggested as much ten years before, that black priests should meet without their white friends and confreres, would have been considered the height of disloyalty. In fact, some still suspect it is today.

Remember when Malcolm X spoke of the Bandung Conference of 1954, when the dark nations of Africa and Asia came together? "Some of them were Buddhists," Malcolm said, "some of them were Christians, some of them were Muslims, some were Confucianists, some were atheists. Despite their religious differences, they came together. . . . The number-one thing that was not allowed to attend the Bandung Conference was the white man. He couldn't come. Once they excluded the white man, they found that they could get together. Once they kept him out, everybody else fell right in and fell in line. This is the thing that you and I have to understand."

It took a great deal for black priests trained in the system to admit to themselves that they had to come together for mutual support and understanding, and to find the strength for their own survival and the survival and salvation of the Church. All our black priests were trained in white institutions; most are members of Southern-based religious institutions, are themselves Southerners and work in the South. Many are assigned to institutions, seminaries and schools in rural settings which limit their experiences of the black people in our large urban centers. Considering all these factors, and that it was the first such meeting, the statement that emerged was an accomplishment.

The three-page statement called the Church a "white racist institution, a part of America's racist society." It suggested that the major contribution the Church could make to the black man's freedom fight was to become a leader in combating attitudes and behavior that tended to maintain white supremacy both within the Church and in the society in which the Church has always been at home. "In the ghettos," it said, "the Church must respond to the new attitudes within the black communities."

The statement closed with a series of nine "urgent" demands of "charity."

1. That there be black priests in decision-making positions on the diocesan level, and above all, in the black community.
2. That a more effective utilization of black priests be made. That the situation where the majority of black priests are in institutions be changed; that black priests be given a choice of assignment on the basis of inclination and talent.
3. That where no black priests belong to the diocese, efforts be made to get them in, or at least consultation with black priests or black-thinking white priests be made.
4. That every effort be made to recruit black men for the priest-hood. Black priests are better qualified for this recruitment at a time when the Catholic Church is almost irrelevant to the young black man.
5. That dioceses provide centers of training for white priests intending to survive in black communities.
6. That within the framework of the United States Catholic Conference, a black-directed department be set up to deal with the Church's role in the struggle of black people for freedom.
7. That in all of these areas, black religious be utilized as much as possible.
8. That black men, married as well as single, be ordained permanent deacons to aid in this work of the Church.
9. That each diocese allocate a substantial fund to be used in establishing and supporting permanent programs for black leadership training.

However, the white man was not really excluded from the Detroit meeting. He couldn't have been: it would have been too much to ask. He was excluded in face only. He still had control over everything we said and thought. It was interesting how, when this group of black men got together, the rightness or wrongness, the appropriateness or inappropriateness, of everything we said had to be judged not in the light of what was right for black people but how white people would feel and respond and what white people, particularly the bishops, would think.

It took until 3:00 A.M. of our last morning together and four separate "final votes" to maintain the word "racist" to describe the present reality in the Church—a term which some white Catholics had already been using to describe the same reality. And at 3:00 A.M. some still wanted to "compromise."

We couldn't go on record to support black "violence" in the light of Christian principles (rather than white interests), and so we supported "black militancy." In fact, when I spoke the first afternoon on "responsible Christian violence," simply requesting that what black people were doing be judged in the light of the theological principles we learned in the seminary—knowing all the while that black people didn't really give a damn what we said about it anyway—one distinguished Divine Word Father leaped to his feet to ask me if I was ready to declare war yet.

The Society of the Divine Word had been accepting Negro candidates before most other groups. A large percentage of America's black priests are members of that Southern-based, German-influenced society. And the S.V.D.'s do deserve credit for producing some of the whitest black men in this country. I often wonder why some of our national Negro leaders have not joined up. You can hardly imagine the pain which the four of us who drafted the statement felt when for six hours ending in the early hours of the morning there was a terrific battle to ward off the attempt led by another distinguished Divine Word Father to weaken everything we had written. Some were even opposed to using the word "demand." Black priests, you see, could not "demand" anything from white bishops.

The second meeting of the Caucus took place November 7–9, 1968, in Washington, D.C. There was a larger attendance including some fifteen black seminarians. Sister Richelle Marie, O.S.P., then of Newark, New Jersey, attended as observer for the Permanent Conference of Black Nuns which had since been formed.

The Caucus had come a long way in seven months from a group of men, some of whom had difficulty using the words "black people" and among whom Black Power was never mentioned. We were angry, as all black people should be. We were outraged at the bishops for ignoring our April message. We wrote all the bishops of the National Conference of Catholic Bishops and told them we were angry and would be impelled to take further action.

We began the spadework to establish the Caucus on a permanent basis. Committees were formed and we divided up into four regions—East, West, Midwest and South—for which chairmen were elected. The chairmen were Father Donald M. Clark of the Archdiocese of Detroit, for the Midwest; Father Rawlin B. Enette, S.S.J., of Baton Rouge, Louisiana, for the South; and myself, for the East. A chairman for the West had not been decided at that time. Then an executive board was established, consisting of Father Rollins Lambert of the Chicago archdiocese as general chairman of the Caucus, Brother Joseph Davis, S.M., of Dayton, Ohio, as Caucus secretary, and the regions' chairmen and representatives.

With the help of Ronnie M. Moore, director of leadership development of the Scholarship, Education and Defense Fund for Racial Equality, Inc., and his able associates, we conducted a "sensitivity program on what it means to be black." We came to the conclusion that it was powerlessness, insecurity and fear which stood in the way of self-identity and responsible black action in our white institutions. We were soon to prove this.

We talked around, under, over, and beneath it, but we simply could not come to a decision on any meaningful confrontation in the event of another silent treatment by the bishops. Not only could we not, we did not want to. As a group we were not ready to pay the price or take the risks that freedom demanded. And so we talked about freedom and about blackness and unity, but we could not and did not want to decide what to do about getting our freedom.

The third meeting of the Caucus, which took place April 24–26, 1969, in New Orleans, found and left us exactly where we had left off after the second meeting —wanting to share in the power of the Church, wanting our freedom, but fearful of the price and the risks and, therefore, ready to compromise the very purpose of our being. This meeting, above all, demonstrated that while we excluded the white man's face, he was there anyhow, controlling our thoughts, and what we said and did.

We talked about "stopping and getting ourselves together," as if one could really stop in order to get himself together. The important thing always was to slow down or stop whenever it came to what we would do in the case of rebuff or a negative response.

Practically the whole meeting was centered around our proposal for a Central Office of Black Catholicism in the United States. You must realize that everything we suggest the white Church will go along with, until it comes to the control and administration of it. The white Church is interested in perpetuating itself as white and is quite willing to take on a little coloration of the situation in which it exists as long as the real control and administration are white. From the opening words of the chairman's report and discussions, all I heard was what the bishops said or wanted. Bishop Gerety, for example, wanted us to "refine the proposal and spell it out in greater detail." The last straw was the listing of all the "help" we were to receive in refining the proposal—the bishops' ad hoc committee, two-thirds white; representatives of religious orders working in black communities, mostly white; diocesan directors of inner-city affairs, almost all white.

Unable to take it any longer, I leaped to my feet. "Whose proposal is this," I shouted, "the bishops' or the Caucus'? White people's or black people's?" Quite frankly, I didn't care about what the bishops wanted; we did not need the help of white people who were soon to outnumber us in the very planning of "our" office. We had given them a twelve-page justification of what we were about. We had given them the proposal in a three-page outline.

At the end of their 1968 meeting and ignoring our demand "that within the framework of the United States Catholic Conference, a black-directed department be set up to deal with the Church's role in the struggle of black people for freedom," the American Catholic bishops had established a "National Task Force on Urban Problems" without a blessed word on a piece of paper. At the height of the *Humanae Vitae** crisis, the American bishops at their November 1968 N.C.C.B. meeting pledged one million dollars for an

* Pope Paul VI's encyclical on human life, called the birth-control encyclical.

"independent, non-profit Human Life Foundation" to study the rhythm method without again a single word on a piece of paper. Yet for some reason, these same bishops became hopelessly immobile and were unable to give any definite answer—except that they were favorable toward it—until they had on paper a proposal with all the operations of an admitted experiment spelled out in minute detail and built-in guarantees of success.

An enthusiastic response of the Catholic liberal press to the bishops' "favorable response" was to be expected. What was not expected was the contentment with that kind of nonsense by a group of intelligent black men who were, presumably, talking about power.

No sooner had the objections been raised and the suggestion made that we thank all the white help offered but refuse it, than a distinguished Negro priest stood up. He told us of the wonderful support we were receiving from the bishops and religious communities working in the black communities. If we proceeded in the direction we seemed to be taking, that support would be in jeopardy. One nun, who should have known better, observed with trepidation that Bishop Gerety might resign from the ad hoc committee. He is known as one of the black man's friends in the hierarchy.

A body of intelligent black men would suddenly become paralyzed if our friend Gerety resigned. The priest who was worried about losing white support had a point. However, he should have been far more worried about the objects of the support. The bishops were so damn favorable, they were unable to give a definite "yes" either to our assumption of power or to granting us a dime.

It was becoming apparent that what the bishops were favorable to, and willing to support, was not a black thing as originally proposed but something that was becoming increasingly white. White people were saying "we like" to our proposal for a Central Office of Black Catholicism, but while they were saying "we like" they were working to take over the planning, the administration and the control. And you can be assured that the whiter this black office became, the more white folks would come to like it. "You're alienating friends and making financial support impossible," objected another. There again was the white man's mind. If my desire for independence alienates my white friends then I am alienating not friends but patrons. If my white friends cannot support anything I control but can support what I do only when they control it and me, then I am alienating not friends but keepers. And I want out from patrons and keepers.

There was an interesting explanation of why we presented our proposal at Houston for general acceptance of the idea of the Central Office, rather than asking for a simple yes-or-no answer without negotiation or elaboration as we had been mandated to do. "The Central Office was the main thing and we did not want to jeopardize our chances." It seemed difficult for some to understand that the Central Office wasn't worth a thing unless it was an exercise of power, a share in power, by black people. Moreover, to allow, much less participate in, something that would be advertised and propagandized as bowing to the legitimate demands of black people, and aiding their independence, while it was really nothing more than the same old white control and white power and white supremacy would be to participate in a lie and a cruel hoax.

The sad shape of the white-wrecked intelligent black men came out poignantly during the whole discussion about power. A body of elite black men was

talking about power and at the same time concerned
about reassuring white bishops and religious superiors
that there would be no limitation on their present
powers.

When dealing with power and black folks, white
priests, like all white folks, are great for theologizing
and philosophizing about power. When dealing with
power and white folks, white priests do not theologize,
philosophize or just talk about power. They get an
issue and in confrontation over that issue, they acquire
power, using all means necessary. At the third meeting,
black priests were perfect examples of the pupil running
before the teacher. We did not have to talk about
power and white folks. Those go together like bread
and butter. But when it came to power and black folks,
black priests went all out for theologizing, philosophizing and talking. Now, I do not have anything against
theology and all the rest. Those who know me know
better. Those who do not will believe what they want to
anyway.

Some of the group began talking about going to
black people, to black Catholics to support the office.
But even if all Negro Catholics were to become black
people overnight, it is hard to imagine that the three
percent of the Catholic population, the lowest on the
economic scale, could support such a project. Besides,
of course, it avoided the issue. The issue was black
people's sharing in the power and resources of the
Church. The issue was whether the tremendous resources—political, moral and financial—of the entire
Church were to be put to the service of freedom for all
black people, or used to support their suppression. If it
were simply a question of doing our little thing alone
with safe Negro Catholics who would be financed by
poor Negro Catholics, we would not have had to go to

the bishops, our financial brokers, in the first place.
Thus, many wanted to define blackness, examine it and
dissect it. Many wanted us to "stop and get ourselves
together"; to define, theologize, philosophize and do
everything about power except exercise it.

The next proposal was still another example of this.
After we had agreed that the board of directors of the
proposed Central Office be black, someone made the
suggestion that Negro bishops should automatically be
on the board. We were playing right into the hands of
the sophisticated white racists who are experts on the
Tom system. You know the way Brother Malcolm used
to describe this system. "The slavemaster," he would
say, "took Tom and dressed him well, fed him well, and
gave him a *little* education; he gave him a long coat and
top hat and made all the other slaves look up to him.
Then he used Tom to control them." And intelligent
black men were telling their slavemasters that all they
had to do was choose *their* Negroes, dress them up
prettily in red, make them celebrities and call them
bishops, and we would automatically put them on our
board. This was the board of a Central Office that was
supposed to give black people power and free them
from white people.

I opposed that motion and said we should make no
distinction between priests and bishops. So far as the
board was concerned, there should be no automatic
membership. We could not afford to have Negro bishops automatically on the board because we do not
choose our own. A black priest rose to remind us that
white priests do not choose their own bishops either.
Aside from the different positions of black and white
priests in the Church, who in the Catholic Church
chooses white bishops but white bishops and influential
white priests? Who in the Catholic Church chooses

Negro bishops but white bishops and influential white priests?

When an intelligent black priest starts talking about how "white priests can't choose their own bishops," it's not that he is crazy or blind. It's simply that we have all been washed but rather than being washed in the blood of the Lord, we've been bathed in the whiteness of the system.

Then there was a major (or senior) seminarian there who was worried. "We've flubbed it," he said. "Nowhere have I heard Christ mentioned." Poor man, he had not come around to being able to recognize Christ operating in, through and with black people. You see, we didn't have to mention Him explicitly. He was there all along just as He is in our cities, involved with what black people are doing. He may have been a little disappointed, though. Perhaps that's why He wasn't recognizable. We were too busy with the white man's hangups about going too far, making waves, rocking the boat, and what we could do and could not do. Christ didn't have those hangups.

The third meeting of the Caucus was not completely disastrous. There were some bright spots. The brightest was a young seminarian from Chicago who was about to organize the black seminarians because, "He didn't want them to be like us." He was a sharp and thinking kid. He was saying things some of us are unable to say even now. He was only in his third year of high school. I remembered that when most of us were his age, we were too busy licking boots to be thinking and saying the things this kid was saying. Our future, if there is one, will be in good hands. On the plus side, too, we did vote to refuse, politely of course, all the white help being offered to "refine" our proposal. Moreover, we voted and directed the Executive

Board to present, again explain, and defend our proposal, but not to negotiate any changes. The bishops had enough right there to give a definite yes-or-no answer if they wanted to, and we were not ready to be treated like children. In the case of a "no" answer, we would decide our next move.

In a resolution attached to the proposal, we agreed that the Central Office must have real power and listed the minimum requirements already noted. We got to the elections and these were interesting because many of the bad guys were nominated for offices. Father Clark and I were the two nominees for chairman. This would have been unthinkable at our first meeting in Detroit. Clark became chairman and Brother Joseph Davis, vice-chairman.

At the convention of the National Black Sisters' Conference in Pittsburgh, Pennsylvania, in August 1968, I was privileged to have several talks with these beautiful black women. It was a week-long event that attracted over a hundred and fifty nuns from seventy-six communities in twenty-two states. They met under the banner of friendship and unity to discuss ways of becoming true to themselves as black women, relevant to the needs, aspirations and happenings in the black community to which they owe their particular being. They confronted one another honestly and talked about the need for black religious to consolidate, about responsible Christian violence, the meaning and importance of Black Power, etc. And they were ready. These black women were getting themselves together in a hurry.

One of the highlights of the meeting was the talk of

Miss Sandra Willingham, formerly Sister Melaine of the Sisters of Notre Dame. "Four months ago, I left the convent," she began. "I left for a variety of reasons, but basically I left because I am black, they are white and ne'er the twain shall meet." She was very frank in speaking of her own shortcomings and her psychological and emotional makeup. She went on, describing how she changed from being completely convinced of the value of the way of life she had chosen, to being completely convinced that it was a way of life for white people only. She made it clear that she had experienced no overt discrimination in her years in the order. "The abuse I suffered was solely psychological . . . all this was not to say that plain old crude racism was entirely absent. It reared its ugly head in most subtle ways, like the convent which I could never visit without being hauled into the kitchen or basement to meet the 'colored help.'" She mentioned that she had been forbidden to participate in any kind of race-relations activity during her first two teaching years. Then, finally, "Slowly, imperceptibly, there was evolving in me the conclusion that in choosing to be a religious sister first and a black woman only second, I was lying about my acceptance of what was culturally mine: I was forfeiting my birthright—selling my soul."

Miss Willingham's experiences, of course, were not unique. Her testimony in Pittsburgh became a lengthy article in the December 1968 issue of *Ebony Magazine*. Well, an Irish Catholic woman from Chicago had this salient advice to offer in the April 1969 issue of the same magazine. Stating that it would be a shame to waste a vocation for "so trivial a reason," she went on to add, "The Church, like the racist society in which we live in America, has made provisions for just such a situation. There are three religious orders that I know of that consist of Negro nuns. The one that I think is closest to her home in Ohio is that of the Franciscan Handmaids of the Most Pure Heart of Mary in New York.

"This is an order of Negro nuns and her superiors are all Negro and she should find happiness among her own people in the religious life, unless, of course, she is neurotic and would object to what she might regard as a segregated community of nuns." The lady concluded by mentioning the Holy Family Sisters in New Orleans and the Oblate Sisters of Providence with headquarters in Baltimore, Maryland, as alternatives, if the Handmaids did not work out.

Apart from the gall, the racism, and the stupidity, the writer was obviously ignorant of the whitewashing power of our racist institution. The Catholic system has done so thorough a job of wrecking black minds that it is far more difficult today to be a black woman in a Negro community than it is to be a black woman in a white community. The one exception is that order of women founded for the colored and Indians, where colonialism reigns supreme. My own experience, involving my younger sister, who is a member of the Franciscan Handmaids of Mary in New York, and hundreds of black nuns in Negro and white communities all over this land, bears this out. When the question was deliberately raised in Pittsburgh, it was the unanimous opinion of the nuns there that under present circumstances, it's easier being black in a white community today than it is in the Negro communities. In fact, the exodus of black women from Negro communities today is a "tribute" to the white system and an irreparable loss to the cause. The more these women leave, the less the chance there is of the reformation of the Catholic Church.

The first meeting together of black nuns in Pittsburgh itself was a living witness to the facts. Most of the white communities encouraged their black members to go and paid the fares. Apart from the Oblate Sisters of Providence, who had twenty-nine members present, both the Handmaids of Mary and the Holy Family Sisters, Negro orders, could muster only two from each community. The number from these groups who attended the conference at the University of Dayton in August 1969 was greatly improved. But the unfavorable attitude of one superior toward the whole business had not changed a bit.

When you stop to think, this state of affairs should not be too surprising. The superiors and the chapters or councils in which authority lies are mostly products of the nineteen-thirties, forties and fifties. Thus, apart from the fact that they labor under the illusions that ignorance is innocence and impotence is virtue; that holiness rises in direct proportion to the loss of humanness; that simplicity is acquired by relegating adult women to the status of children; that authority is exercised in regard to adults exactly as it is in regard to infants and, correspondingly, that obedience in adults is exactly the same as obedience in children; that the job of a superior is to make sin and imperfection impossible; apart from all these illusions (which they share with their white counterparts), Negro superiors have other problems.

Many of them were around when their particular communities came into existence out of the segregation policies of the white, Catholic, Christian orders which simply would not accept Negro vocations. For all of them, their coming into being, their continued existence and, in fact, much of their present support is due to some benign white patron. For many of these patrons, supporting Negro communities was an easy way of easing their consciences for not having lifted a finger against the segregated and bigoted system. Others were genuinely concerned and interested, and in the face of their inability to change the patterns, they saw these communities as the next best thing. Now that a new day has dawned, and black power is here to stay, these communities that could be the source of revitalizing religious life in this country and the world are shackled by superiors from a bygone day. The people in power have always been used to the Great White Father's bringing them forth, nurturing and protecting them; guiding, advising and leading them and, above all, paying the bills. These superiors now feel seriously threatened. Any attempt to break away from dependency upon white patrons is a sign of the grossest ingratitude. They can't understand that past and/or present kindnesses are not legitimate justifications for blocking a mature independence that allows growth. One Mother General I know shudders at the mere mention of "black" or "black power." The very words mean betrayal of past friends. Immediately we are told how good this cardinal or that monsignor or father was to us. "We can't let them down now." This is what women who desire to be black are running into. Some Negro superiors have become so whitewashed that they are using the same excuses to harass and damp the hopes of the future that white "religious" used to keep out or limit Negro membership.

Every time I see a Negro Catholic congregation at Mass (like most any kind of Negro congregation gathered in church) I immediately want to hum "Bringing in the Sheep." Here are all these lovely black sheep in their Sunday best. Unfortunately, they are not being brought in to be fed. The poor, unsuspecting sheep are being brought in to be fleeced of their God-given minds, their courage, and their ability to act as and for black people. And so I sing "Bringing in the Sheep," but I sing it with pain.

Black Catholics think that there is something irreligious in recognizing the fact that they are an oppressed group in the Church. They think it's immoral to admit that those who oppress them are the enemy. They think charity demands that they consider the man who is enslaving them a benign benefactor. But, when Christ said, "Love your enemy and do good to those who persecute you," He was not saying, "Do not see your enemy for what he is." He was identifying His enemies all over the New Testament. Nor was Christ telling us, "Let your enemy brutalize and kill you and oppress you; and yo' jus sho' him yo' smiling white teeth which matches yo' unthinking white mind." Being unable to see the truth is not love but insanity. It is going against the instinct He gave us, the natural instinct for self-preservation.

White folks love to quote to black folks (but not to white folks) the words of Christ to Peter the night He was arrested: "Put your sword back where it belongs! Those who use the sword are all destroyed by the sword" (Matthew: 26:52). They forget to remind black folks that on another occasion He had this interchange with His disciples: "When I sent you out without purse or haversack or sandals, were you short of anything?" "No," they said. He said to them, "But now if you have a purse, take it; if you have a haversack, do the same; if you have no *sword,* sell your cloak and buy one, because I tell you the words of Scripture have to be fulfilled in me: He let himself be taken for a criminal. Yes, what Scripture says about Me is even now reaching its fulfillment." "Lord," they said, "there are two swords here now." He said to them, "That is enough" (Luke 22:35–38).

Now unless you believe that Peter and some of the other disciples carried swords—obviously with Christ's approval—in order to clean their fingernails or to earn their living by pulling monthly heists at the Galilean National Bank, the only explanation for their customary sword-carrying is self-defense. They were prepared to defend themselves against the unjust aggressor who would brutalize, oppress or kill them. Christ simply reserved the right to decide when He would legitimately defend Himself and when for a greater good, when His hour had come, He would not defend Himself.

You see, Negro Catholics get all hung up on the nonsense white people tell them. They let white people fool them into putting all violence under the same hat. When black people engage in a little violence to defend themselves against the enormous violence of white suppression, Negro Catholics are "objective" and condemn all violence, meaning black and white violence.

I remember speaking to a Catholic Interracial Council after an incident at Cornell University in April 1969. I have, as I think I've said, a thing against interracial societies. They do a lot for white people but precious little for black people. A prominent Negro Catholic lady arose to ask me, "What do you as a Catholic priest think about the Cornell situation?" Her tone of voice told me exactly what she thought I should think. "I was horrified at the sight of those kids with guns. I don't see how that kind of behavior can be justified and how it helps the cause." She was applauded. One knows who and what white Catholic liberals applaud. Always concerned with winning friends and influencing people, I hastened to reassure her. I admitted that I, too, was horrified at the sight of the guns. It was not the guns, precisely, that frightened me. Evil men, or crazy men, or irresponsible men with guns horrify me. Good and sane and responsible men with guns do not automatically horrify me. Well, anyway, I told this woman that I was horrified at the pictures at Cornell, but not by the sight of the young men with their two shotguns and three rifles whose pictures were all over our television, newspapers and magazines. What horrified me was the guns that were loaded into the cars of the white kids, pictures the white press missed and white-operated television cameras could not pick up. Black kids did not first enter Willard Straight Hall with guns in their hands. Twice white kids attempted to oust them by force and were rebuffed. Only when word was brought that white students were bringing guns on the campus did those black students leave and reenter with the means of defending themselves.

I told the Catholic Negro woman that I was able to justify what those young black students had done and precisely as a priest. I believed I had learned the principles of legitimate self-defense taught me by my white professors. They had not told me that these principles were not applicable to black people. As to the cause, I told her that Cornell could be the beginning of a new day in regard to the cause. Let Father Theodore Hesburg, president of Notre Dame, make his naïve speeches in view of the relatively few, safe, and status-preserving Negroes he's got there. Let Mr. Nixon, the President of the white establishment, talk his silly talk about backbone and stuff: "There can be no compromise with lawlessness and no surrender to power if free education is to survive in America. When students terrorize other students, when they engage in violence, when they carry guns and knives in the classrooms, then

I say it's time for the faculties, boards of trustees and school administrators to have the backbone to stand up against this kind of situation." Mr. Nixon had no difficulty compromising with the lawlessness of the university in discriminating against blacks. Nor did he spell out that there can be no surrender to *black* power if free education for *white people* is to survive in America. After all, white people did not put the likes of Nixon and Agnew in the White House to mess up the good thing they had going in America.

"Did you realize what happened at Cornell?" I asked. "A handful of black students got their goals—goals with which white liberals agreed 'while disapproving of their techniques'—in a few short days. Above all, they accomplished this with no violence and not one drop of black blood being spilt."

There was news the press missed while concentrating on responsible black kids with guns and ignoring white kids with guns. Congress and state legislatures immediately caught on to the implications and roused themselves to push legislation outlawing guns on college campuses. Let's see what they do about the R.O.T.C.'s guns and the "peace-keepers'" guns. The President, the attorney general, and all good white folks condemned the Cornell students. It wasn't long before their Toms got into the act, too.

The whole pattern of Negro "progress" in this country was being put in jeopardy. You are quite familiar with that pattern. It goes like this: Defenseless black people march, pray, beg and sway back and forth singing "We Shall Overcome" for justice. White people "nonviolently" attack, brutalize, turn dogs on and kill these "violent" Negro singers and marchers. Then other white folks shed a few tears over the rich black blood flowing in the streets and pass another law which we really do not need and which they have no intention of enforcing.

At Cornell, white students had begun to arm themselves to keep the pattern going. At the University of Texas last year, six black students were killed by irresponsible policemen. You know what happens all over this land when black people are not prepared to defend themselves. They are massacred. But at Cornell, black students got ready. And when white students saw they were ready, they figured it was not worth the price of white blood. That decision upset the whole pattern of "Negro progress" in America. There were no black bodies over which white liberals could pour forth insincere words in funeral orations. And a Negro Catholic woman, to the applause of her white liberal friends, could not see how what happened at Cornell really helped the cause. I told the lady and her applauding friends that I could not understand their misgivings and disturbance. I thought they should be happy. I thought that progress without violence is what everybody wants.

Father James LaChapelle, S.V.D., a black priest at the Negro St. Elizabeth's parish in Chicago, told me about one of his parishioners pulling him to a corner of the sacristy one Sunday morning after Mass. He said, "Father, you speak well. You lift us up to the heavens. But talk to us of sanctification. Talk to us about Jesus Christ and heaven. Don't tell us about being black. Every time you say the word 'black,' you bring way down all those beautiful things you are talking about. You lower yourself." That is not unique. For years Negro Catholics have heard sermons in Church about Jesus, about sanctification and all about heaven. It was a sanctification, a heaven and a Jesus that did not get upset about black servitude, white racism in and outside of the Church.

In a survey taken among the elders at the same St. Elizabeth's—whose makeup is the same as that of most Negro Catholic parishes I know—LaChapelle found that to talk about being black and proud of it indicates to his parishioners: "Disrespect and vulgar language used by the young in the presence of middle-aged Negro men and women. To rob, rape, murder black and white indiscriminately. To bust whites over the head just because they are white. To loot and burn black and white stores indiscriminately, even if it means putting nine or ten soul brothers out of a job. To be dirty and stinky. To wear the natural. To be loud, noisy and undisciplined. To be a member of the Blackstone Rangers, Disciples, Black Panthers." Could George Wallace say it better?

The words of Father Vernon Moore, a young black, intellectual priest, are to the point. "It has been shown," he says, "very conclusively that the more Negroes identified with the Catholic Church and the longer they were a part of it, the less militant, less vocal, less strong they have been in their concern for civil and human rights and the less they have identified with their down-and-out black brothers and sisters."

Part of the tragedy is that these are the people who give the most "moral" and financial support to the white Catholic Church. These are the people the white system programs and produces, whom white priests train and are proud of. These are the responsible Negro Catholics out of whom white priests and bishops make "Negro leaders" and whom they consult *post factum* in order to say "we have touched bases with the black community."

After reading Albert Cleage's *The Black Messiah,* which discusses in biblical terms the building of a black nation, I asked Catholics in the neighborhood what they thought of it. Only several had even heard of it, and the story was pretty much the same when I asked other church-going Negroes. It was quite different when I asked the same question of people I know who have stopped going to church or are not affiliated with organized "Christianity." What are the chances that Catholics could understand, much less relate affectionately to, Stokely Carmichael, Albert Cleage, James Forman, Eldridge Cleaver? They are very slim. White control of the Negro Catholic's mind is behind the question that suggested this book: "Why is Father Lucas so bitter?" The fact that anyone could be wondering why a black man in America or in the Church is angry or bitter is amazing.

Another Negro Catholic woman, a friend of mine, was upset when a white priest in Harlem referred to me as a "black militant and radical." Catholics pray daily at Mass to join the "militant host of heaven singing, holy, holy, holy. . . ." The word "militant" and its derivatives, such as "military"—which my cardinal archbishop, as military vicar, wears with distinction— have a positive value connotation in almost any circumstance except one. I'd have to be dead not to be a "militant" today. But, my friend was well trained. A white priest called me a "black militant"; she knew that was bad. Ditto "radical," which simply means getting to the root of things. It never dawned on my friend that maybe there are some people by comparison with whom I am happy, and she should be happy, that I am a radical. Where would I be if I were not radical in reference to Cardinals McIntyre or Krol or some Harlem priests? But all this lady could think about was what a white priest called me. I have meant much to this Negro Catholic woman. She loved me and wanted to continue to do so, so she wanted someone to tell her it wasn't true. She looked for another white priest to tell her I wasn't a black militant. She has not gotten to the stage, where we all have to get, of not caring about what any white priest has to say about black people.

After a recent lecture, when I talked about how Negro "leaders" in the Church are selected, a young Catholic Negro woman approached me. She had agreed with everything I had said, but was a little upset over what I had said about the methods. She thought it was an attack on a particular person. "What we need now is unity. We have no choice now but to support him" (the particular person she thought I had in mind). She found it difficult to distinguish between an attack on the process and an attack on a person. The process is that the man chooses black leadership for black people on the basis of whom he considers a Tom. But even if he goofed and came up with a Malcolm, the process is wrong. But the man has got Negroes so hung up on the individual rather than the people, that the individual must always come first. It was like that in Chicago. Some were against doing anything because it might look like a personal attack on Father Lambert. The man pretends your complaint is a personal attack on Father Lambert, whom he so loves. If the man really loved Lambert he wouldn't try to make him a Tom. He would not have tried to use him against black people.

After appointing his Tom, the man tells black people that they must support him, because "black people need unity." Watch the man. When John or Robert Kennedy, or Viola Liuzzo threaten the interests of white people or white supremacy, the white man doesn't sit around talking nonsense about supporting them for the sake of white unity.

Frank Testa is a Roman Catholic priest of the Archdiocese of Newark. He is white and of Italian descent. His crime was being one of the twenty signers of the Newark statement about racism in the Church. At the time he was an assistant priest at St. Bernard's parish in Plainfield, New Jersey, and was the only priest in Plainfield to sign the statement. Plainfield has a large percentage of Roman Catholics of whom a large number are of Italian descent. So you know what happened when Father Testa signed the statement? Neither Anthony Imperiale, a councilman at large for Newark and living in Plainfield, nor any of the others ran around telling people in Plainfield, "You have to support Father Testa; he is white, Italian and one of us." His fellow priests in the rectory, good Catholic Christian gentlemen, stopped speaking to him. The people picketed; the good Catholic, Christian, white people began picketing the Church for the removal of their white, Italian brother, a Roman Catholic priest. Moreover, they threatened. They threatened to hit the Church in the collection basket. There was no appeal to have Testa removed on religious or moral grounds. There was just a demand. Frank Testa had to go. If he did not, they'd stop putting in their money. A white Italian priest signed a statement which offended white parishioners in a white, largely Italian community. The white Italian priest had to go. He now has a different assignment.

So it seems the young woman has been had. She thinks black unity compels her to support "dark pigmentation." I told her how the man gets to the white man who betrays white supremacy. Unity is neither virtue nor vice. Virtue or vice depends on the circumstances. Black people must recognize that unity is good when it serves the interests and goals of black people. Otherwise, it is bad.

I have no obligation to support a certain pigmentation. I support all blacks who serve and work for the freedom of black people. I do not, unless I am crazy, support anyone white or black who hinders black freedom. I am not supporting color, but mind, heart and will. If a mind, heart and will do not work for black people, they do not deserve support simply because their face is dark. Don't argue that Tom is not trying to kill you. Whether he is aware of it or not, the man is using him to kill you. If he is not killing you personally, he is killing black people, he is destroying the black nation. And if he is destroying the nation, he is destroying you personally.

The white man has no illusions on this matter. Anyone who dares to threaten seriously his interests must be stopped and eliminated. This is not a question for debate. But, when he appoints his dark-skinned tool to impede black interest and to maintain black slavery, he runs around telling black people with all the force he can muster, "support this man, 'my man'; black people need unity; they must support their own."

The Republican party during the 1968 presidential campaign had Senator Edward Brooke, a Republican from Massachusetts, trotting around telling black people to vote for the Republican ticket. "Support your senator" was the motto. The Republican party may have done a lot for Senator Brooke, and it's obvious it wants him to do a lot more for the Republican party. To support Brooke just because he had dark skin would be to say that black people needed Richard Nixon and Spiro Agnew. To say that black people stood to profit with this team, you'd have to be blind, deaf, dumb and dead.

Negro Catholics need to straighten out their minds. When the man appoints a Negro whom he thinks is a Tom, blacks must stop the nonsense of running around shouting, "We have to support him, he is one of us." He may not be one of us. The first question one must ask is, Is the man right, is he really a Tom? If he is, no matter what shade his skin is, he is not one of us. He is not for black people, but against them. He may be unconscious or ignorant. The question then is, Can he be helped, can he be enlightened, can he be made to serve the interests of black people? He cannot be helped unless he wants to be. He can be forced, but this depends on how much the man is willing to tip his hand and counter the force. Sometimes he will stand aside and let the Tom go down. He can always find other Toms. If he wants to be helped and can be, he should be helped, brought along, and supported. That's the only kind of support that makes sense, helping him to be a man that is out to free black people. There are cautions, of course. It is not a question of simply saying he needs and wants help. There must be definite signs given. And the revolution cannot be stopped or slowed down until his heart and head catch up. The nation must be built, black people must be gathered around their Christ with all deliberate speed.

When the announcement was made of my assignment as assistant at St. Joseph's in Harlem, it had been assumed that I would be made a pastor in one of the Harlem parishes. There had been many people asking for that and a lot of people were upset when it wasn't done. Letters were written to the archbishop stating that my assignment was one more example of white

Catholic backlash against a black man who says anything that displeases the establishment. One lady called
me in Indianapolis in tears. She told me a small group
had gathered at her house to discuss my returning as
assistant pastor at St. Joseph's. She said they all understood what the situation was. What got her so upset
was the realization of how "really brainwashed we
Catholics are." One of the group, she said, had felt obliged to observe that while she knew what was behind
it, "in fairness to the white priests, they did say that
Father Lucas was difficult to live with." She was repeat-
ing the words of one of the priests in Harlem, a man
who is ridden with misunderstanding, fear, and dislike
of the new movement. "Father Lucas was not liked by
those he lived with and was difficult to live with."

My friend asked her gently, "If that is true, don't
you think our priests are among some of the world's
great hypocrites from the way they act when Father
Lucas is around? You'd never guess some of them dislike him the way they do." The thing was whether some
white priests Lucas lived with liked or disliked him.
This was the criterion of a black man's acceptability in
a black community. Nothing was said about the reaction of the people in those parishes to Lucas. They do
not count. One would think that a black man who is a
priest in a black community is there on the sufferance of
the white priests with whom he is to live. Obviously,
there is no question of the white priests' having to live
with him.

To be honest, I must admit that I am difficult for
some white priests to live with. And unless some of
them are willing or capable of making some adjustments, I can frankly say I will continue to be rather
difficult. Let me tell you about this "difficult to live
with" bit. You have to understand my initial approach.

Catholic priests are normally ordained after four years of graduate work in a seminary. The usual age of ordination, then, is around twenty-five or twenty-six years of age. I had not bought or subscribed to the general belief that being newly ordained was equivalent to being newly born. I have always assumed that at twenty-five or twenty-six one is a grown man. This seems to me to be an ordinary presumption. I am of the school that believes authority is not exercised in exactly the same manner in regard to an adult as it is to a child. Obedience is not the same cup of tea for an adult as for a child. My pastor was a grown man and so was I. He had authority to exercise over another adult. His authority was limited by canon law, diocesan law and statute, custom, common sense, and the fact that two adults were involved.

It was with such a mentality that I approached my first assignment as a priest. It immediately struck me as ludicrous when many of my priest friends began to feel sorry for me. All kinds of well-meaning advice on how I should adjust was forthcoming. My pastor-to-be had a reputation in the archdiocese of being "difficult to live with." Apparently, white people, too, can be difficult to live with. All the advice concentrated on how I should adjust to him. There was not a word about his adjusting to me, though he was known to be difficult. At that time, they didn't know me yet. Unfortunately for me, I had never bought the idea that the pastor-assistant relationship, even in the Catholic Church, was identical with the father–little boy relationship. I had assumed that like marriage, this relationship also involved two adults. So one day I broke up just such a confab about my having to live with Monsignor Nevin by saying, "Here, wait a minute! What's all this about my having to live with him? We is got to live with each other and so we is got to adjust to each other." I left for Croton Falls with dire predictions and friends greatly concerned.

Three months later I was transferred. We had mutually adjusted to each other and were getting along reasonably well. What happened was that the good intentions of the archdiocese fell victim to the almighty dollar. In this country, the dollar only looks green; in reality it is white. And my Church has a long history in America of adjusting to white people with money.

Another example of "being difficult to live with" was my relationship with a pastor in Harlem. He had spent most of his over twenty-five years of priesthood in Harlem. In fact, I had known him as a youngster when he was assistant in a neighboring parish. I came to him in the middle sixties. He is a very kind man, the type who, if I were to find myself short and ask him for a shirt, would give me not only the shirt off his back but the five in his bureau as well.

Strange as it may seem, the problem lies precisely there. It is not his kindness that is at fault but a deep-rooted inability to deal with a Negro on any level other than the Negro's being in some need, the Negro's begging or requesting something he is able to bestow. It is this type of missionary that is too often found in the black community representing the Catholic Church. The Negro's *need* of him, whether it be of the social, intellectual or economic order, is the basis of the relationship. When the relationship is firmly established and accepted (that is, the superior white man doles out patronage out of largess to the inferior Negro) he is at home. He is happy; he is cheerful; he is well. He is extremely kind and generous. Everything is in its proper order. That's the way things should be. That's the way God always wanted it between white and black.

So he was happy when things were going according to God's plan. More than the Negro, he loved the situation when he would have to give one of them who was short a five-dollar bill. He was right at home when he was making decisions for one Negro, telling another what must be done. He sermonized brilliantly before an audience of elderly people, mostly women, on crime, dope addicts and prostitutes in Harlem. Never once did I hear him mention the complex causes that created the environment that made these escapes necessary. That would have led to questions; it would have endangered the myths of the white man's virtues. So on big feasts he spoke of the drunks, the dope addicts and the prostitutes in Harlem. There was no one else. There are almost three hundred thousand of them in Central Harlem.

There were sermons on love but somehow even this disturbed me. It kept coming through that even here we were miles apart. The love he demanded of whites for blacks was able to exist apart from freedom, real equality and justice for blacks. To my mixed-up mind, that was not love but patronage. The love demanded of blacks for whites seemed a combination of patience, forbearance, forgiveness and ignoring enemies, long-suffering and nonviolence, of course. To my mixed-up mind, this seemed more a tonic for servitude. That's the way it was. That's the way it is. That's the way it must always be. It's the only kind of black/white relationship he understands and knows. Always it must be the Great White Father making decisions for the ignorant and unintelligent Negro child.

Heaven help the black man who does not see the relationship quite like that. Of course I was difficult for him to live with. I hope to remain impossible. There was no way possible for that man to live with me in

perfect harmony and tranquillity. He used to come up
with all kinds of inexplicable maladies, none of which
have returned since we parted. He had never been
prepared to deal, much less live, with a black man.
Negro Catholics, too, have been conditioned. When a
white man says a black man is difficult to live with,
Negro Catholics know immediately that there is something wrong with that black man. The thought that
something is wrong with the white man cannot enter
their minds. And so Negro Catholics worry about me
as they are worrying about the Clementses, the Da-
vises, the Martin de Porres Grays everywhere. They
are worrying about me because the white man says I am
difficult to live with. I pray to myself, "Thank you,
Lord, for the George Wallaces all over this land.
Thank you, Lord, for it might take the Wallaces to
open the eyes of my folks. You know, Lord, George
would find it difficult to live with the original Uncle
Tom."

Some of my friends are anxious to get some racist
white priests to say that they like me.

A funny thing happened recently after I had appeared on a radio program. A lady I had known from a
former parish got very excited. She decided with several others that she had to do something to get my column in the archdiocesan newspaper. The next day she
went to an inter-parish Mass and came back completely
reoriented. "His column would be good for white
people but not for ours." When asked why, she replied,
"Our folks might leave the Church." She sees the drop
in attendance and is worried. But she has her vision all
mixed up. Black people are not leaving the Church.
They are waking up to the reality that the Church has
left them and is not making any steps toward them. So
they have stopped running after the white Church just

as they have the white-everything-else. She was like someone waiting at the bus stop behaving herself so the nice busman will stop. Meantime, the bus is heading away from her at fifty miles per hour.

A young black Catholic lady who attends one of our neighboring white Catholic colleges called me last year. She had heard me speak on several occasions and was wondering if I would speak at the kickoff of the semester programs of the Afro-American Cultural Society they had formed at the school. She was delighted when I told her I normally try to make myself available to black people at any and all times and would be able to make the intended date. Then she went on to add, "The last time I heard you, you spoke on racism; I wonder if you might speak on something positive like, for example, the contributions of Negroes to this country?"

I assured her that that approach would be fine with me. "But sweetheart," I asked, "whose understanding of what is negative and what is positive will I use—the oppressor's or the oppressed's, the white man's or the black man's?" One of the escapes, you see, for white folks when they don't want to hear or consider something is to label it negative. And as usual, they have whitewashed the Negroes who imitated them.

While white people play semantic games with "negative" versus "positive," racism is a very positive reality for black people. The recognition, understanding and eradication of it is of supreme importance. The attitude and behavior whereby it is better, more propitious, to be white than black in America and in the Church must be changed. There is a general intellectual acceptance of white superiority and supremacy in America and in the Church. In both societies white people have so completely put this attitude into practice on all levels—social, economic, political—that it is really better to be white than black. A human way of life is far more attainable in our nation and our Church if you're white than if you're black. Changing this reality could be regarded as "negative" if you're white; it's very positive if you're black. Racism is the chain around the neck, head, feet, arms and legs of black people and we will have to shout and fight and do whatever we can to break it.

There are really two major tasks confronting the black man. This racist society and its institutions must be drastically changed. What can be changed more immediately and effectively is how people behave rather than their attitudes and beliefs. This is not to say that in the long run real changes in attitude and belief are not more important but I would much rather first stop the man who is hitting me over the head with a stick before I try to alter his attitude about where I belong.

The second task of the black man is nation-building. These two necessities cannot be seen as a game of the "chicken and the egg." If buildings must be destroyed in order for human dwellings to be built, and if the destruction and the building cannot be done at the same time, the destruction will come first. Black people have no such option. They must deal with the destruction of racism and the creation and building of a black nation at the same time. There is a need in the black community for revolutionaries. There is a need to destroy and change what must be destroyed and changed. But revolutionaries must also be involved in the building of a black nation and ultimately an American nation. Together they make a very positive program. It's a program that is positive for black people, for white people, for the Church and for America.

Black people, like white people, do not achieve or fail to achieve in a vacuum. This book is concerned with the institution of the Roman Catholic Church in America. Like the overall society, its context is white and racist.

I celebrated a Mass in Newark one day. The occasion had been initiated by a group of black Catholic teenagers who made the preparations and invited adults from all the inner-city parishes and nearby areas. I was asked to be celebrant or president that afternoon and we did all we could to show how the Catholic liturgy can involve worship not limited to white culture but including Afro-American culture as well. The homily was a dialogue in which many people expressed their views on the scriptural and other readings at the Mass. For my part, I spoke briefly of the need of black Christians to get a clear picture of a black Jesus, interested in and concerned with the present interests and concerns of black people; a Jesus who is involved and part of what is happening in the black communities, calling into being a black nation through which will be achieved its own salvation and the salvation of the whole Church and mankind. "An appreciation of this kind of a Jesus engaged in this kind of a struggle," I said, "has been denied us by white 'Christians' for too long. We will have to do the job ourselves."

I had scarcely finished when a middle-aged Negro woman arose with tears in her eyes. She said she was a "born Catholic" and "had never had any trouble with white people." She "couldn't understand or appreciate all this talk about a black Christ. Couldn't we all go back to worshiping a colorless Christ?" She was roundly applauded by many blacks and whites who were there. (It shows that even some white folks have a natural inclination to shout and respond in Church.) My heart went out to that lady and all who applauded. She was a "born Catholic" and probably had no trouble with white people all her life. The poor soul has never begun to realize how she accomplished that feat by twisting and distorting herself. The changes and adjustments she had to make in order to be "loved" by white Catholics had never dawned on her.

The opening hymn was "Walking the Walk and Talking the Talk." These kids realized that for too long they had been talking the talk of the oppressed and walking the walk of slaves. And they had been doing this to please, to have no trouble with, and to get along with white people, white Jews and white Protestants and white Catholics. They had done this in order to survive. Now these kids had dropped that talk and ceased that walk of the past. They were singing with gusto, for they were talking the talk of freedom and were walking the walk of men.

That's what the older woman could not realize. She never had trouble with white folks. As a "born Catholic," she had had a head start in getting along with white Christians. She learned how to talk as they wanted her to, and walk the walk they bequeathed her. She knew how to voice their ideas and talk their talk. Moreover, she deluded herself into believing that they believed their talk. For years white Catholics have been talking about a "colorless Christ" who was Savior of all men and open to receive and relate to all men. And the more they said this, the harder they fed black people a lily-white Jesus, concerned only with white interests, who could justify anything done by white people, who was displeased with whatever black people did apart from what white people told them to do. This white Jesus loved black people who desired and strove to be white. If they continued trying to be white, and behaving like white folks told them to behave, after a brief period of peaceful, patient and nonviolent loving of white folks, this Jesus would take these black-skinned folks with lily-white souls and lily-white minds and lily-white hearts to a lily-white heaven. In this lily-white heaven, white folks would dole out to them some of their white goodies in a patronizing manner and the blacks would be colorlessly happy for all eternity.

If you cannot see my color, you are color-blind and should seek help. What is important to me is what my color says to you. What ideas, emotions, feelings, values and expectations well up within you? What actions or behavior patterns does it lead you to? At least equally, if not more, important is what my color says to me. What ideas, emotions, values, expectations its recognition gives rise to within myself. What actions and behavior patterns it occasions in me. The American fault, the Catholic fault, the you-name-it fault is not the absence of color blindness. It is that "blackness" and "whiteness" have been saying the wrong things to and precipitating the wrong kinds of behavior in black and white individuals and in the black and white communities. This is what must change, not the ability to distinguish color.

The goal is not to be blind to differences or to deny differences. Like the other goods God has given me, I love and appreciate my blackness. I do not want you to miss it, to deny it or try to separate it from me. I do not want you to hate it, lie about it, subjugate it, treat it as inferior, tolerate it or patronize it. What I do want is that you recognize it, appreciate it, love it and treat it fairly. That blackness is also me. I want it and God wants it.

Just a few years ago Father John Curry, a white priest who was trying hard to understand and relate to the now generation of black people was, after much frustration, being transferred from my home parish, where he had been stationed. Well, the folks got upset and angry and decided to do something about it. Sure enough, with the aid of their white advisers, these good Negro Catholics got all hung up on all those techniques —petitions, talk, "peaceful" marching, begging the bishops—techniques long distinguished for their ability to entertain white folks and their inability to move them. Needless to say, none of it worked. Curry went to Scarsdale, New York, where he is angering white Catholics by telling them they must become Christians.

White Catholics love to talk to black people about being calm and cool, not too forward in speaking lest they antagonize white liberal friends; be diplomatic and sweet and use the proper channels and, above all, nonviolent. Of course, white folks must tell black folks about this. Black people have only been doing all this for hundreds of years. White Catholics, like other white people, have never experienced those virtues. They simply talk about them to black folks. And if these virtues are so great for black people who have always exercised them, they ought to be able to do something for white people who, at best, have only talked about them. Any white person who really believes in them should not be wasting his time talking to black people, who know all about it. He should be telling all the whites he can find about tolerance and patience and understanding, about nonviolence and long-suffering. Then, if he can convince a sizeable portion of whites he will be rendering a great service.

White people win elections by appealing to the lowest prejudices and fears of ignorant whites; send out *their* police and F.B.I. to raid Panther headquarters, to shoot black teenage "looters," and to brutalize college students who rebel against their oppression. Then to give it the smell of respectability, white folks send for *their* religious leaders and their white-people President and Vice-President to glorify and urge the crushing of those who are dissenting against the wonderful system we have going. "And you young whites must remember you will soon inherit and be the establishment of this American way of life, this white way of life. So stick with us."

And you colored Catholics are in such a bag, you run around talking the same white garbage to your brothers while the man laughs and pats you on the backside. Do you really believe the man who is your enemy, who has been oppressing you all your life, will tell you who *your* good guys are and who your bad ones are? Is he the one to tell you whom you should listen to and whom you should follow?

Listen to him, fools that the white system has made us! Who else will inform us best how to defeat him than the oppressor himself?

6

My Lord, What Must They Do?

In the light of the preceding, Lord, it is necessary to say something about what must be done. Since we have been talking about a white racist Church made thus by a majority of white racist people, we have to speak in terms of what must be done by white people. There is a great deal for black people to be doing, but that is not the topic for this book.

Nor is this, Lord, a kind of magic pill, which if enough people swallow painlessly with a glass of cold water, they will go to bed tonight and awake tomorrow to a brand new world. In fact, things may get a great deal worse before they start to get better. And if whites keep electing racist comedians to high offices, and if we continue getting the type of leadership we have in the Church, we may have a major disaster on our hands.

Usually when whites ask, "What can we do to help the racial problem?" they really don't mean precisely that. What they mean is, "What can we do that won't cost very much, that will not be difficult, that won't upset or embarrass whites or change their basic pattern of doing things?" And that won't upset the essential black/white relationship? And that will be something, anyhow, for which Negroes will be eternally grateful?

This chapter is not intended to be a blueprint for the improvement of race relations. Throughout I have defined racism as an attitude of mind—white is by nature superior and must therefore control inferior black —and have described the patterns of behavior that reinforce this attitude. I have described and proven that the Roman Catholic Church in America is a white racist institution. It looks white, thinks white, acts white. Insensitive to black people, white interests control its every move and decision. Black people are a tolerated and controlled group that have no power. The question that faces the Catholic Church with regard to black people is not integration. It is whether the Church will survive in the black community and among black people.

If I judge from my experience in Harlem and other black communities and take into account what black lay people, religious and priests are finding all over this land, there is one trend that is emerging rather clearly: the black Catholic population is increasing in age and decreasing in numbers. The most generous figure estimates that roughly four percent of the black population is Catholic. This is about the same as the estimate made by the Second Council of Baltimore in 1866. If one counts in addition to the number of black heads over which the waters of baptism are poured in a given year—which is extremely few in our large Northern cities—the number of black people defecting from or simply having nothing to do with the Church, three percent would be nearer the truth; and that figure is decreasing rapidly.

The reasons which attracted Negroes to the Catholic Church in the twenties, thirties and forties either no longer exist or are fast disappearing. One of these was the Catholic school, especially in view of the disaster that was and is the public school in the black ghetto. Now, some schools are accepting non-Catholic kids. Moreover, parents are getting more conscious of the whitening of black kids which takes place in even the Negro Catholic schools. Finally, with community control of schools which is so important to the blacks, they realize this will be accomplished in the public schools long before the Catholic school system—if it still exists—will even want to begin talking about it.

Another reason for convert-making in the past was the prestige of belonging to a white organization. Except for places like New Orleans, and among the real old guard, this motivation is now happily buried. It was part of the old and now-dead dream of integration. Negro Catholics always knew that they would be going to segregated churches and church schools. Nonetheless, they were members of a white organization and a privileged and prestigious few, that much closer to "integration." What took so long to find out and longer to admit (some still refuse to consider it) is that the Church had no intention whatever of integrating. The same superior/inferior relationship of whites and blacks was embedded in a paternalism so deeply rooted that in many cases it remained subconscious.

At best, Church people—priests, religious and some laymen—fought for and enabled individual Negroes to escape the ghetto and to achieve integration in the typical American fashion. The exceptional Negro "of whom whites could be proud" often was helped by some influential white priest to obtain a job where he was the first or only one, or helped to "integrate" a school or neighborhood, or even pushed in politics. Many times, the type of Negro so helped was delighted to remain the first or only one, etc., and was to remain eternally grateful to his white patron. This gratitude oftentimes meant that that Negro allow himself to be exploited for personal prestige and the satisfaction of individual priests and sometimes to push the Church's interest. Rarely was the advancement of the black people a consideration.

The Negro Catholic schools to which he went merely supported the racist society. Often they were staffed by inferior or non-producing personnel who would not be watched and checked upon as they would be in white schools. The expectations of the children were none too high.

As more and more black people recognize this state of affairs, more and more drop out of the Catholic Church. That they do not go to Mass is simply a more recognizable aspect of the trend, though many white priests have not caught up with it as they complain about Negro Mass attendance. This situation not only explains why Negro Catholics are decreasing in numbers but why they are increasing in age; why the Negro Catholic population (apart from the grade-school children who will disappear as soon as they graduate) is

looking ever more clearly like a Negro senior citizens
or middle-age club. Many of these have grown accustomed to their Church's being supported by charitable
white friends of the white pastor or religious order.
They are told of the graciousness and concern of their
white ordinaries. They have never considered that this
is not what Catholicism is really all about and that they
have a stake in its existence and growth. Young black
people recognize all of this. They see clearly that the
Catholic Church as it exists among blacks has yet to become a truly black institution, that is, one that belongs
to black people. They see it has no intention of so
becoming. They identify Catholicism as a foreign or
white religion serviced primarily by whites for the ultimate interests of whites. And they are not interested.

These young blacks understand clearly that what
the Catholic Church offers for integration is exactly the
same as what the rest of white America has been offering
for centuries. They know that an integrated or racially
open Church—which the Catholic Church is not—can
go hand in hand with a very racist Church—which the
Catholic Church is. If at best integration means mixing
white and black people together on a more mathemati-
cal basis than one pea in a whole big pot of rice, you
may have a physically integrated institution. But it may
be equally racist.

There are further questions of social, psychological
and political integration. Young blacks are interested in
many other questions. What limitations will be put
upon the possibilities of integration? Any limitation is
no integration but a sham and pretense. How are blacks
and whites to be related in the setup? Will the relationship be of equals or of superior and inferior? Will mutual love and respect or white patronage of black dependency be the keystone of that relationship? What

will be the power factor, white power controlling and directing black powerlessness or power mutually shared and responsibly exercised?

All of these questions will have to be answered for black youth. They will have to be answered by more than words. Young blacks are as conscious of the issue of colonialism as the American colonists were. You remember the issue which arose in each former British colony when the Union Jack came down and government was handed over to the natives. Time and again a highly qualified British civil servant who was perhaps doing an excellent job was replaced by a native of less experience. The quality of the work may have declined for a time. But the self-respect and self-esteem of the native community went up. Black youth sees the colonial status of black people in the Catholic Church. They see their powerlessness. They recognize the failure of white Church leaders to place black clergy—especially "militants"—in positions of real responsibility. They see the token titles given with little or no power attached and recognize that most are for the white man's showcase to keep the natives happy. And black youth is saying, "To hell with this nonsense."

Because young blacks are revolted by what they see in the Church, the crisis of black vocations is acute. Not only are blacks not interested in the priesthood or religious life, but those already in are having serious problems. In the last year no less than twenty black seminarians from all over the country have been in touch with me to discuss the continuation of their studies in the face of present realities. If it comes to such a choice, they are determined not to betray their heritage or forsake their culture in order to "qualify." Young black women thinking about the religious life, in addition to the problems they share with women, feel the same crisis. Negro communities are not the answer. Some of these communities are currently considering merging with white communities and real black women are being weeded out, pressured out, or simply leaving in disgust. Their whitened Negro superiors are delighted with the situation. They want to rid themselves of those who will embarrass them when they merge with the white folks.

The number of black priests who are leaving the priesthood outright or are taking leaves of absence is alarming. I know twelve personally who have left since 1964. In view of the small number of black priests in this country, the situation is desperate. Many of these men are questioning the very meaning and possibility of their total dedication to an institution that alienates them from their people and subjects them to racism and a colonial status.

Brother Joseph Davis, S.M., in a "Position of the Catholic Church in the Black Community" paper he prepared for the U.S. Bishops' Conference before one of its last year's meetings put the matter well:

> In instances which may not be rare, it would even seem that obstacles are directly put in the way to make their [black priests'] association with blacks and the black movement next to impossible. They are expected to maintain an almost non-partisan neutrality in the black/white problems of America. . . . The greater number of black priests and religious find that while their skin is black their mentality, customs, and habits have become white. They find this no longer desirable or acceptable. They see themselves as persons who potentially have the most to offer to their black brothers and sisters through selfless dedication to the community, yet they among all others have the least contact with their brethren.
>
> That black priests and religious have much to offer to the white community in terms of witness, understanding and as instruments of building racial compatibility cannot be doubted. However, the assignment of black personnel to white communi-

ties is viewed frankly as being put on public display, indications of the largess and liberalness of their white brethren. The black clergy view it as a disservice to them at a critical time in their history.

Many of these men and women who are coming to grips with themselves and their black community find themselves labeled by whites and white-Negroes as troublemakers, a euphemism for bad nigger. Not all are able to ignore the nonsense and continue being themselves. Because of this the vocations of black priests and religious are becoming extremely tenuous.

White Catholics and their white bishops must know that the question now is whether in the next two decades the Catholic Church will be anything more than a memory—an unpleasant one at that—in the black community. *If they care.*

At the heart of the problem is, of course, white racism. It is to no avail getting upset, angered or emotional when you hear it. Talking a lot of nonsense about communism and black racism is stalling. You know that communism has made less inroads among black people than among any other group in this country and that neither the Church nor American society has allowed black equality, much less tolerated black racism. You must understand precisely where this black/white problem lies. It is amusing to see some well-intentioned white religious flocking into the black ghettos to do their white thing for black people. Oftentimes they are "just being, oozing out luv," without a blessed worthwhile thing to do. They expect black people to become completely enthralled with their white presence. In the meantime, they are the only ones who gain in terms of emotional and psychological well-being.

It is important to see the problem in terms of the effects of white racism. The problem lies precisely with those nice middle-class, law-abiding, segregated and insensitive white communities in which the Church is so at home and whose interests she serves best. It is in these areas that white Catholics who know and care, including white religious and priests, can make the greatest contribution. It is there they can work to change the attitudes and acts that beget the Harlems and much of the poverty of this country. It is there they would be attacking the problem at its roots. If one understands this, he will not make the same mistake as the priest in Morristown, New Jersey who (as many do) kept asking me all night, "What are you and black people going to do about racism?" He did not see that racism is the white man's problem. He will have to answer to what *he* is going to do. Nobody can force him to change his mind. Black people are just taking less and less from him.

Moreover, if these dedicated persons really mean it when they talk about "taking up the cross and following Him," there is no more guaranteed place for a white Christian to find a cross than in a white, especially Catholic, community. It is relatively easy for a white nun or priest, for example, to say and do the right or Christian thing in a black community. Try it in a white community or a white Catholic community and that's something else.

I am not, however, advocating a wholesale pullout of all white religious and clerical personnel from the black communities. Thanks mainly to the patterns of discrimination regarding Negro vocations in the past and to the overall irrelevancy of the Church to black people now, black priests and religious are scarce and the future looks bleak. Thus, on this score there must remain for some time a place for white religious and other people in the black communities. Moreover, apart from this, I believe there must be some white presence in the black community just as there must be some black presence in the white community to serve as a reminder of what the Church might be and isn't and to provide some kind of continuity if we should ever come together as Christians. It is the manner of this presence that must change, however.

Rather than the customary chauffeur, gardener, houseman or super-nigger, better educated and employed than his white neighbors and showing how white he has actually become, the black presence in the white community will have to be that of a black person on an equal footing, proud of his blackness and occupying a position of prestige, honor and responsibility. Likewise, the white presence in the black community will have to change radically from its father/mother role. This is going to be extremely difficult for white religious and priests, who have been psychologically and historically conditioned to assume that especially in the black community, they are automatically to function as leaders of and spokesmen for their constituents. Instead of leader, teacher and spokesman, the white religious must be willing to see his place as learner, helper and supporter of whatever the black thing is. This will be the white role—if there is to be a meaningful one—in the black community.

Whites who wish to remain among blacks will have to appreciate the growing call for control by black people of all programs—including Church programs—in the black communities and meaningful participation in making decisions in whatever affects black lives. This means *all* Church matters. Black people feel that none or very few of the experimental urban ministries run by the white clergy over the last thirty years have paid off. They have produced only black dependency.

This determination on the part of black people to control institutions operating in the black communities should not be too difficult for Irish, Italian, German or Polish priests and religious to understand. It was not too long ago—in fact, in some places it is still true— that an Irish pastor was not expected to be most successful in a German parish, or an Italian pastor in an Irish parish, etc. The history of the American Catholic Church shows that at the height of each group's ethnic consciousness, such mixings often proved disastrous.

You must understand what support of the black thing means. Some time ago, I was at a small meeting with a group of whites who wanted to support the *Black Manifesto* and devise ways of so doing. We simply could not come together. They all thought they agreed with the second part, the demand for five hundred million dollars to be used for programs like a black university, investment in farming, black publishing and communication facilities, etc. It was the first part or the rationale, including the concept of reparation, which has been called revolutionary, destructive, radical and, of course, communistic, that caused the problem.

I am not suggesting that many blacks have had no difficulty there. The interesting thing is that they felt able to get more white support if certain words, ideas and phrases were to be changed to be a bit more acceptable to white people. Some were indeed hurt when after an hour and a half I rose to leave, telling them I had done all I came to do; the problem was from that point theirs and no further help was really possible from me. One asked me rather pointedly, "Then white support is not important to you?"

The answer, of course, was not the kind of support that a black thing can get so long as it becomes a white thing. I had come to explain and try to clarify the *Manifesto* for them. I had no authority to change a word in it. Nor did I have any desire to do so. As a black man and a Christian, I have no difficulty with it. Responsible black people had gotten this thing together. I had explained it as best I could. It was their problem to determine whether and to what extent they were able to support this black thing. I listened sympathetically to their difficulties and criticized their suggested changes. "But, here is the *Manifesto*," I said, "the difficulties are yours; I cannot solve them on your terms. Now I will leave you to wrestle with your problem."

Especially white religious and clerics should not come or remain in the black community primarily or exclusively to "bring Christ to black people." Come or be there to *find* Jesus Christ in these black communities where He lives in His poverty, His suffering and His love. You might even be able to find Him in yourselves, relating to and respecting black people as human beings equally beloved by the Trinity; and you might find you can respect your own humanity more.

Apart from basic understanding, if white Catholics are going to get their minds in order, they will have to rid themselves of some strongly held myths. One of these is the idea that all that is required of the brave souls who are daring enough to consider what their role has been in the present position of black people is a *mea culpa* or, more often, a *nostra culpa*. "I am guilty" is heard more infrequently than "we are guilty." Some might even add a minor flagellation. Acknowledging guilt is only a first step. The greater difficulty is in recognizing one's own responsibility for something that should not have been. The determination to remedy as much of the harm as one has caused and to correct the situation goes beyond mere guilt feelings. Action that results only from guilt may well find the length of its life span coinciding with the end of that feeling, and feelings are notoriously short-lived and unreliable.

There is also the myth that one can get up some bright morning and simply wish away long centuries of history and by that act avoid the unpleasant consequences of the past. White Catholics must understand that simply regretting certain things is not going to save them the price of past behavior or present behavior.

Several months ago I was talking to some good friends of mine who are white, Irish and Catholic. They work in a religious retail store in New York with which I have been dealing since my high school days. We were discussing the racial problem. One of the men, who doesn't have a speck of malice in his bones, began talking about the Negro middle class or "those Negroes who have gotten ahead." He referred to a Long Island community of predominantly middle-class Negroes. "They have made it," he said, "they have comfortable homes and two-car garages. Yet, they have not raised a finger to help their own. Why don't these people think of others and try to help them?"

I did not, nor do I, deny that, particularly in the past, the Negro middle class has remained generally aloof from the black revolution, especially in some of its more aggressive manifestations. Thank God, this is changing. What I told my friend was that white people have no right to make this criticism. Only black people do. You see, white society set up the criteria or rules by which some few special Negroes are able to escape the typical experience of black people in America and make some limited inroads into "white society." The man set up the rules—come on your own, for yourself, and the hell with the rest—by which a Negro might pass through the white barriers. A Negro seeking to "better himself" obeys these rules and squeezes through. Then the man who established the entrance requirements turns around and criticizes the Negro who fulfilled the entrance requirements. The Negro middle class is what it is because the white man made it this way.

Take the whole area of so-called preferential treatment and quotas. I was in a group recently discussing the demands of the City University of New York students. They were demanding a school of black and Puerto Rican studies; that students in S.E.E.K. (which was a special program for recruiting and preparing minority youngsters for college) have a determining voice in the program; that the racial composition of freshman classes reflect the city high-school ratios; that all students in the School of Education take Spanish and black studies.

One priest rose to say that all preferential treatment and all quotas are morally wrong. This is nonsense, of course. One does not treat a pregnant woman on a bus or a man in a wheel chair boarding a plane the same as anybody else. What he could not stomach was that white people should suffer some consequences of centuries of repression. For centuries, white people have had preferred treatment in regard to housing, education, employment and social status. City University, like most schools, has always had quotas. These quotas do not disturb most white people. They are fighting to maintain them. Black people have been put at a great disadvantage because of the white preferential quota system. As soon as they begin to demand redress white priests develop consciences about "all quotas and preferred treatment." Imagine priests, of all people, being upset about preferred treatment!

It's like the remark made about Regis High School in New York City, a rather exclusive and scholarship Jesuit institution: "All right, if they lower their standards to take in Negroes, they're taking the heart out of Regis." Whatever kind of heart it is, it certainly wasn't a Christian heart when I wasn't even allowed to take the exam in spite of my being at the top of my graduating class. What has been good enough for most black children for centuries in order to maintain white supremacy is unthinkable for relatively few white children for a few years in order to eradicate the effects of white behavior on black youngsters.

Another myth that must be eliminated is the one expressed by a young lady at International House of Columbia University after I had spoken one evening. She identified herself as Irish and Catholic and spoke of how the Irish had been received in this country, and how many poor whites there are still. "And yet," she concluded, "they do not go around acting like you people." I frequently hear this sort of thing from Catholics who note that other groups in this country have been oppressed and have raised themselves up, so "What's wrong with Negroes," or that poverty is no more black than white in America. This of course, is not the place for a history lesson, though it is obvious that this myth is related to the first two.

It completely ignores, for example, how the Irish arrived in this country as contrasted with the blacks;

how slavery systematically destroyed black family life; and how blacks were denied from the start such aids as the Irish had in family stability, Church and clergy. It ignores the post-Civil War slavery which still endures. It ignores the fact that Irish behavior has not drastically changed. In the nineteenth century they acted violently against "law and order" in order to throw off oppression. The black man today has a long way to go to match that violence. Now that they have made it, many Irish are quite violent in defense of "law and order"—on our police forces, in the F.B.I., etc. The black man also looks toward the time when he need not be fighting oppression.

As part of this is the belief that poverty in America knows no color. There are more poor white people in America than there are poor black, I am often reminded. In numerical numbers, this is true. It is also true that there are more white people in America than black people—roughly ten times as many. Proportionately, poverty claims about ten to fifteen percent of white Americans while it claims about forty-five to fifty percent of black Americans. Moreover, there is hardly a white American who is poor because he is white. The black are poor because they are black. Whereas white minorities have overcome certain barriers by a simple change in name or address, that same "opportunity" is not afforded the black man. He can be spotted miles away on a clear day. It is myth to claim that poverty knows no color in this country.

Another great myth that Catholics must rid themselves of is that of Negro progress. One type of letter I receive frequently in answer to my columns reminds me of the great progress Negroes have been making in the past ten or twenty years. They point to—apart from our national heroes, whom they have created—"your senator and mayors," "your congresswoman," "the growing number of television personalities that are black." All of this is clear indication of the great progress Negroes are making in this country. In fact, they might be moving "too fast."

There are individual blacks who have broken many barriers recently and are making it not only in the traditional fields of athletics and entertainment but also in television, technology, politics, etc. On the basis of these marginal individual successes, a myth is created, sometimes even going so far as to suggest that we have an open society with equal opportunities, and that any man—black or white—can make it if he tries hard enough. Individual breakthroughs hardly reflect the conditions of the masses of black people in this country. And further, one must distinguish between progress in terms of overall betterment of blacks and progress in terms of lessening the gap between black and white in a racist society where it is preferable to be white. On the first score, according to standard indices, the objective conditions of blacks have been improving on an absolute scale, particularly in education. This, of course, is relative. To take one black in where there had been none may be a hundred-percent improvement on a statistical survey. It's still only one. In terms of the black-and-white gap, the condition of blacks has been deteriorating relative to whites. The disparity between black and white America in education, income, employment, health and housing is wider today than it was ten years ago. What is more significant is that the widening of the income gap in the past ten years has occurred in spite of a great improvement in non-white educational attainment. Perhaps one of the best refutations of the progress myth concerning black America is the fact that a black child about to be born today has less chance of seeing his first birthday than he did in 1960.

It is the system that has created and is widening this gap that must be changed. Such a change will be truly revolutionary in this country. That is why the letter from the gentleman in New Orleans (when *The Clarion* was carrying my column) was so far from the mark. He thought I was not "sufficiently aware of the great strides that were being made by Negroes." Apparently a sports devotee and fan of Willie Mays, he told me, "I should be really proud of our great athletes and entertainers." So many white Catholics live in a world of myths, particularly regarding this black/white thing. Black people are talking about revolution. We are trying to get out of slavery. And white Catholics think the Negroes should be proud. Negroes should stand up and applaud because some Negroes can run faster, jump higher, sing louder—and better—hit the ball farther than some white people. And the white man will reward them handsomely for their ability to entertain and excite him. And this is progress!

Another myth that white Catholics must abandon is that of the "Black excesses and white sympathy" syndrome. Several months ago one of our *Catholic News* columnists, Father Marvin O'Connell, wrote a piece entitled "Black Excesses Erode Sympathy for Black America." Like the lament I am hearing everywhere, it demonstrates how far from reality white Catholics are in this matter. Father O'Connell's thesis was clear. "Norman Mailer and Roy Wilkins," he stated, "are not the only ones fed up with the arrogance and hooliganism of a destructive minority of Negroes. White racists around the country are jubilant over recent black excesses while sympathy for the Negro cause among millions of ordinary people has clearly begun to erode." The clear implication of the article was for blacks to check those "excesses" or face the loss of valuable white sympathy.

The author pointed out Mr. Mailer's weariness of the "internal power struggle in the civil rights movement." This weariness was brought to a head because of the "annoyance and discomfort" which Mailer experienced when "he and a hundred other reporters were kept waiting forty minutes in a sweltering anteroom for an audience with Dr. Ralph Abernathy." Apparently this was an unusual and unthinkable experience for Mailer and those reporters. Good thing they are not black and have to wait for emergency treatment at New York's Harlem Hospital or for a policeman to respond to calls in Negro neighborhoods where whites are not involved. Father O'Connell went on to quote from Roy Wilkins, whom he described as "among the most distinguished and thoughtful Americans of our generation." Well, the "distinguished" is very true and the "thoughtful" may be true, even though the thinking is rather dated. One wonders, however, if that characterization is due to the fact that Wilkins often sounds like O'Connell. He quoted Wilkins as saying, "The supine attitude of white academic officialdom—administration and faculty—to the violent immaturity of a handful of black students reflects the height of irresponsibility . . . surrenders by a university on such matters as all-black dormitories, courses, departments and control of scholarship programs would only feed the flames."

Father O'Connell's conclusion was: "I think in their different ways, Mr. Mailer and Mr. Wilkins are testifying to the same fact, that the solution to the race problem rests ultimately with the white masses. In the past couple of decades, most white men have become aware of the debt of shame and exploitation they owe to Negroes. Nothing, however, will make them forget that unpleasant debt faster than pictures on the television news of black racists swaggering through the rubble of alma mater's administration building."

In his conclusion lies a myth. The excess alluded to was at Cornell. The myth is two-pronged. The first is that most white men are aware of the debt of shame and exploitation—recall the response to the *Black Manifesto*—they owe black people. The second is that white sympathy has meant something to the black cause and that its loss means a damn.

If whatever sympathy whites can muster is limited to the unproductive programs of the past, and is so easily lost, then it is worthless in any case. If it can be measured in terms of liberal statements and signed petitions but nothing more, then the erosion of this sympathy for black America will be a boon for black America.

The "proper channels" illusion is another that must go. It is amusing to hear some Negro leaders and concerned whites wax eloquently about proper channels. This invariably means channels that exist or are said to exist for the adjudication of rights. What they long for are the good ole days of the Negroes' law-abiding, peace-loving, nonviolent, sweet-singing and on-the-knee begging of the establishment for his due. No white man need tell black people about proper channels. They know them well.

The joker is that some channels were there but others were merely fictitious. None of them worked for black people in any case because white people refused to let them. Even the channels of the courts, which have done much in terms of legislation, were stymied by the length of time involved and even more by the lack or the manner of implementation of their decisions. Yes, there were some channels, not as many as we were led to believe. They may be proper for white people. They haven't changed much the black man's condition in America; they have been very improper for him.

In the Church, "proper channels" are just as useful. Proper channels are still working over the proposal of the National Black Catholic Clergy Caucus. Proper channels are not changing Church priorities in regard to black people.

Two events closely following upon each other in New York have still not enlightened Negro Catholics about this fact. Both involve the transfer of young white priests from Harlem parishes. Apparently white priests who try to relate to black people on other than the superior-patron-versus-inferior-dependent basis find the going rough. Father John Curry at All Saints was learning to do this rapidly. Difficulty with the pastor, a man of another long-dead era, regarding the relationship of black and white, brought no support from the chancery. When Curry offered to accept a new assignment if it would result in certain meaningful changes including a black priest at All Saints, the archdiocese forgot the "if" clause but transferred him anyhow. Some people got together to try to do something about it. They used the proper channels—speaking to the pastor who couldn't even understand what they were talking about in their suggesting that perhaps the people should have some voice in who was to serve them. They received a cordial reception from the chancellor and some other diocesan officials who heard them politely and even went out to tell one of their leaders, Mrs. Lorez Harden, that Father Curry had requested a change. That, of course, was not exactly the height of honesty. After more weeks of proper channels, the parishioners gave up. Father Curry remained in Scarsdale learning how difficult it is to talk Christianity in realistic terms to white Catholics. And at All Saints, more people simply stopped coming and more got more disgusted.

About two years later, in early 1969, the same situation developed at St. Mark the Evangelist in Harlem. The two figures involved were Fathers Edward Hearn and his pastor, Robert McCraley, C.S.Sp. Again, the situation was a young Hearn, trying to relate to black youngsters in terms of present realities, and a pastor supported by the old guard, not comprehending and actively resisting. In the middle was a somewhat vacillating "parish council," almost handpicked by the pastor, caught between conflicting aspirations and norms of propriety.

When word got out that Father Hearn was to be changed, a group got together to object. From the start it was made clear that Hearn had to go because of his inability to get along with the pastor.

The group, in a well-worded position paper, expressed their feeling that they were not looking upon this as a matter of conflict of personalities, as some were trying to make it. They mentioned the effectiveness of Father Hearn "not only in his duties to the parish in the regular sense," but in his having been "instrumental in breaking down the sense of isolation and clannishness that has heretofore existed in our parish." They pointed out that the most important matter was: "The need to develop a realistic and meaningful role for the black Christian laity that will give a sharing of power and a sense of self-determination; to extract from the structure of the Church, by any means necessary, an open and irrevocable commitment to discontinue the duplicity and condescension that have been the rule in dealing with black people in the past; to obtain the right of the black laity to share the decision as to who will administer to them in matters spiritual as well as temporal; to force the Church to abandon its method of token or fake compliance with the desires of black people and to meet and deal with the real needs of the laity." In the light of those needs, they issued an immediate demand that "Father Edward Hearn remain in the parish according to our wishes as indicating a response to those needs."

Constrained by the older parishioners and the council, the group used proper channels, going to the pastor, who would hardly recognize them; Harlem's vicar-delegate, who got the transfer postponed for a time; the provincial of the Holy Ghost Fathers, who was most arrogant and saw this as strictly an affair for the Holy Ghost Fathers, and a question of Father Hearn's vow of obedience. The people had no say in the matter and were told they had "no right to interfere." Mind you, from the other side of the mouth people are told that priests are for their service. Yet the service of the people and whether or how the people feel they are being served have nothing to do with the assigning and transferring of personnel. The question is rather, how a priest gets on with his pastor, or a childish interpretation of obedience which makes such things a purely private matter between a priest and a bishop or provincial. That is why Father McCraley considered it most natural when he met with the parish council to reveal the written terms under which *he* would keep Father Hearn.

Finally, they went to the chancellor who was rather polite and seemed sympathetic. They were unable to see the cardinal. When threats of using "improper channels" were voiced, promises were made that Father Hearn would remain and the matter would be closed. Four months later, at the beginning of June, Father Hearn was persuaded to "go on vacation." He has been "vacationing" in a new assignment in Virginia since. I called him at St. Mark's on July 29 and was politely but dishonestly told by the pastor, "he is still on vacation." The parish council decided to make a mild protest to themselves and carry the matter no further.

White folks must understand that if they are to talk about "proper channels," they must be willing to make such channels work for black people, too. Otherwise to talk of "proper channels" to black people is only a myth. They may be "proper" for whites or some whites. They are unworkable and improper for blacks and the latter would be fools to get hung up on the white man's proper channels.

In speaking to a group of nuns one evening in New York, I was confronted with the question, "I agree with all you said, Father, but does that justify hatred? And if it does not, what are you going to do about black hatred?"

Realizing that she was being choked by the myth of black hatred which I find in so many Catholics, I asked her, "What do you mean by hatred, Sister?" "You know," she replied, "this teaching that white people are your enemies and black anti-Semitism and that kind of thing."

This was at the time when Albert Shanker and the U.F.T. were getting desperate in their illegal strike to break the back of community control of schools where black and Puerto Rican parents are concerned. All it took was a few unfortunate remarks from two black teachers in Brooklyn for Mr. Shanker to blow them up to such proportions that the whole city, including

Mayor Lindsay and Manhattan's Negro borough president, got up-tight and B'nai B'rith started issuing reports about black anti-Semitism in the city.

When it comes to "black hatred," I said that when black people begin hating whites, then we will really have something going. No slaves have really loved their masters more than black people in loving whites in this country. An honest recognition of facts and a determination to eradicate injustice is not equivalent to wishing others evil. Perhaps whites do believe that putting an end to the exploitation of blacks is an evil and so by wanting that, blacks are thinking evil thoughts or hating whites. Moreover, I suggested that if the way white people feel toward and have been behaving toward black people is an expression of their love, then maybe black people will be much better off with white people hating them. One of the major things black people can do now, I told her, is to stop letting whites show them their present kind of love.

Closely related to the preceding myth is the one that says white people have anything to teach black people about patience and love. I remember when Cardinal John Wright, then Archbishop of Pittsburgh and a man I admire in many ways, preached the opening Mass sermon at the first National Black Sisters' Conference. He spoke about the need of the Sisters to be there and his joy in seeing them in Pittsburgh. Then he spoke eloquently about the need for patience and love.

One would think that black people had just started migrating to this country about thirty or forty years ago because of terrible conditions back home. One would think that black people began fighting as soon as they got off the boats. You would never guess that black people have been begging, praying, singing, toiling and fighting for their freedom and the rights of human beings from the moment they were enchained by white Christians. White Catholics and their white bishops are obsessed with the myth that they are in a position to talk to black people about love and patience. Instead, they should all be running up and down white neighborhoods, especially white Catholic neighborhoods, talking and shouting to white people about patience and love. They should beg black people, who are expert at it, to come in and tell them about it. They should know that blacks now feel they have given all the time they are going to give.

The final myth, and one of the greatest, is what I call the separation/polarization complex. The tragedy is that there are many Negroes—colored Catholics, Negroes like Roy Wilkins, Bayard Rustin, so many Negro ministers—who believe in it. This is why one priest kept asking me after a talk, "Is separation going to help Negroes?" It is why I get so many letters asking me about black separatism. There has always been separation between black and white in this country, and it has always served white interests. The white man separated black people from him for his own economic interests. To justify this, and to keep black people in line, the myth of white superiority and black inferiority was created. Many—even liberal—Catholics talk as if separation is not a fact. Moreover, they forget that neither separation nor polarization has any value in itself. "Remember," I reminded a group one evening, "we are all going to separate ourselves as we return to our respective homes this evening." What gives a moral flavor or value to separation is the why, the wherefore and the how of separation, the circumstances and goals. More and more black people realize all this. That is why the black power movement—or whatever you want to call it—is so relevant. Black power implies separation. But this does not mean that racial separation is taken as an ultimate goal.

There is a minority view in the black community which sees racial separation as most desirable. Some have replaced a long-enduring and all-pervasive white superiority complex with a black superiority complex. Many whites, on the other hand, think that any black who doesn't fall in line with a white superiority complex is "preaching black superiority." Some blacks have been led to the conclusion that white folks just aren't worth living with anyway. Most of those I know who hold this view are despairing of America's willingness or ability to seriously integrate black people into our society. In any case, a growing number of black people, like myself, see separation as a means to an end. This is a somewhat tricky position which can be easily misunderstood. Black people are beginning to admit to themselves and others that they are separated and that their separation, established centuries ago, has been reaffirmed time and time again. The question now is what to do with our basically if not totally separated selves.

Black Power says to black people: take the situation, this separate situation as we now find it; in these circumstances, let us build ourselves up to the point where we can confront the other America on the only terms to which it responds: power—economic, political, educational. The task of the black community is to redefine itself, to set up new values and goals and to organize and act around them. Inherent in this concept is the development of a community-oriented attitude in individuals. The reestablishment of pride in being black and an acceptance of the forces from which we came are the means by which we can restore the self-respect that was destroyed by centuries of systematic white psychological violence against the black psyche. Black Power wants to reduce black dependency and put the black community in a position to bargain rather than to beg.

One area of separation that black people can and should push is what I call psychological separation, or freeing the black mind from the white man's bag. It is white control of the black mind that has immobilized so many Negroes in thought and action and has produced a large number of white Negroes (or Negro whites, depending on where the emphasis should go). By Negro whites I mean those who look like me but think like, feel like, respond to, view things, and talk like white people. Black people should create, promote and nourish psychological separation.

When Ron Karenga says, "We're not for isolation, but interdependence. But we can't become interdependent unless we have something to offer. We can live with whites interdependently once we have black power," it does not have to mean that before integration, there must be a chronologically first, hypothetical black power ghetto *totally* black in every way. The position is better understood in terms of priorities. It need not insist on a two-step theory: first, requiring separation so that black people can regroup, unify, and gain a positive self-image and identity; and second, real integration. What many like myself who hold that position are saying is that "step one," separation, has long been a reality. That, while efforts to further interracial contact need not be abandoned or delayed, the greater emphasis by far should be placed on building the black community, or re-creating the "ghettos" since they will be with us for some time to come. That present coalitions with whites, and any integrated efforts, must right now be based on true integration that the society can only hope to achieve at some future time.

Coalitions between blacks and whites must be beneficial to blacks. Coalitions where blacks are merely used by whites are out. Integrated situations cannot be black dependency upon a white paternalism which assumes white superiority and black inferiority. It is important that a false myth of black separatism be squashed. It is important that certain "Negro leaders" understand this separation business and stop making silly statements. When black students demand their own lunchrooms and dormitories, they are not doing what white segregationists have always done. They are not trying to demonstrate assumed superiority over another group. They are simply refusing to accept black inferiority. They are saying to hell with an integration that says a closely controlled number of you may sit in chemistry or sociology or mathematics classes and take exams and be marked, but stay clear of the rest of our lives and goods.

The Southern region of the National Black Catholic Clergy Caucus, at their January 1969 meeting in New Orleans, rejected white-led integration. The whites were talking about a kind of integration that said, for example, when there are two Churches—one black and one white—you integrate by closing the black Church and "letting them come over to our Church." "Integration on white terms is toleration," said Father Rawlin Enette, S.S.J., chairman of the Southern region. And Father August Thompson of the Alexandria, Louisiana, diocese said, "We want integration but not as the white man decides he wants it."

But the white man has given no sign that he is ready for integration. Enlightened black folks are not about to discuss the nonsense and play the games that whites and some middle-class Negroes call integration. Time is too precious. To call this approach separation or separatist and to pretend that "Black extremists" are re-

sponsible for separation is another myth. The sooner
the myth goes, the sooner we can get serious about integration.

You should be able to ask yourself with regard to
blacks, "What would *I* have done and what would I do
now if *I* were in the same situation?" Once you can honestly ask yourself that question, you may change your
attitudes. You will realize that black people today in
their struggle for power and inclusion in America, in the
Catholic Church, in any institution whatever, are not
going to be much different from the Irish, Polish, German and Italian people in their struggles for the same
goals. Right now, for example, if white people insist
that violence is still the key factor, black people will be
as nonviolent as they can and as violent as they must.

Catholics will have to change a lot of their attitudes
about religion, the Church and role of the Church.
They will have to stop thinking that religion is that
something which one does one day a week. They will
have to see that religion is the daily, hourly relationship
with God through Christ in the Spirit; that this relation
involves and is part of one's relationships with other
human beings directly or indirectly; that it is not the
mumbling of words that sound like prayers or the mul-
tiplication of "pious practices."

Sunday Mass, Christianity, religion, should not be
the great escapes from the real world, but a source and
a means of greater and more fruitful involvement in all
areas of human existence. Catholics avoid many important concerns and questions today by calling them "politics" and unworthy of religion. Draining religion of its
essence, they have identified it with trivialities, banali-

ties and nonsense. It was not too long ago that Catholics called being a good Catholic going to Mass on Sundays—that is, just being physically present—not eating meat on Friday, and saying nice things about "purity." Today, if you exclude those "way-out folks" who prefer Saturday Mass and those who do not feel bad about eating chicken on Friday, most would feel the same. It was not surprising that while Governor Rockefeller of New York in 1969 was "balancing the State budget" by cutting welfare and medicare payments and reducing services for the poor, Catholics in New York were busy being upset over their never-were saints, George and his novena, and what to do with their St. Christopher medals. During Lent, a time for penance and renewal, Catholics can limit it to, and find its fulfillment by, merely going to Mass more often (but just as routinely), saying a few more "prayers" and giving up candy, cigarettes, movies and liquor. This is their total response to starving people, to daily injustices, to failing schools in the slums that turn out more failures, etc. The basic issue is whether religion is going to be preached in its hard, realistic demands on our daily life—including decisions on real estate, welfare, taxes, police behavior, employment practices and the like—or whether it can be nicely tucked away into the fifty minutes for Sunday Mass, twenty minutes for Monday night novena and the social contribution of the weekly envelope.

After eight months in St. Joseph's Parish in Harlem—magnificently run according to eighteenth-century standards—I received my first indication that life was present. Four of the parishioners had a spirited discussion one Sunday morning in the rear of the Church. The difficulty and dispute was over what color cassock the altar boys should have worn—red or black.

The mentality that the major role of the Church is to support and maintain what is, regardless of how foul what is is, must go. It is frightening how many ordinaries and pastors and priests and religious and lay people have dedicated themselves to the dubious goals of not being controversial, of not upsetting the establishment. They see this as the primary role of the Church. This attitude must go.

White Catholics and especially the power structure must give up the attitude that all we are going to have to deal with are the nice safe Negro Catholics the Church has programmed so beautifully. Sooner or later they will have to deal with the black community at large and not only in terms of little nothing programs and gestures toward colored Catholics.

In line with this, we will have to stop deluding ourselves that meaningless tidbits like "jazzing up the Mass" will satisfy those folks. We will have to realize that we will never really have a liturgy, no matter what gimmicks we use, until we get a Church that is relevant to black people. To think that relating superficially to people on one level of their lives can blind them to the absence of relations on all other levels is an illusion.

A while ago a lady from another parish in the Archdiocese of New York came to me with a letter from her pastor refusing to admit her twins back into school unless she brought a letter from a priest substantiating her summer Mass attendance. She was furious. I had long ago refused to write such letters. It's awful enough to show children such distrust. It's disgusting to ask an adult to submit to such humiliation.

I called the pastor and told him I simply refused to take part in such degrading nonsense. He told me the old story about the need for parents to give a good example to the children. What kind of example and what value is that, I asked, when the kids know their parents are simply going through an empty and despised, because forced, endurance session simply to avoid the children's being thrown out of school? You should be far more upset, I said, about why she doesn't go than the fact of her not going.

Why should black folks go to Mass at all? Their going demands a faith and theological understanding of the Mass that is lacking in many of us priests. Is religion only to be these fifty or sixty minutes per week? The Mass is supposed to be the sacrament or *effective symbol* of the Church. But where is the Church for black people in your area? The pastor of that particular parish, like so many of them, would not think of involving himself in community affairs. And priests in general never visit with the people. The people have no say regarding what is done in the parish and no control or influence in the school. There is a parents' association (the teachers do not have to come) with elected offices; yet the pastor runs the entire meeting.

When black Catholics go to Mass, they are usually subjected to unprepared sermons that are either downright silly or are so general that they can be given in Texas or China. There isn't even a pretext of the preacher's being aware of the gut issues touching the people's lives. In other churches many of the relatively few priests who are daring to speak about present problems are substituting for, or are putting secular reading on a par with, the Scripture selections for Mass. This is not to say that other readings have no place in the Sunday Mass homily. They can be, for example, excellent illustration of a Scripture text which is the subject matter for the homily. But when they are put on the same level with or are substituted for Scripture, apart from creating theological difficulties this lends credence to the assumption that Scripture has nothing to do with social concerns. Such concerns are above and beyond the call of duty for Catholics. The point, however, is that Catholics, and especially priests, will have to realize that it is going to require a great deal more than guitars, nice music, threats about hell, and connecting parents' and childrens' Mass obligation with staying in the parochial school to fill our churches with black people.

The Church must be willing to use all its resources in behalf of black people—moral, financial, political, whatever it has until it hurts. If the Church is going to continue claiming to be Christ in the world, it will have to start being just that, even if it means taking up the cross. It will be setting itself new priorities.

The Church will have to function as a moral agent using its moral power. It will have to tell its white, middle-class constituency and others that religion is more than just going to Mass on Sunday, wearing a medal, lighting a candle and fingering beads. It must challenge their racist attitudes and assumptions. It must shatter the illusion that the moral law is synonymous with sexual morality and can be totally fulfilled by not publicly violating the sixth and ninth commandments. It must shout from the rooftops that sins requiring knowledge and deliberation, like sins against justice, are far more serious than those which result from passion; that it is a sin to segregate blacks and consider them inferior; that it is a sin to keep blacks out of "your" neighborhoods, denying them the possibility of decent housing; that it is a sin to force and maintain them in failing schools. It is a sin not to employ or to underemploy blacks: it is a sin to exploit their labor; it is a sin to overcharge for food or charge exorbitant interests for loans and credit; it is a sin to deny or not to care about the absence of essential human services in black neighborhoods; it is a sin to vote white supremacy and oppression of black people.

The Church must do more than talk about these things. It must live them. It must condemn those institutions and organizations, including its own, that say through discrimination that blacks are inferior. Priests, for example, will have to stop trying to rationalize their membership in athletic clubs, notorious for discrimination, on the basis that they are private. It is not a question of legality but of morality and example. To be authentic, the Church cannot take the attitude recently expressed by some officials of the New York archdiocese when approached by a priest to discuss the diocesan support of a group calling itself Human Interests Regarding Employment. It is a coalition of churchmen, university students and faculty, and civil rights groups from metropolitan areas of New York State who are concerned about the lack of minority group members, particularly blacks, in the work forces of major construction projects which involve state contracts. Their appeal was met with the response: It's all right for Protestants [many upstate Protestant clergymen are involved], but these are *our* [italics mine] people who have carved out an empire for themselves in the construction industry. When the Protestants attack Wall Street and the Jews the school establishment, we'll go along. But just to hit the construction industry which is almost ninety percent Catholic here is not fair.

When it comes to financial resources, the Church will have to make a major change in its priorities and behavior. It will have to make a serious attempt to use its buying power to enforce fair treatment of black people. Moreover, regarding its own spending, it can no longer look for some small expenditure in a ghetto here and another one there for which it will reap the maximum publicity. The Church will have to earmark a *major part* of its finances for meeting the needs of the poor, especially the black poor and to help defray the cost of the black man's struggle for freedom. Two years ago, I spoke about this need to priests of the Hartford, Connecticut diocese during their retreat. I told them parish and diocesan money and landholdings could be used to set up a central fund to provide seed money for housing programs. Parishes and dioceses can act as nonprofit sponsors for housing under federal programs :

—investing certain percentages of their funds to help develop black businesses ;

—establishing credit unions where the poor can borrow without paying exorbitant interests ;

—setting up funds to help defray the legal expenses of those imprisoned and harassed for their activities in the freedom fight ;

—making some of their landholdings available for low-income housing or for black farmers in the South.

One of the priests, a pastor, asked me, "Suppose the bishop objects to my spending parish money that way?" "Are you asking me what you are to do if the bishop objects to your being a Christian?" I asked in reply. "Why do you have to ask the bishop about such things in the first place? When was the last time you asked him how much can the rectory spend of parish money for liquor? In fact, if enough pastors and people were to get together and urge this kind of thing, many more bishops would be doing it on a diocesan level."

Catholics will have to learn to run the risk of letting black people control what Catholics are helping to finance. They will have to give without strings and without white control and support the possibility of black failure and not just black successes.

The Church will have to abandon its lack of realism toward political action. Politics is a fact of life which can be used for good or harm. It will have to discuss issues like police/community relations, community control of schools, welfare, employment even during election years, and call its members' attention to their civic responsibility in terms of their vote. In many of our large cities, the Catholic Church wields tremendous political power. We must get away from the idea that we are doing something with our Christmas, Thanksgiving or Easter baskets handouts. Black people want the Church to help them so that they won't need those damn baskets. We must get away from the suburbanites coming down in Harlem accompanied by the press and television men to clean a street once a year. Black people want them to use their political power to insist on the kind of services needed every day of the year. In short, the Church must be willing to make its political power, like all of its resources, work for black people.

The Church will have to stop trying to control black people. It must be able to overcome its fears and trust black people to the extent that it just might be possible that there is something a black man or woman or a group of black people could do without some white's deciding what, how, when and why. To do this, the Church must stop its subterfuges in making black "leadership," in "consulting" with blacks after decisions have already been made. As the superintendent of Catholic schools in New Orleans told a nun after a few meetings with black parents discussing school integration (New Orleans fashion), "We will listen to them, but of course we will do what's best for them."

The Church is going to have to accommodate itself to black people's exercising power on all levels. The Church and white Catholics will have to learn to live with and accept black people's saying and describing things as they see them whether or not white people agree or like it, and whether or not the findings concur with all the studies white folks are making about black folks—for money.

7

Lawd, What About Me?

One of the most frequent reactions I get these days is, "If you feel this way about the Church, Father, why do you stay in?" Black people put it somewhat differently, like the Muslim who stopped me on the street several months ago and said, "How the hell did you get stuck in this bag?" pointing to my Roman collar. It's a question many black Catholics are struggling with today. I have wrestled with it, but at the moment I still feel justified in remaining within the Church. I can only try to help others, but each person must make his own decision.

Racism is so deeply rooted in the Catholic Church

—like other white institutions—that it is often found to be worse or more open to exposure in religious orders, among priests and lay people who have a "special commitment to Negroes." Communities like the Sisters of the Blessed Sacrament or priests working in the inner cities often present the fiercest opposition to black people's desire for self-determination. They act as if there is an eternal decree demanding that black people must always and in all matters be completely dependent upon them.

Some of the priests in Harlem with whom I have lived are the most racist priests in the archdiocese. In many cases, it is unconscious racism. This, of course, is understandable since racism is part of the socialization process of white Americans that begins from birth. Most of it is very conscious. Unlike the twenty Newark priests who were able to recognize the racism in their archdiocese, Harlem priests were very upset over the April 1968 statement of the National Black Catholic Clergy Caucus. Most of them fell in love with the "minority opinion" (the attempt to soften the statement). Apart from my own sermons, a Harlem Catholic churchgoer would be unlikely to hear that white racism is a problem in America and essentially a moral one. This, in spite of the fact that it's easy for a white priest to speak about white racism in Harlem. For my efforts I have been branded "extreme, difficult, militant, radical."

Older priests and a frightening number of younger ones still have a hero or martyr complex. They feel they are really great to spend their time among these "trying and sick" people of Harlem, as one publicly spoke of them. There are nothing programs and superficialities. In one parish where some imaginative innovations are being tried in the school, the rectory is still staffed by a black cook and black housekeepers, and white secretaries. In most, the attitude of white superiority is manifest. Many, like so many white liberals, seem ready to fight for my right to see things the way they see them, and for my right to respond to events and things as they think I should respond to them.

Needless to say, I do not fit into the scheme. In the past, it was relatively easy to take care of troublesome black priests. All that was required was to see (or say one saw) an uppity guy with a glass (containing alcohol) in his hand, or speaking to a woman as if she was a human being and not poison. It was not long before stories got around about his being a drunkard, or that allusions were made about his association with the woman. The rest was left to the imagination. It may be that for years he had been putting some white confrere to bed ossified and would not think of being as free with women as some whites assume they have a right to be with black women. But that was all it took to get the nigger transferred or disciplined. This technique died in the fifties. Black priests I know would not bat an eye about suing for libel or slander in such situations today. There is now a more subtle approach. If they cannot completely ignore you, they wonder out loud.

"Where does Lucas get the money to fly around the country giving speeches?" asks one. One would never suppose that it's customary to pay a speaker's expenses when he is invited. "Isn't Lucas neglecting his parish?" One priest laughingly criticized my going to a meeting on a day I was on duty. He himself thinks nothing of going to Jones Beach (about thirty miles away) on a duty-day, leaving a kid in the rectory. Nine years ago they didn't care about where Lucas was when he was wasting time with them, or what Lucas said when he was saying what they wanted to hear. Another Harlem priest wondered where I got the time when I went to Chicago to speak for Father Clements' installation. That particular year he had taken five vacations, including an eight-day cruise. He still found time to go to Rome and Ireland with Archbishop Cooke when Cooke was made a cardinal.

There are three alternatives I see for a black man in the Catholic Church. He can say the hell with it and leave it. Many I know see this as the only answer. "Get out, otherwise you'll be tainted," they say. To me this is no answer. America is a racist society and so are all her institutions, including the churches and synagogues. But twenty-two million Americans cannot pack up and go to Africa or to the moon. If they remain, it is a choice of to which racist institution(s) they will belong in this racist society and what they will do.

The second alternative is to stay in and "adjust." It is not too difficult for a Negro, especially one with talent, to be someone besides himself, to allow himself to be used in return for personal rewards from whitey. This is what some white priests have in mind when they ask, "What does Lucas want?" or hint about making him this or that "in order to shut him up." Everyone has a price, they believe. It would be easy to rationalize the second choice. I can delude myself that in getting a little prestige and allowing myself to be used, I am really helping black people. After a while, they might even call me a "good and distinguished Negro priest." Remember when the Newark priests made their statement? Archbishop Boland described as "a distinguished and good Negro Catholic," some damn fool who said, "I simply cannot go along with the priests and those who are attacking the Church. I have never known it to practice discrimination or to be insensitive to the black community. I'm not sure that the priests don't have some other reason for doing this. It's a terrible accusation." The woman was identified simply as a "newswoman of one of the major Negro newspapers in Newark" because, "I don't think I ought to get involved, in my position." (Too many Negroes are in positions which don't allow them to get involved with black people.) But this alternative makes me vomit.

The final alternative, the one I've chosen, is to stay and fight. It involves using all the talents one has. I intend to be a black man and remain a priest in a white racist Church. I will caucus, organize, plan with black people and accept white support to make real a black Jesus Who will call together and form a black people through whom He will save the Church and America. Like others, I will continue to speak out—-to retrieve the minds of Negro Catholics from the man's captivity, and to encourage white Catholics to start believing what they say they do and to start behaving the way they talk. When white Catholics start acting toward black people the way they teach black people to act toward them, the problem will be solved. If we black people fail, all—black and white—will go down together.

I have made this choice because I feel there is more to the Catholic Church than white racists. I still believe the Church is a divine *and* human, a free and responsible community of faith, hope and charity called into being, nourished, sustained and missioned by Father, Son and Spirit. I believe the community is to be achieved by sacrament, word, and ministry and that it is called to be the Sacrament of the saving unity and presence of Jesus Christ in the world today and until all is reconciled to the Father.

Well, it is the human aspect with which I have difficulty. Particularly with regard to black people, this community has limited itself to perfunctory and mechanical sacraments, irrelevant words or none at all, and little ministry. The Church has substituted financial interest for faith, platitudes for bases of hope, and self-centered patronage for love. But I believe the human distortion of this community can go only so far, that it cannot destroy or completely overshadow the Divine reality. As long as this is so, there is hope.

I am further encouraged by the many blacks who are coming to their senses and who will remain to work for change. I am encouraged by thousands of whites who understand and are in the forefront of the struggle. For every one I know—Tom Buck (author of *An Open Letter to the U.S. Bishops,* who urged me and started the ball rolling toward this book); Robert and Zil Groux; Matthew Ahmann; James Groppi; the Newark twenty; James Sugrue; Sisters Maria Mercedes and Catherine Clough, both S.B.S.; Patrick and Jeanne Ryan; the Lees and parishioners like them from St. Francis in Indianapolis; the excellent white priests I have lived and worked with, like the late Monsignor Joseph Walsh; Fathers Charles McSween and Lawrence Pushor—for all of these and more whom I know, there are thousands I do not know. There are many who, when given the opportunity to face the truth, are truly responding in words and deeds to my and others' written and spoken words. They indicate a growth in understanding and a desire to change. While all of these number in the thousands, there is need for millions like them. But these are the yeast in the three measures of flour.

In my own archdiocese, Cardinal Cooke and other diocesan officials are now discussing some things they would not have wanted to hear a few years ago. Several

months ago Cooke introduced a committee on financing
which is hopefully a first step toward getting wealthier
parishes to share some of their abundance with poorer
ones. How well it will be pushed remains to be seen. My
own appointment as pastor, the second of two black
pastors in the archdiocese and the state, is also encouraging.

It is a challenge for which I am grateful. Many will
criticize the move negatively. Some of my Negro parishioners are not yet ready for me. Years of being told by
word and deed that to be black is to be inferior and
incapable have left some feeling insulted and apprehen-
sive about any black person in a leadership role. Some,
immediately on the announcement, began talking about,
"They didn't ask for a black pastor; they were happy
with what they have had." There are still places in our
land where Negro Catholics would reject a black pastor
because of this conditioning. But these are the facts of
life that must be changed. At thirty-seven, I am the
youngest pastor in the archdiocese. On the other hand,
thirty-seven is not exactly a little boy.

While discussing the promotion, Monsignor O'Brien,
the vicar-general, assured me that the archdiocese
is committed to the principle of black leadership in
the black community. How well this principle and its
implications are understood remains to be seen. It is not
a question of what is done or is not done for Lawrence
Lucas, nor of attempts or lack of attempts to tie me
down, or shut me up. Rather it will be in the sincere
effort by the Church to understand and relate to black
people differently than in the past, and to use all its resources for their liberation and spiritual-human development. In short, it must be part of a gigantic effort to
cast a Christian light on American life, including black

life, through Christian love, and to do it effectively. And it must be understood that this light must radically challenge existing systems and structures.

To the extent that *Black Priest/White Church* can help the cause, it will have served a purpose. In the meantime, there will be all kinds of people, including good Catholic Negro laymen, religious, and priests who will divorce themselves from Lucas' views, and be upset about his "badmouthing" the Church. Some will really be sincere, others not. Some will be terrified. They want what I want, but they are not ready to pay the price and run the risks. Lucas will discomfort and annoy them, making them feel threatened. This, too, should not be too surprising. It was Christ's own folks, as with many nonconformists after Him, who did Him in. They took Him to the Romans complaining that He was radical, seditious, subversive and causing trouble with our people and stirring up revolt against you good Romans.

Thus, if Lawrence Lucas is to be hated, vilified and persecuted by white racists, and Negroes programmed by such people and centuries of oppression, so be it. There remain the words of Christ: "Happy are you when people hate you, drive you out, abuse you, denounce your name as criminal, on account of the Son of Man. Rejoice when that day comes and dance for joy, for then your reward will be great in heaven" (Luke 6:22–23). The thing is to make sure I am being persecuted for His sake.

ABOUT THE AUTHOR

LAWRENCE LUCAS was born in New York City
in 1933. He was educated in public and parochial
schools in Harlem and at Cathedral College and
St. Joseph's Seminary in Dunwoodie, New York.
Ordained for the New York Archdiocese in 1959,
Father Lucas is at present pastor of Resurrection
Parish in Harlem, and is the only black pastor
in the New York Archdiocese.

Father Lucas lectures widely, writes a nationally
syndicated column called *The Black Voice,*
and has contributed articles to numerous newspapers
and magazines, including *The Commonweal,
National Catholic Reporter,* and *Ave Maria*.
He is Chairman of the Eastern Region of
the National Black Catholic Clergy Caucus,
is on the Board of Directors of the National
Conference of Black Churchmen, and is on
the Steering Committee of the Black Economic
Development Council, of which James Foreman
is probably the best-known representative.